The Art of Visualizing

Black

&

White

A Guide to Intuitive Drawing

This is a how to draw art book. All images were created solely by the artist/author. Some strictly for the purpose of this book.

© 2012

Michael Csontos
currently resides outside of Prescott, Arizona

Dedication:

For my son Shane. The most imaginative and spontaneous line artist I have known.

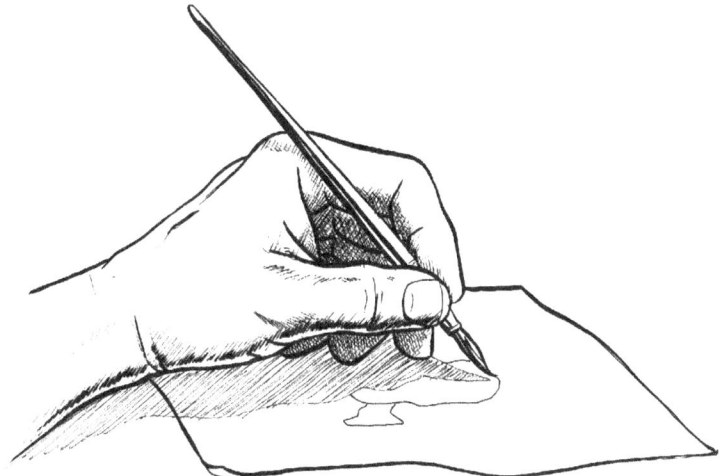

Preface

Artwork is the main construct to social communication, but I have always felt that the act of creating artwork should also be a free flowing of self expression. I have also believed that any art should convey the thought behind it easily or at least be fascinating in its interpretation and execution. If it is too haphazardly composed then how could anyone construe it as anything but a casual approach to what I believe should be a genuine attempt at creating a work of art that is meant to last for the ages or at least evoke some type of enlightening emotional response. In any event this volume of work reasonably expresses the way I create art in the linear genre of drawing and inking in black and white. It is also my hope that it helps artists realize that it is not necessary to initially concentrate on anatomical accuracy. Just draw, and eventually your mind's eye will tell you what, if anything, needs adjusting. It is next to impossible to turn off your mind's eye, so you might as well use it. The entire scope of this book could be explained very easily: Let your mind's eye create for you. Do not force it, just allow it to happen.

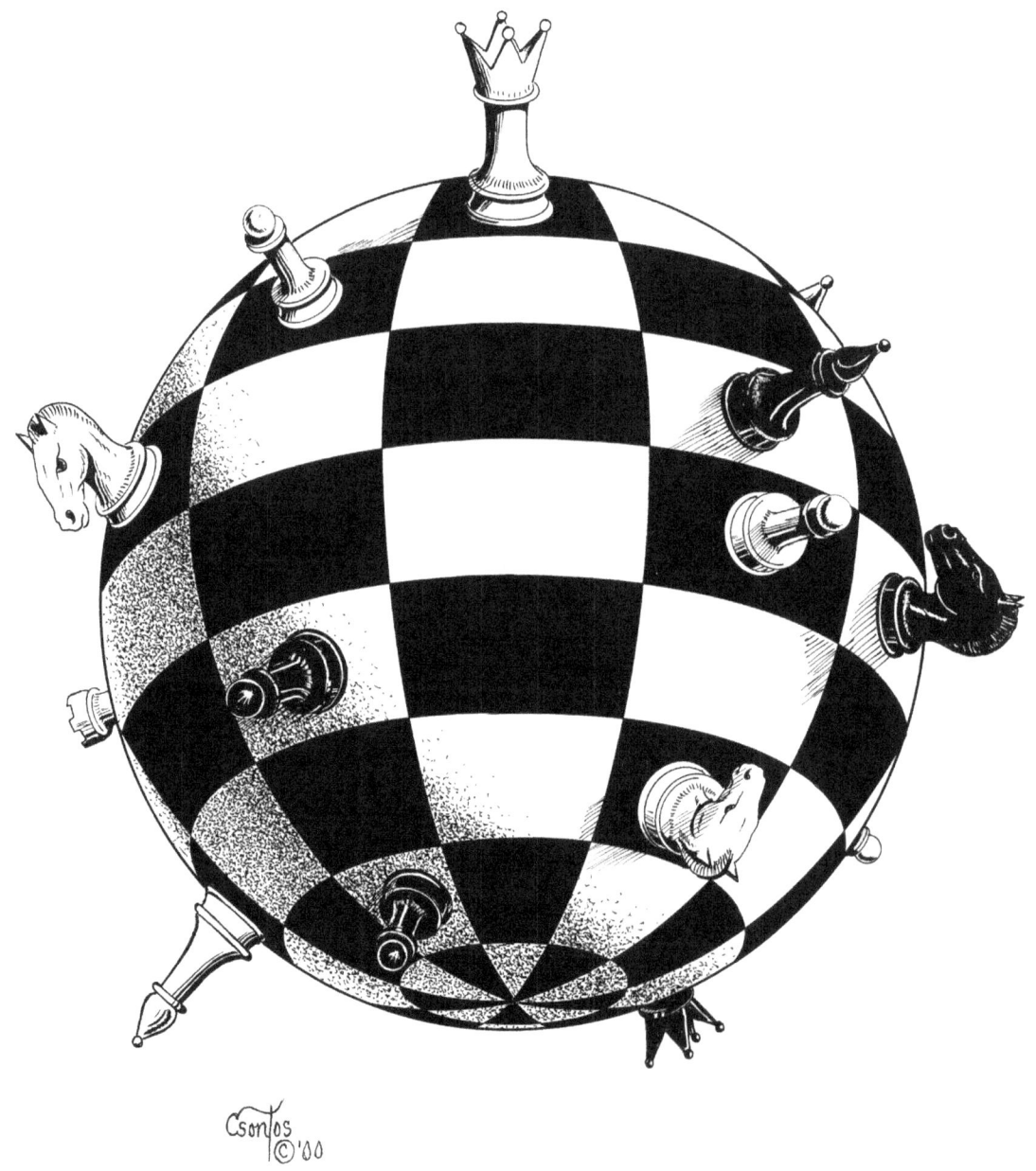

"It's Your Move"
Ink - pen and brush.

TABLE OF CONTENTS

Introduction

Even though visualizing is the main reason behind this book I will also be primarily concerned with ink as a finish because it reproduces cleanly and it has excellent contrast. It also works well with direct to plate printing and any other contemporary printing and copying method. However I always use pencil to start any linear imagery. There are also several finished pencil and computer illustrations as they also include the art of visualizing in black and white.

There are two basic types of illustrations that I would like to present. One is my favorite and that is a spontaneous, autonomous approach with no preconceived idea. I'd like to believe that these works are fine art. The other (and this style usually pays the bills) is preconceived which is either based on a word, an idea, a subject matter or even just a phrase. This style is sketched to comply with a customers request and sometimes critiqued and sketched again until it conveys the feeling or objective it is supposed to.

I will constantly refer to how or why any preconceived image was developed and brought to a finish.

Visualizing

For any artwork that is not a commission, visualizing is a way of letting the artwork create itself. Obviously the imagery comes from your mind

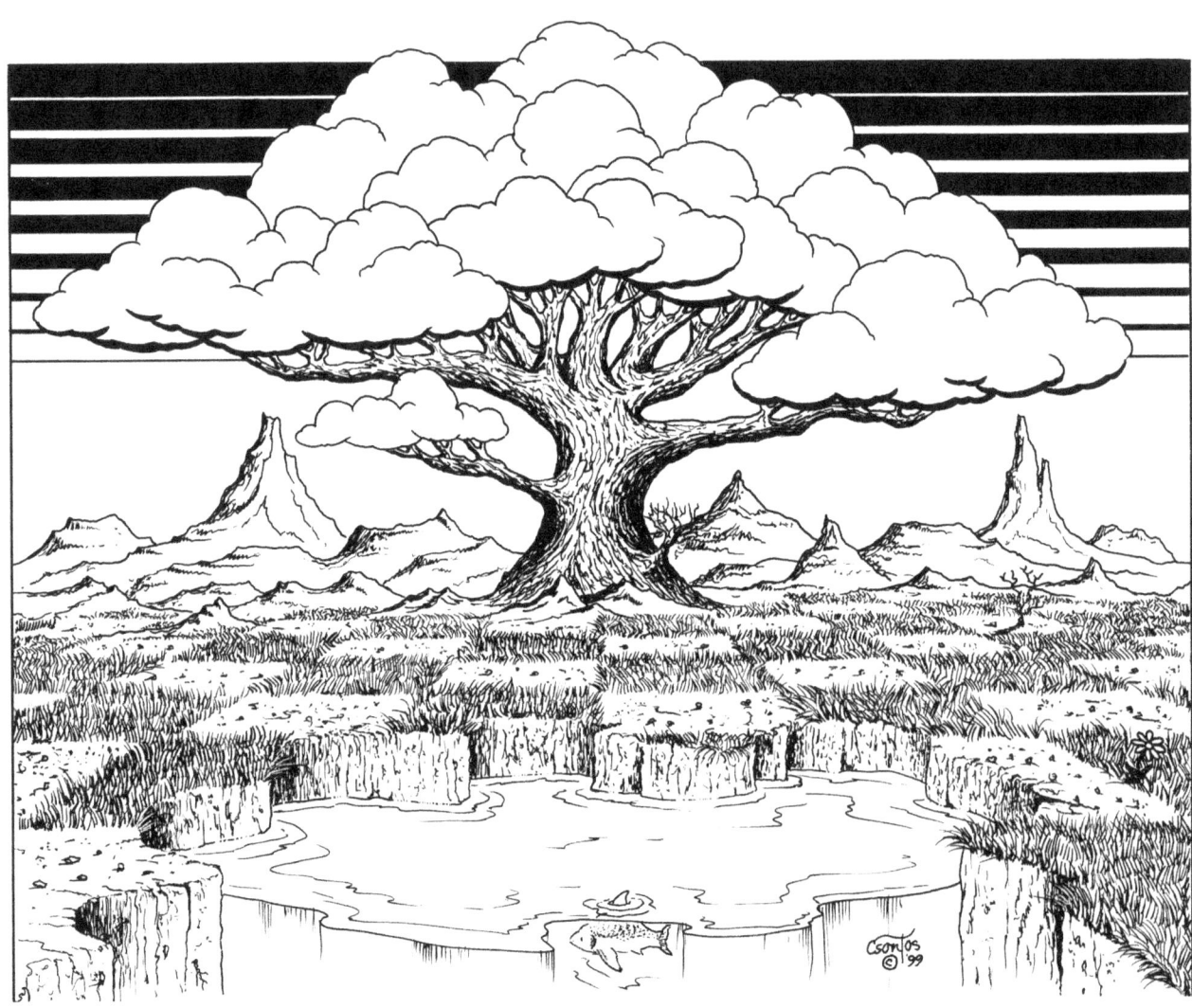

"Tree With Its Head in the Clouds"
Ink - pen and brush.

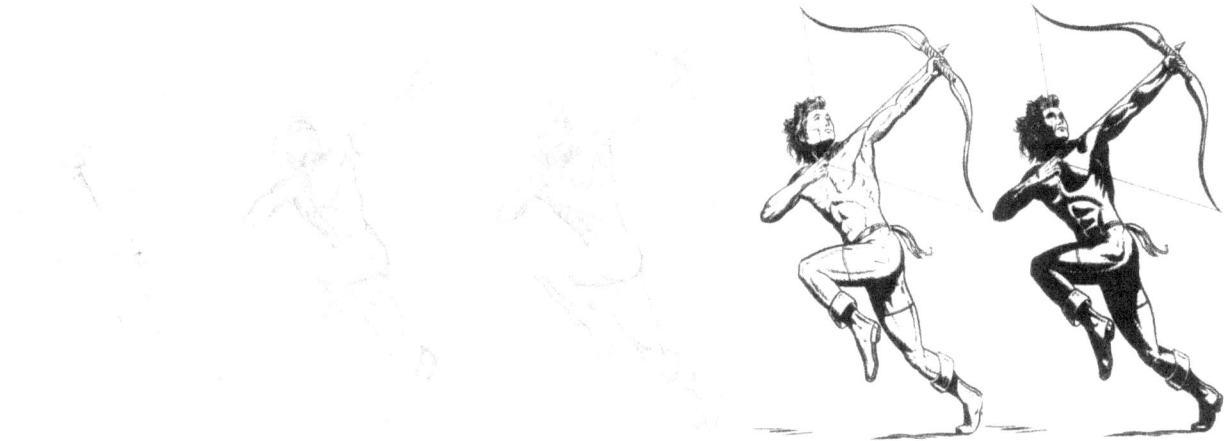

An archer in five steps with a pencil for the first three steps through two samples of inking. First a small brush then additional tone was added with a larger brush.

and your imagination but it is not originated by means of a direct external input. Once the idea develops, rendering takes over and then experience will bring the piece to a relatable comprehensible finish. Whether it be in pencil, ink or even a grayscale image produced on the computer.

When I compose a personal linear work I approach it with a loose an unstructured manner using spontaneous and fluid movement of a pencil. I usually do not see anything in my mind or on the paper until there is an adequate amount of linework or tone to give me the ability to visualize an idea or a theme. Considering the low cost of plain paper, if after a few minutes of sketching an idea does not emerge, I will usually start again. It rarely makes sense to erase as plain paper does not hold up very well to erasing unless it is just a few simple lines. If I am starting a linear work of art on an illustration board then

I would obviously erase as that surface is more durable.

With a commission type of work visualizing is also used. The only difference is that the image is conceived first and the sketching is then brought to the level of the mental image. At least that is my procedure. I have included dozens of commissioned pieces in this volume to give you an idea. The difference is obvious as a commissioned work has a theme that is related to a particular subject matter it is in reference to, usually for a book or magazine illustration along with hundreds of other applications.

As for works of a personal nature they seem to have more of a surreal, fantasy or conceptual perception imagery and theme. I am always intrigued when an idea develops more and more detail and substance after I have realized the initial imagery. It seems, like I said, to draw itself.

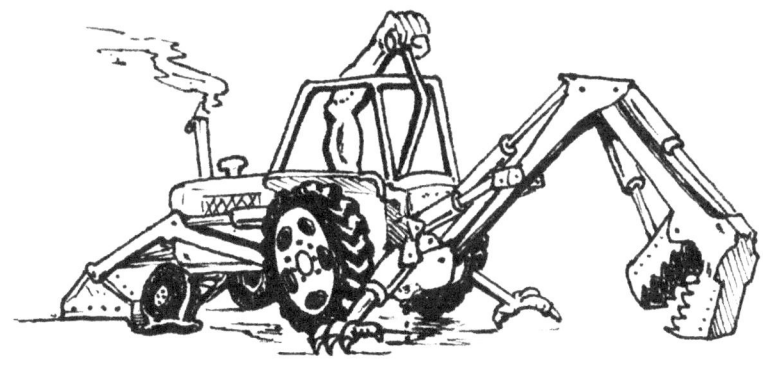

This inking for a t-shirt was developed for a customer that had a backhoe service. Her only request was that she wanted an idea similar to the muscle car t-shirts from the late sixties. Once she said that the idea popped into my head immediately. So I just drew it out. Felt tip pen.

Texture and technique

Being as how there are a multitude of 'How to Ink Comic Books' on the market I will not be redundant and delve into more of the same. I have purchased several of these and they are excellent at giving you the basics on using different types of pens and brushes. In my opinion there is only one way to become proficient at inking and that is to practice, copy, practice.

I have used crowquill type pens, felt tip pens, brushes, drawing type pens (these pens use a waterproof ink with a straight nib) of which there are several brands and sizes on the market, sponges (natural are the best - available in the water color painting section) and anything else I could think of. I have pretty much stuck with the drawing pens and brushes. I have been spoiled with new brushes as they go to a razor sharp point just like a crowquill. My only problem with crowquill pens is that I am a backwards left hander and I tend to dig the tip into the paper instead of letting it float over the paper. When a brush gets old from wear it gets chopped down to be used for textures such as leaves on bushes, dirt, bark on trees, volcanic type rocks, splashing water and other objects rather than just lines.

For studying contrasts, one trick I used in the past years was to use black and white film. I took pictures of everything you could imagine. I then used a copy machine and adjusted the contrast to get a copy that had the grays removed and replaced with black. Then it was just a matter of experimenting with techniques that simulated the effect I was going after.

Nowadays with computers, Photoshop and digital cameras it is almost too easy to get high contrast study references of just about anything. I have also used Photoshop for toning in combination with linework.

Once you've gotten the technique down that you prefer for any particular texture it makes visualizing even more fun. Because now the mental struggle of wondering how to portray a particular subject has been removed.

It seems that most of my personal work relies on the imagery being unusual, so not a lot of savvy is needed to portray the objects. And it seems that most of the commercial or commissioned work only needs linework with brush and pen. In my 35 years of illustrating I have never been asked to do a commercial project in pencil.

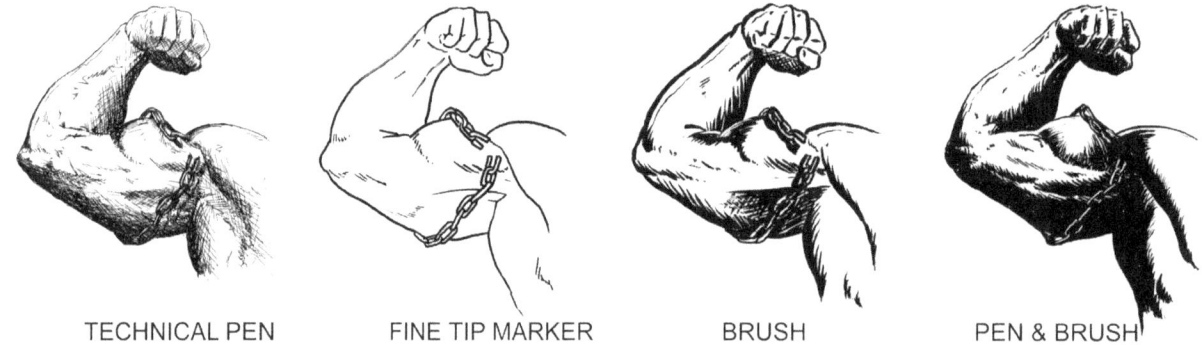

TECHNICAL PEN   FINE TIP MARKER   BRUSH   PEN & BRUSH

Different ink techniques of the same object. Sometimes it's not always easy to decide on which technique to use. And when you do decide, the customer may change your mind for you.

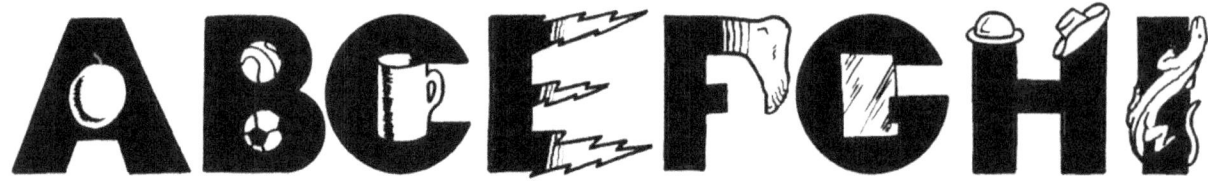

An alphabet of clip art. Every letter of the alphabet was drawn with a corresponding image that related to the first letter of that image's word. Color was then laid in on the computer.

Visualizing with a spontaneous technique in pencil and ink.

There are a few similarities to my inking technique when compared to my painting technique. The obvious initial one is trying to aimlessly doodle with no preconceived thoughts or imagery. In this case I used a #8B sketching pencil for the first four stages. Some of the time when doing pencils for an inking I will go through up

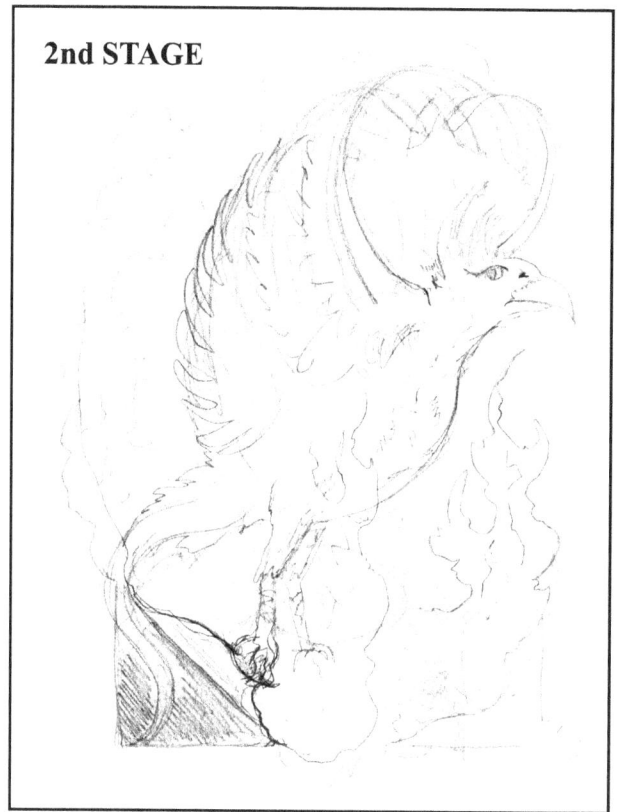

2nd STAGE

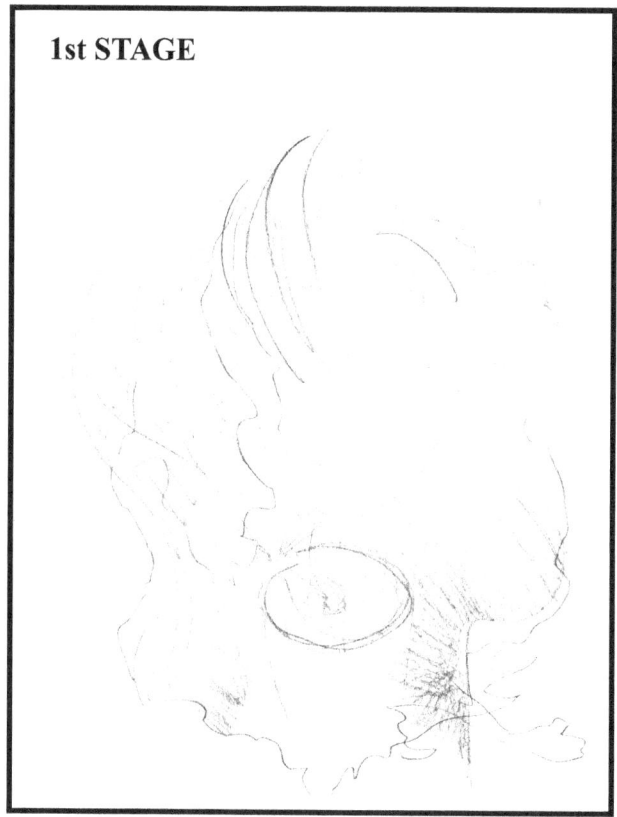

1st STAGE

stage. If I need to understand the toning better in certain areas then I will adjust those areas with more penciling. If I wanted the artwork to be a finished penciling then I would have started with either illustration board or with a heavier and

to about five sketches before one of them starts to give an indication of imagery that I would like to finish as an inking. If I was using an illustration board then I would obviously erase instead of starting over.

For this piece I only did two spontaneous original sketches before I settled on this one (1st Stage) that I would take to an inking finish.

Now that my brain sees an image coming out of the sketch (2nd Stage) I'll refine it with more toning and control. It's not necessary to bring it to a degree where the penciling looks like the finished stage because the inking will be the final

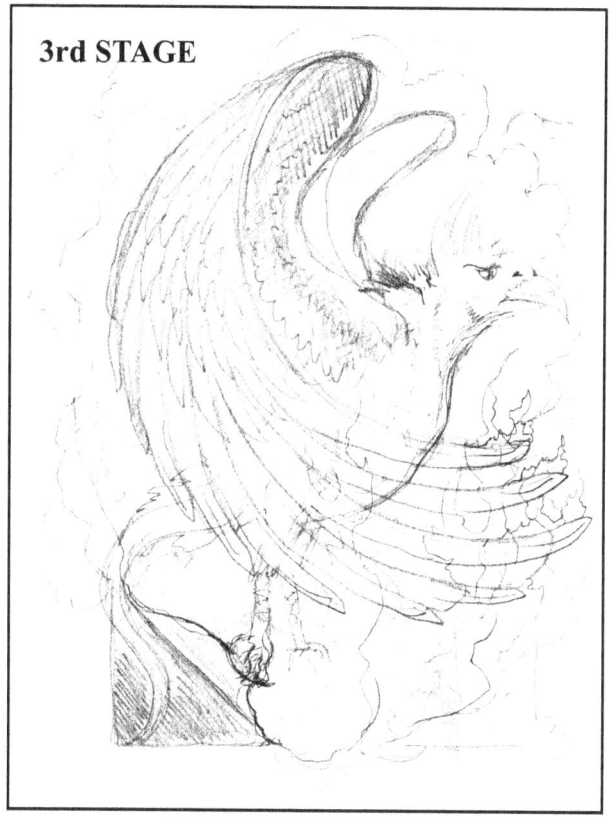

3rd STAGE

4th STAGE

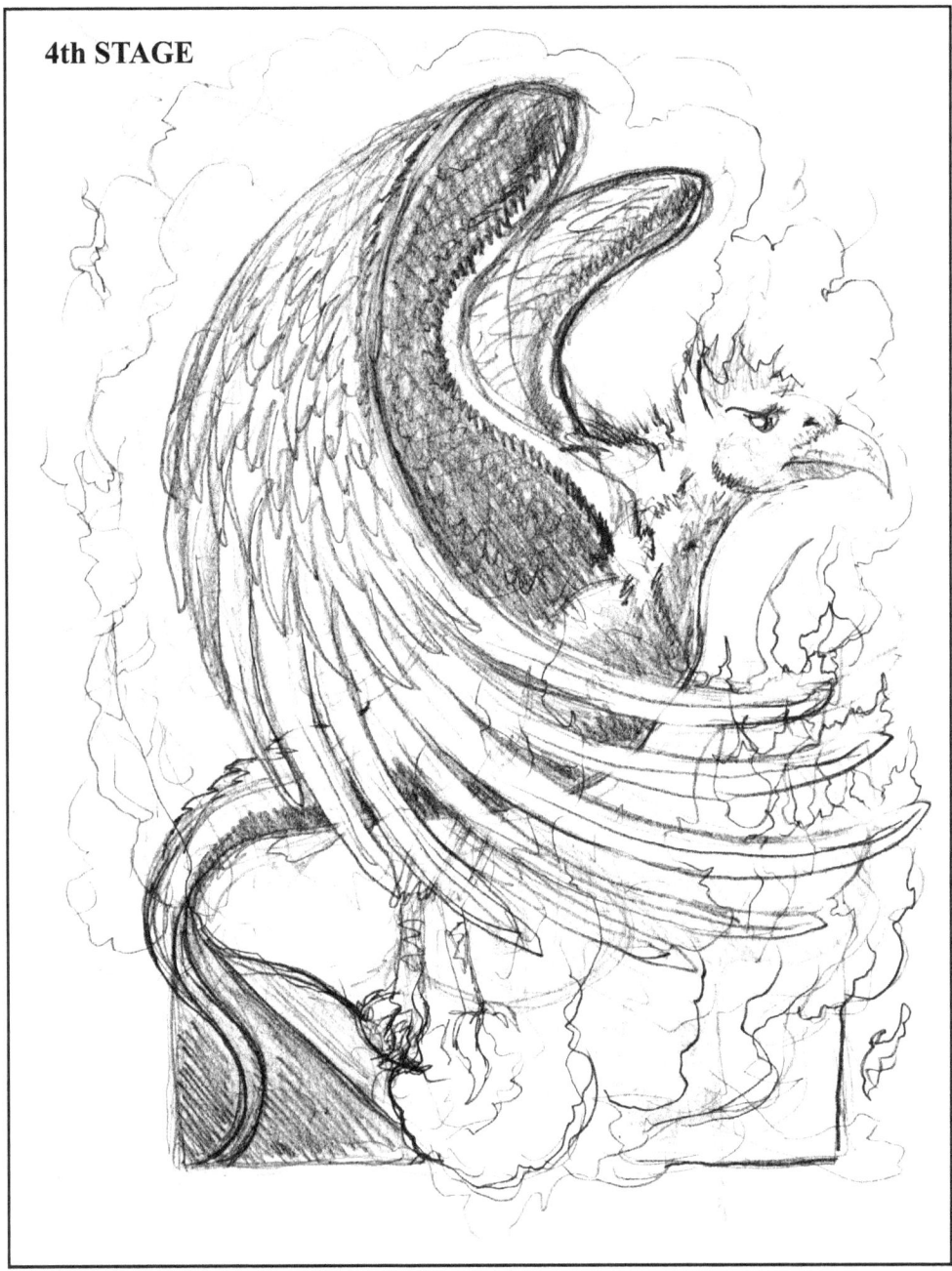

table and a #HB pencil. My reasons being; I had quite a mess with using the #8B pencil and it was getting hard to see the detail which means it would of been even harder to see through the paper even though using a light table; and this way I would have the toned sketch off to the side so I could compare the inking progression with the toned sketch a lot easier. The problem with using regular copy paper with such a soft lead is that it does not lend itself well to repeated erasing and redrawing.

Stage 5 shows the pencil outline I redid that will be under the inking on the light table. It's not overly spectacular but it is enough to give me the basics.

better grade of paper. But for this image I definitely wanted the finish to be ink. As I brought this sketch to the second phase of rendition, I thought it had potential but my mind's eye had some objection to the curve of the wings. So in this case I did erase with a kneadable eraser just enough to be able to re-sketch the wings with a more desirable curve (3rd Stage). Now I like it a little better. Sometimes once I have the idea, I may re-sketch on fresh paper using a light table, just to have a cleaner copy.

After adding the toning that I wanted (4th Stage) I did decide to redraw the image using my light

One of the fairly consistent things I do when I go to ink with a light table is that I use a coated paper. It's super smooth finish gives a beautiful crisp pen line when using Pigma pens and equally crisp lines when using a brush. That being said, those aren't even the main reasons I use coated paper. The real reason is that as I ink a drawing I try to still be spontaneous with detail, texture and toning and that leads to a few blips, blobs, goof-ups, mind changes and just plain old mistakes. The coated paper allows me to scrape (very gently) with an X-acto knife (I prefer a #16) any lines I want removed. I try to wait until I'm all done because even though this

10

5th STAGE

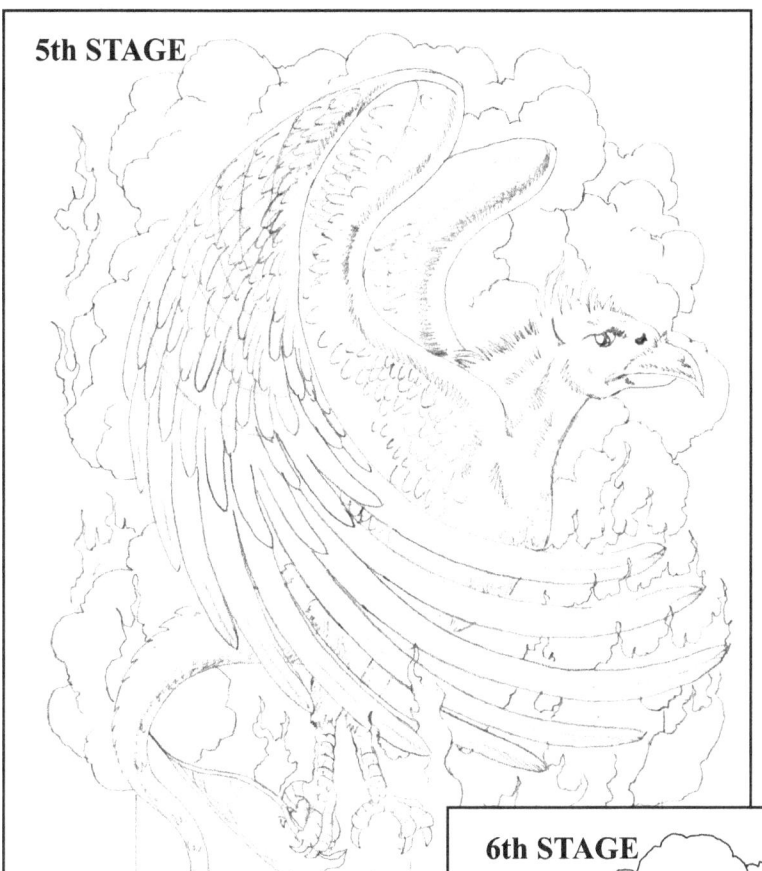

could always go over areas and edges with a brush later to build contrast and shadow. Plus the pen came in useful for all the feathers. As I went along it became apparent that I was using the pen for everything. I found that interesting because I enjoy the variety of line a brush gives.

Stage 7 shows the finished inking. I did complete the entire piece using just a few drawing pens. I guess it just matters what kind of feeling the imagery has. Another good aspect of using a light table is that I don't have to erase the penciling. When I work on illustration board and do have to erase, it seems the erasing tends to remove some of the ink as well. I believe that is because the ink is not sufficiently

technique makes it quite easy and clean to remove ink, it does not prove very compatible with re-inking, because now the surface is no longer coated where I scraped and is down to the fibers of the paper. One of the paper brands I use is Utopia Gloss Coated 80# Text Bright White. Heavy brushed areas do not scrape as good probably because the ink is different or more concentrated because it comes from a jar whereas the pens need to be able to maintain a draw from their reservoir.

Stage 6 shows the inking about 50% underway. I opted to use a pen to start with because I could jiggle it to give a rougher edge to simulate feathered profiles. I

6th STAGE

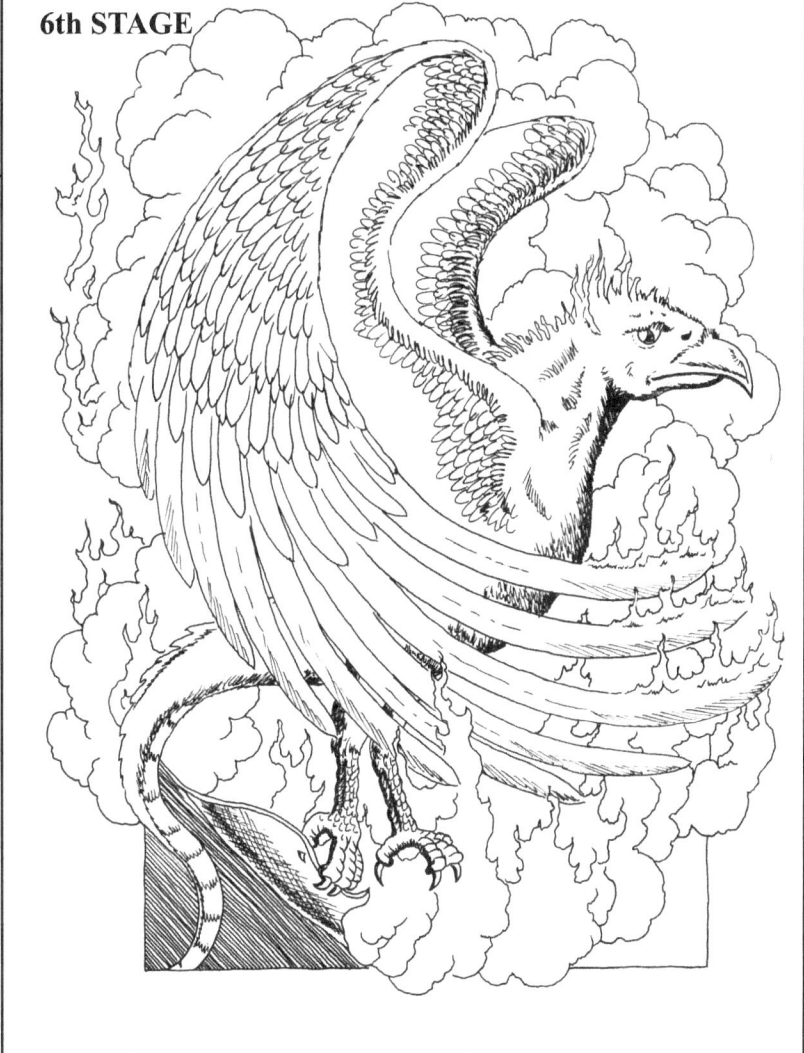

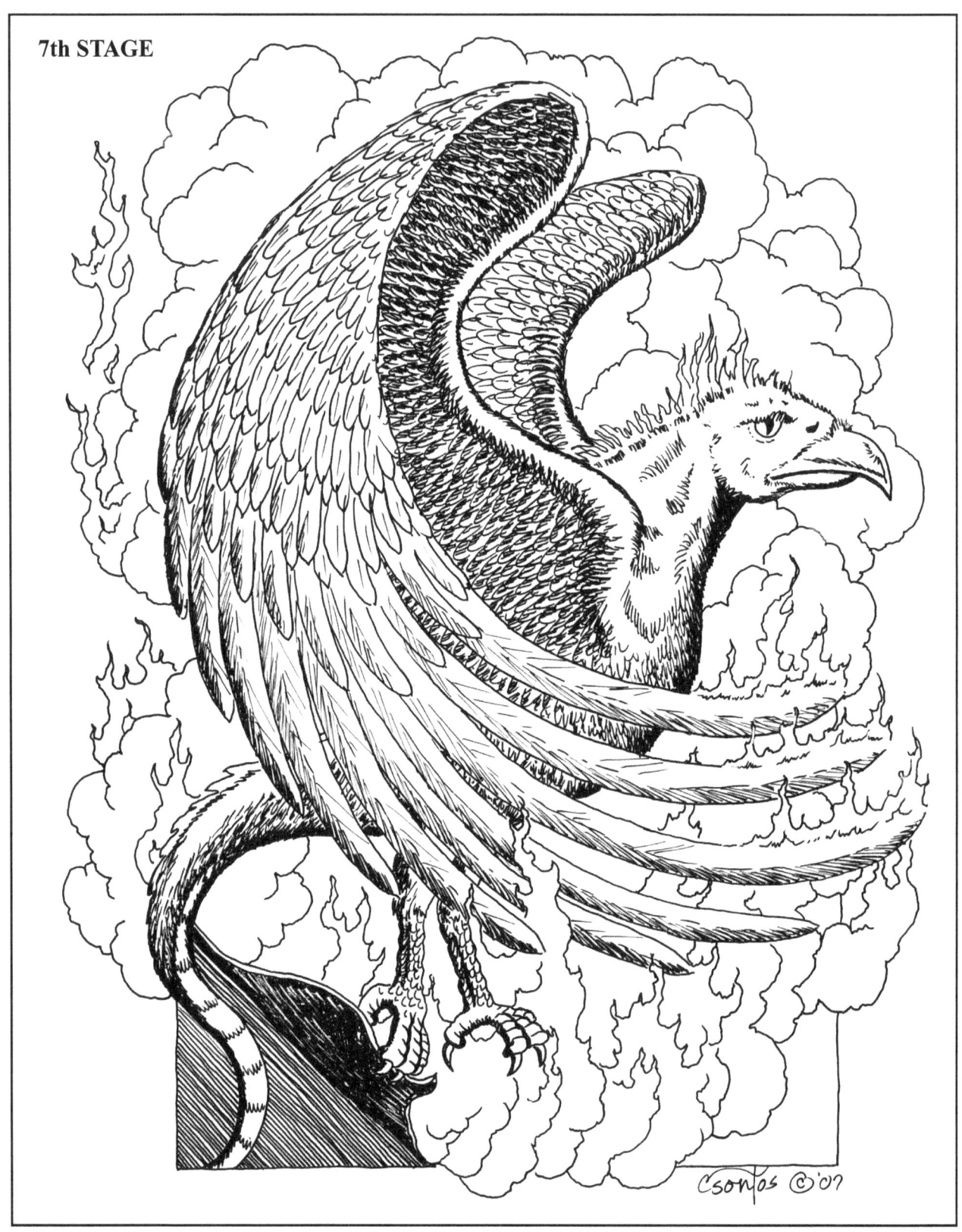

"Phoenix"
Ink - pen.

attached to the fibers of the paper but rather sits on the surface of the pencil so it ends up being minimally absorbed into the paper. I must say the most fun part of this project was the time spent developing the idea with contrast and tone in pencil as in Stage 4.

Samples of spontaneous illustrations.

Now that I've shown you the approach for one of my personal images, here are a few more with the original sketch that prompted the finished image. I almost always use a coated paper and a light table for the finished inkings. Especially if I have absolutely no idea what the imagery will be. There are however, exceptions, such as the space and pencil images later in this book.

Preliminary sketch

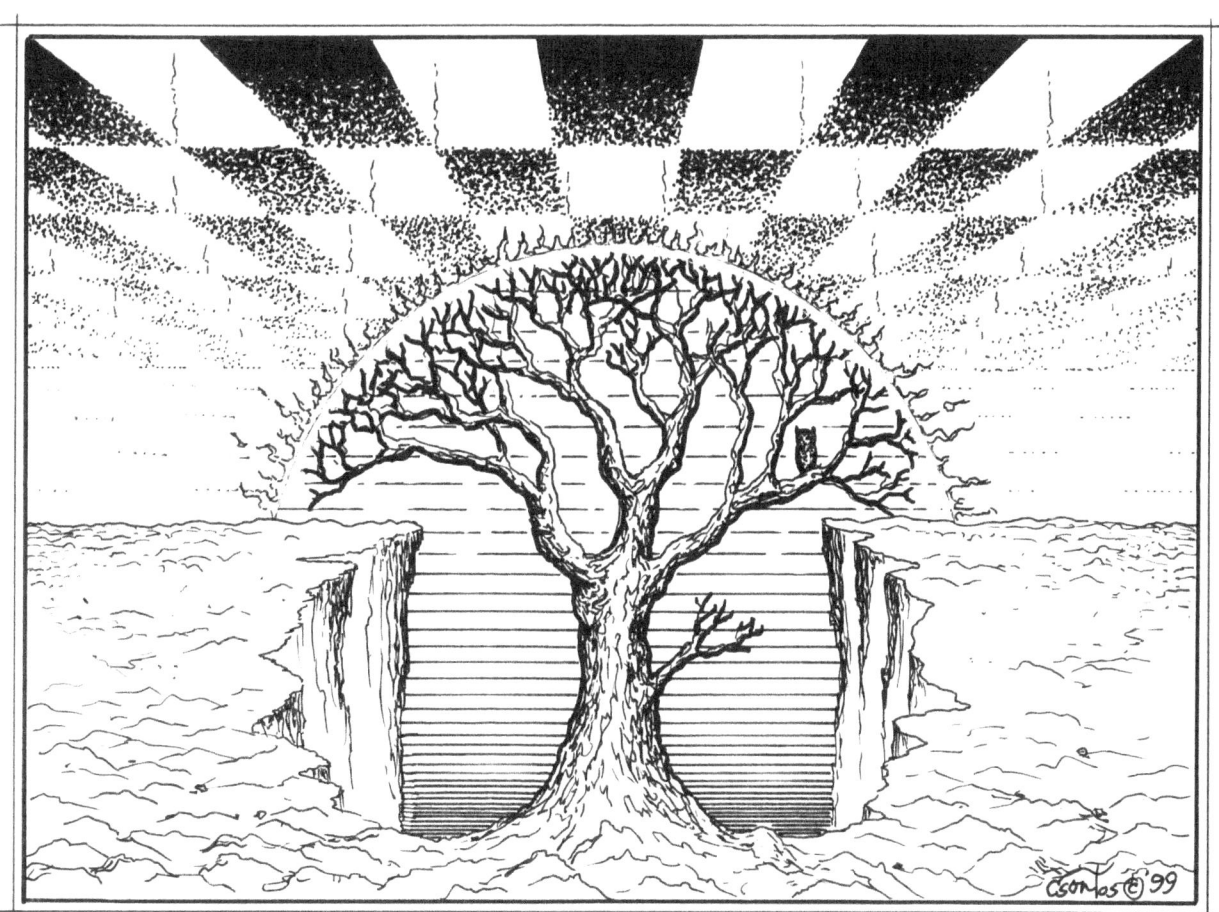

"Substance of Light and Form"

As you can tell, I seem to have this thing for a checkerboard effect. Ink - felt tip pen.

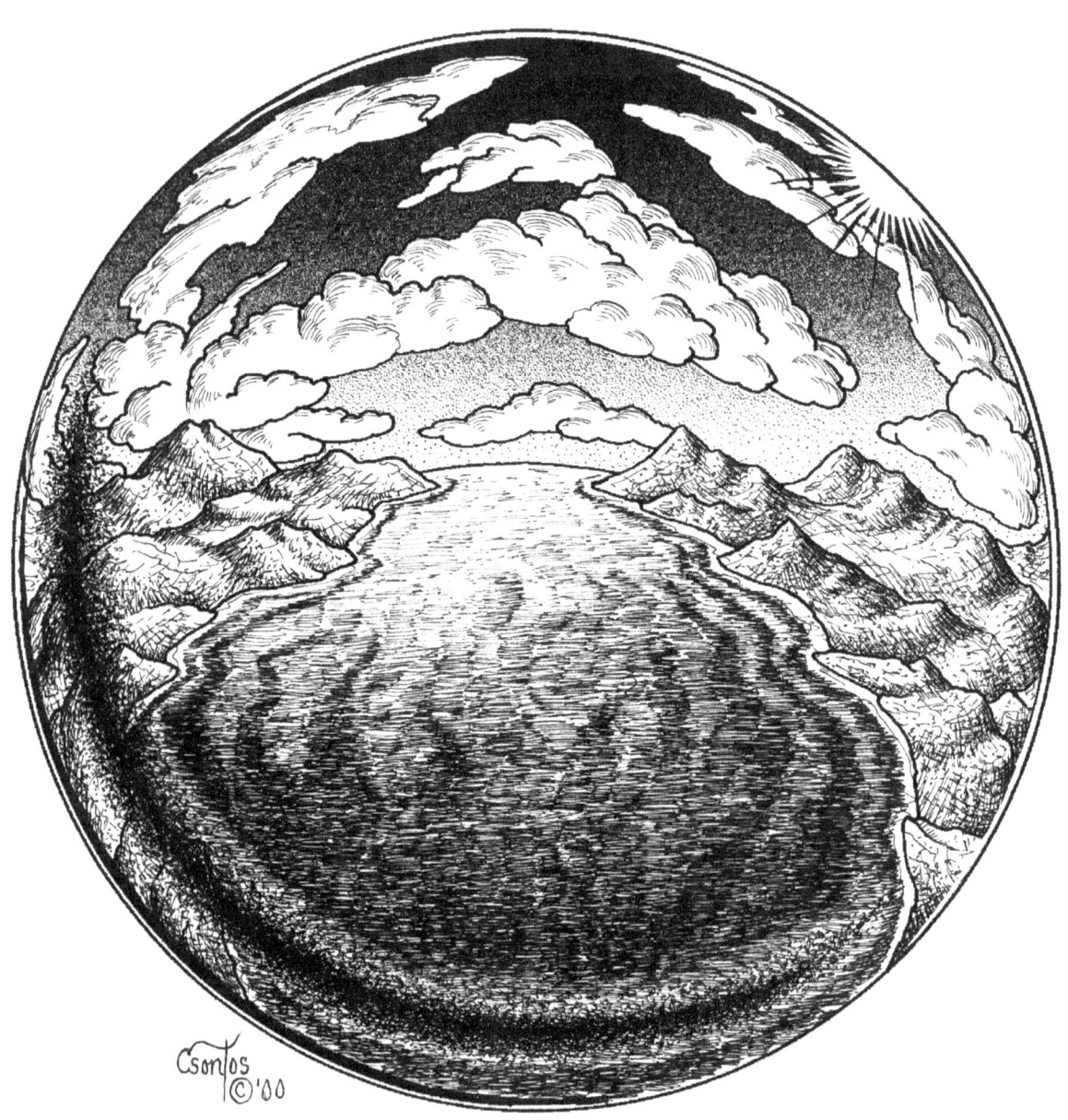

"Mirror, Mirror, on the Ball"
Ink - drawing pens. A personal tribute to M.C. Escher.

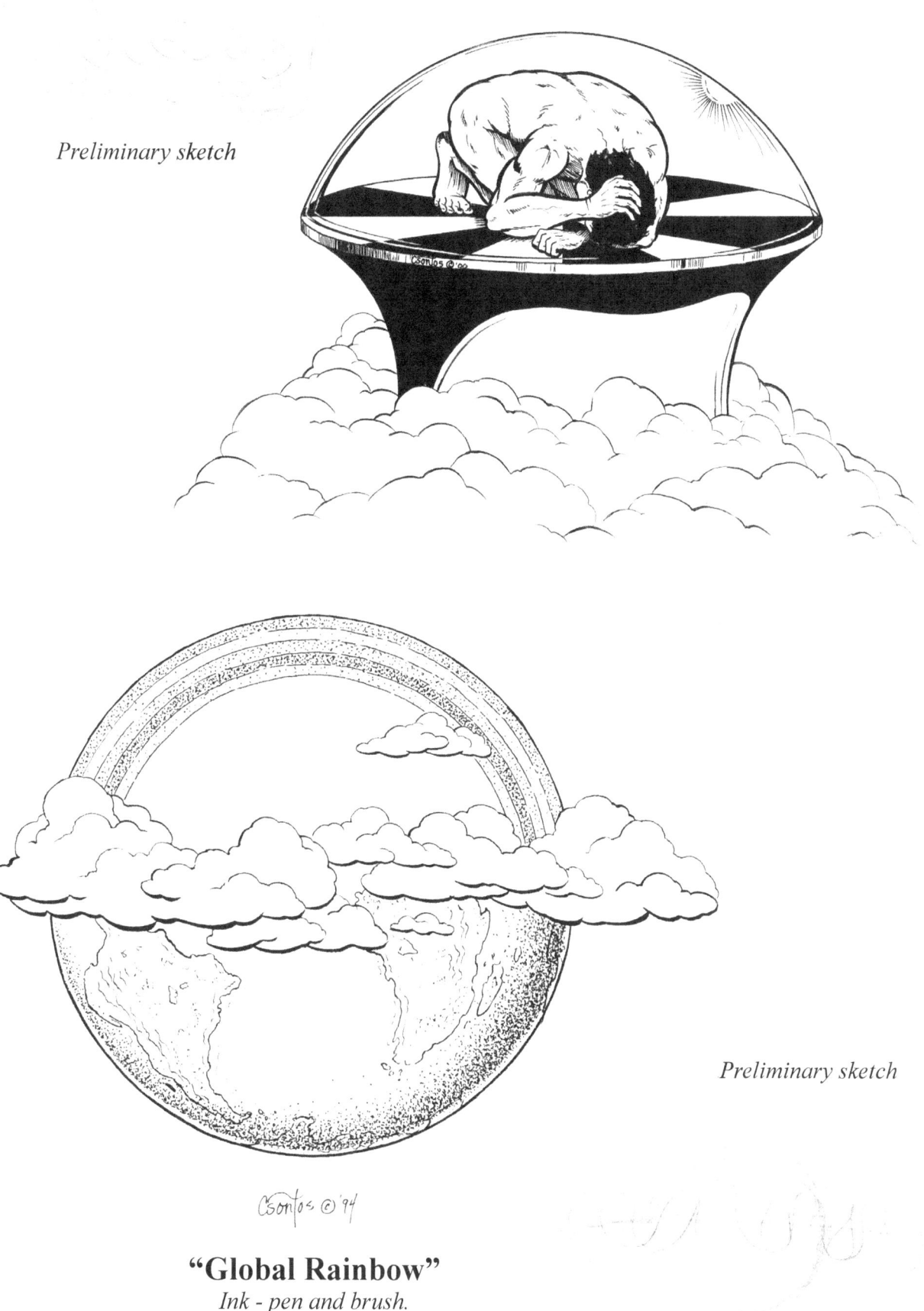

"Purgatory Chamber"
*Ink - pen and brush. Sometimes I get the feeling
this is me. But only sometimes.*

Preliminary sketch

Preliminary sketch

"Global Rainbow"
Ink - pen and brush.

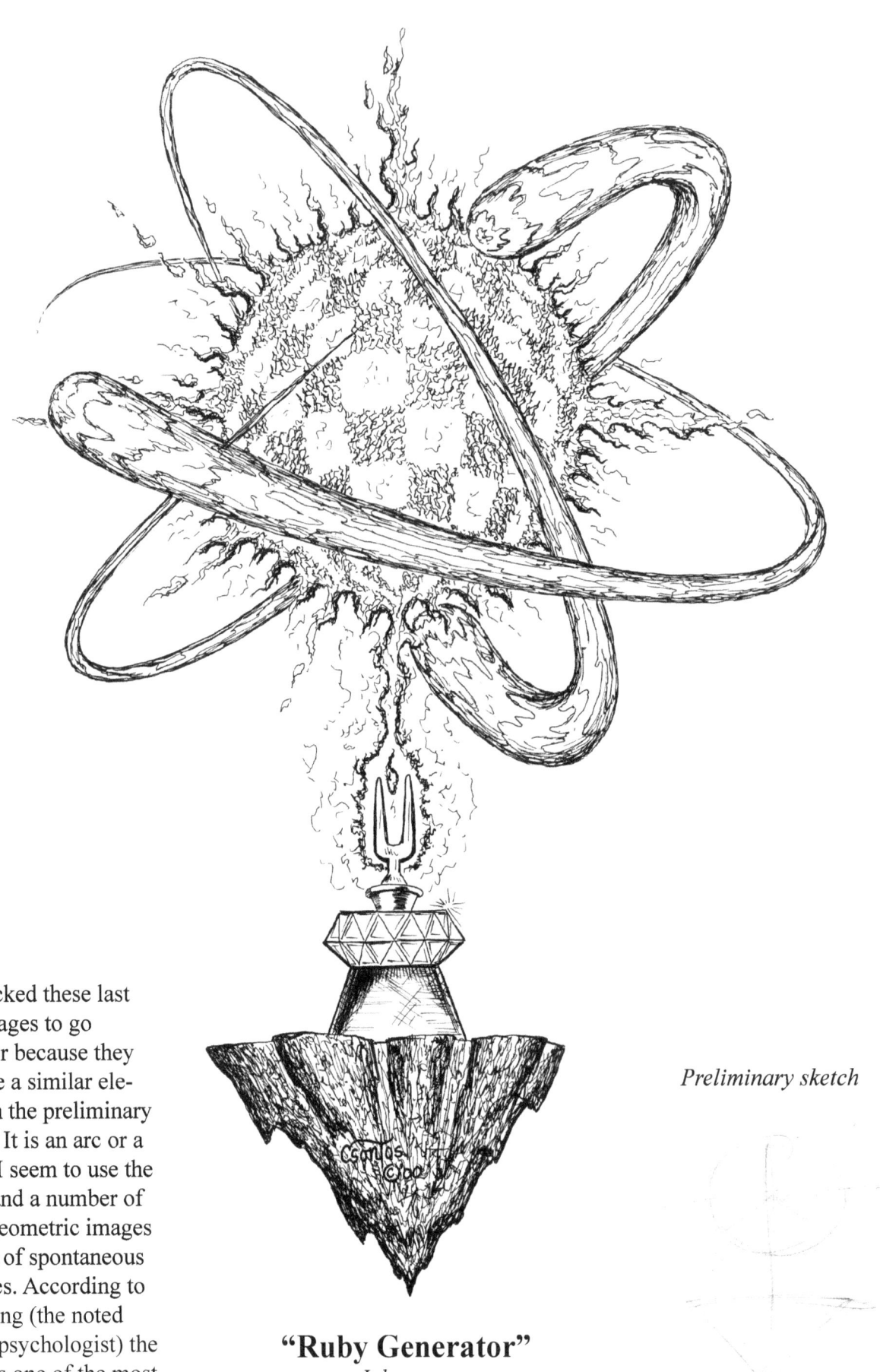

I've picked these last five images to go together because they all have a similar element in the preliminary sketch. It is an arc or a circle. I seem to use the circle and a number of other geometric images in a lot of spontaneous sketches. According to Carl Jung (the noted dream psychologist) the circle is one of the most widely used symbols.

Preliminary sketch

"Ruby Generator"
Ink - pen.

16

Visualizing with pencil and ink for preconceived commissions or commercial projects.

This assignment was quite enjoyable to do. I was asked to do the cover for a telephone directory in the town where I used to live. It was a small town (only 3000 residents) but the landscape was beautiful, surrounded on two sides by canyon walls, with the other two sides leading the way in and the way out. The request was an inking depicting some of the natural landscape aspects of the area.

The canyon area happened to be the last stronghold of saguaro cacti which decreased in numbers as you drove up out of the canyon. There were also buttes of solid rock. Two rivers also merged with the smaller one stopping (in name) at the intersection of the larger one. I hiked for about two miles east from downtown and when I found the right place I began sketching. As you

The preliminary pencil sketch.

can see from the sketches I included a saguaro, a prickly pear cactus, (which I added later because there was not one directly at the sketch site), a river which I could see parts of, and a butte with distant foothills and mesas. There were also a few turkey vultures in the sky. I photographed the butte in the direction I was interested in for an additional reference. You'll also notice I took the liberty to change the perspective and the placements of objects, being careful not to change the main focus of the butte which was the landmark of interest.

I refined the preliminary pencil just a tad in the studio and then rubbed charcoal over the back

The finished pencil sketch completed in the studio on illustration board.

so I could transfer my sketch to the surface of an illustration board, which I redrew for the inking.

I was so confident of the imagery I chose that I didn't even bother having the community association (the customer) critique the refined pencil sketch. I did have them review the finished inking. And when they did I inquired about the lettering necessary to complete the cover. At that time the only venue for me was press lettering, which I did on an acetate overlay.

I also inquired about the color of the paper to be used as that helped to tell me to what degree I should take the detail and shading. The paper color was to be a light olive green. That being the case I choose not to add an overbearing amount of texturing for I felt it would of ruined the finished effect. The small size of the cover (7" x 8.5") and the type of paper was another consideration not to over indulge the detail.

I was fortunate that the community association liked the piece because not all commissions go that smoothly. As you can see from the finished stage there was not a great deal of time in the finished inking part. Maybe two hours at most. So that might have been the subconscious reason I went ahead with the assignment without having the penciling critiqued. I believe that

I had the imagery I wanted in my mind all the time, (mainly because I had hiked all over the place). All I had to do was find the right spot that coincided with that visual thought and adjust it until it felt just right.

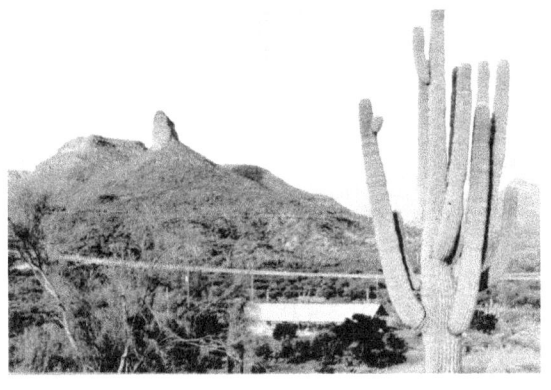

The photograph I used as a reference.

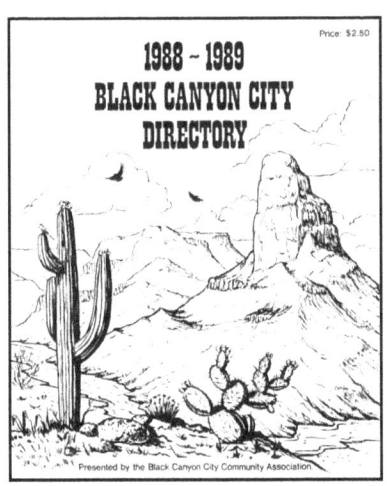

The cover complete with lettering.

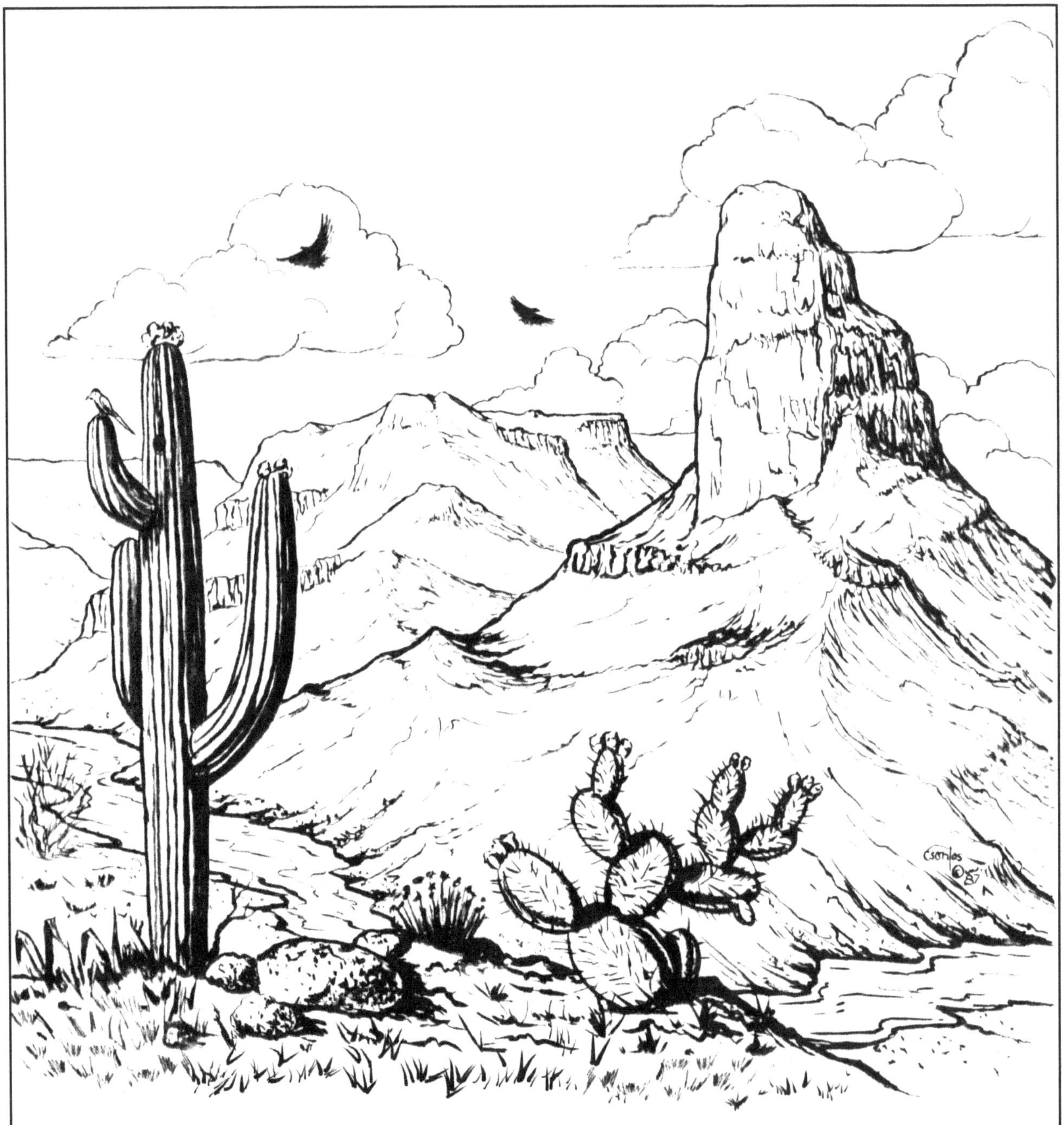

The completed inking done over the penciling on illustration board. Brush.

Samples of preconceived commercial projects.

Sometimes it is necessary to use photo references like the preceding sample because of the request. These next two pages are samples of illustrations that were partially visualized (without photos) before any drawing took place. They were all done in ink by hand with either pens or brush. They are also all assignments or commissions for commercial applications. All I needed was a few comments or suggestions from the customer. Once that happens I just pay attention to what imagery forms in my head. If the customer critiques it, then new images form.

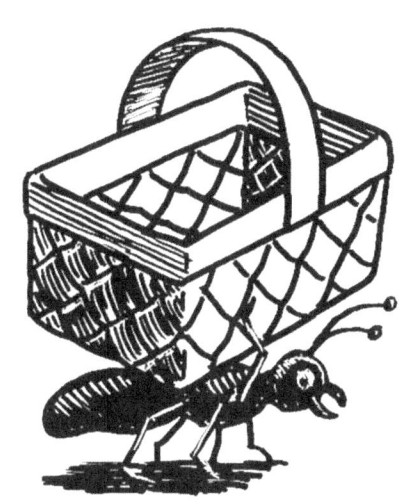

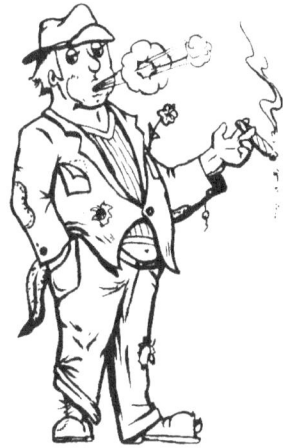

This inking was for a flyer advertising a picnic get together for some of the town folk. They were commenting on the fact that the ants won't be taking away your lunch at their particular event. Drawing pens

'Crazy Horse Feed & Tack'

The name of this business was all I needed to get the imagery going. I love having customers with a sense of humor. Drawing pen.

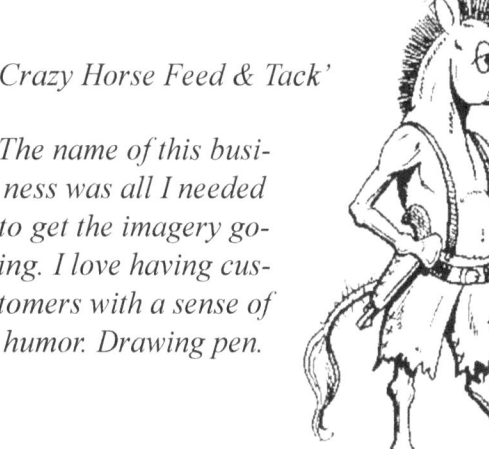

I'm not sure why this customer wanted an image of a bum. She had a delivery service, a real estate business, a landscaping materials business and numerous others. This bum was the logo image for all of them in different positions. Once she told me what she wanted I did one sketch and as it developed I added the flower, the puff of smoke and the hole in the shoe. Felt tip pen.

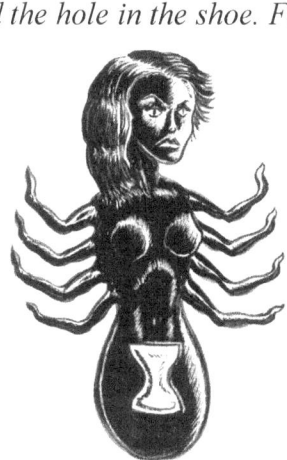

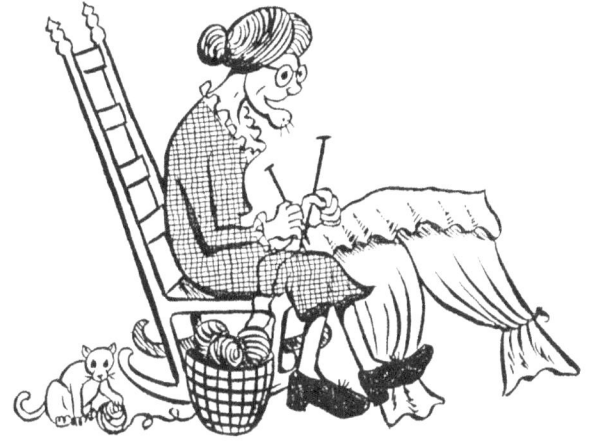

A humorous illustration for the local spider farm that bred spiders for anti-venom. The customer mentioned he was having marital problems. Brush.

This illustration was for 'Grandma's Window Shades'. An elderly lady that could make window shades from scratch. The cat was my idea because we have always had mischievous cats. Drawing pens.

19

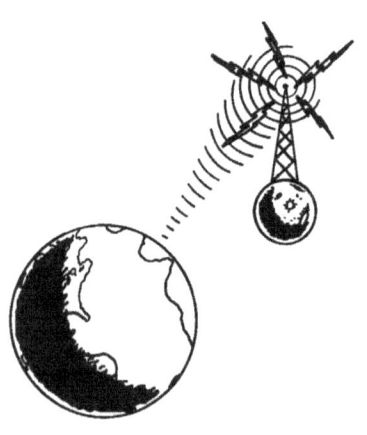

This is an image for a web site that tells of the future of communication on a moon colony. Drawing pen.

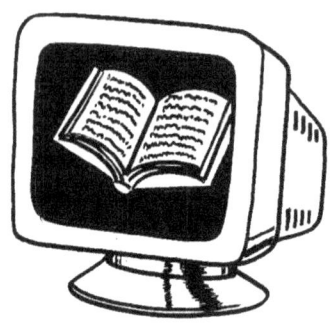

Another web image for reading e-books on line. Drawing pen.

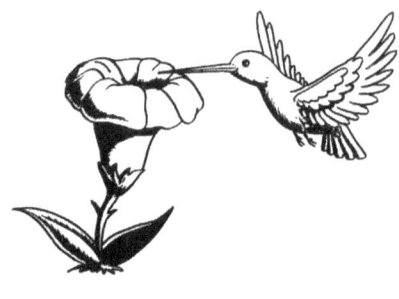

This image was for a seed sale for spring planting. Telling of the possibilities of visiting hummingbirds. Drawing pen.

Even though I enjoy the spontaneous type of personal artwork the best it is always nice to have the experience that comes from being able to do illustrations that are of a commercial nature. They teach me artistic discipline, they give me an opportunity to pay attention to what the customer needs and is trying to say, which is the main aspect of commercial visualizing, and I get the chance to use other media when the need arises. I believe it is my sense of humor that brings some of these customers to my studio especially when some of the projects are not even close to being serious.

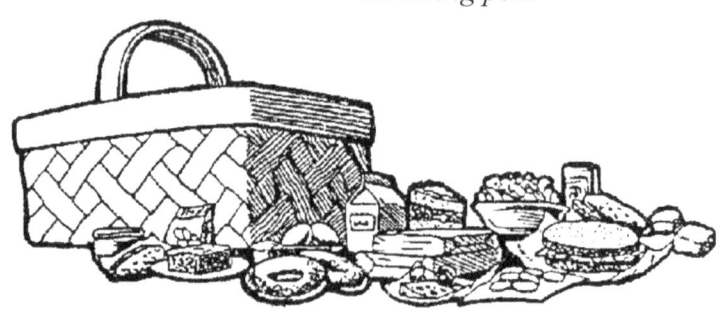

A picnic basket image for a brochure that advertised a new chuck wagon in an area that was mostly manufacturing. The customer suggested the imagery. About six years after I did this drawing I came across similar looking clip art. I am sometimes amazed at the number of assignments I get considering the millions of clip art on the market. Drawing pens.

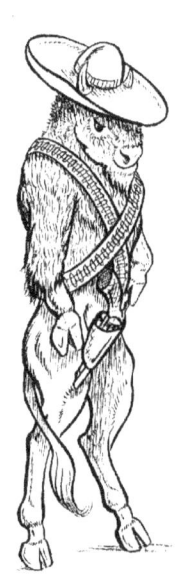

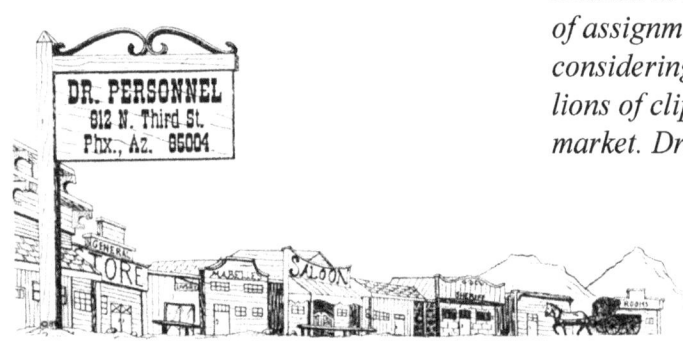

This is an envelope illustration for a business that placed medical personnel. I also did the letterhead and business card with the same look. The customer asked me if I could draw an old west town. That's all he had to say. Each one was different. Drawing pens.

This buffalo desperado image was created for a restaurant owner who had a pet buffalo. It was to advertise the house brand of salsa. The comment was, 'Can you make him look like a bandito?' I also used his buffalo on the front of their menu. I had to go through several sketches as no one knew his buffalo as well as he did. There are also several t-shirt designs with buffaloes later in this book. Felt tip pens.

Preconceived commercial projects that utilize perspectives.

Perspectives are used quite a bit when it comes to images that are renditions of man made objects, such as furniture, buildings, city scenes, architectural renderings and the like. I have done so many furniture illustrations (literally hundreds) that I felt it necessary to build a perspective drawing table attachment.

The first one was a board about one foot high and four feet wide. I just laid it on the regular table and drilled some small holes at the left and right outside edges. These holes were spaced equally so that any two (a left and a right) were on the same horizon line. I could then place the paper (almost always 8½" x 11") anywhere on that board. I then placed a pin (I used a pop rivet) in the corresponding left and right holes. I was then able to use a straight edge (I drilled a

hole in a corner of a metal yardstick) and placed it over either the left or right pin, keeping the hole up, to give me the lines necessary to draw the object in perspective. If I sketched enough lines then I could also sketch the object properly. Considering where the perspective points would be was the main thing to take into account for the placement of the paper. I had to be able to do various layouts with a variety of positions.

After the first hundred drawings I felt the table could be revised. My next perspective board was basically the same, just larger. It was 72" long and 18" high. Same holes as the first one only I added several columns of holes spaced about four inches in from each column. Sometimes I would vary the layouts so much that I had the paper over one of the holes and I would end up poking through the paper with the pencil if I wasn't careful. Even though this second version proved useful for the next hundred draw-

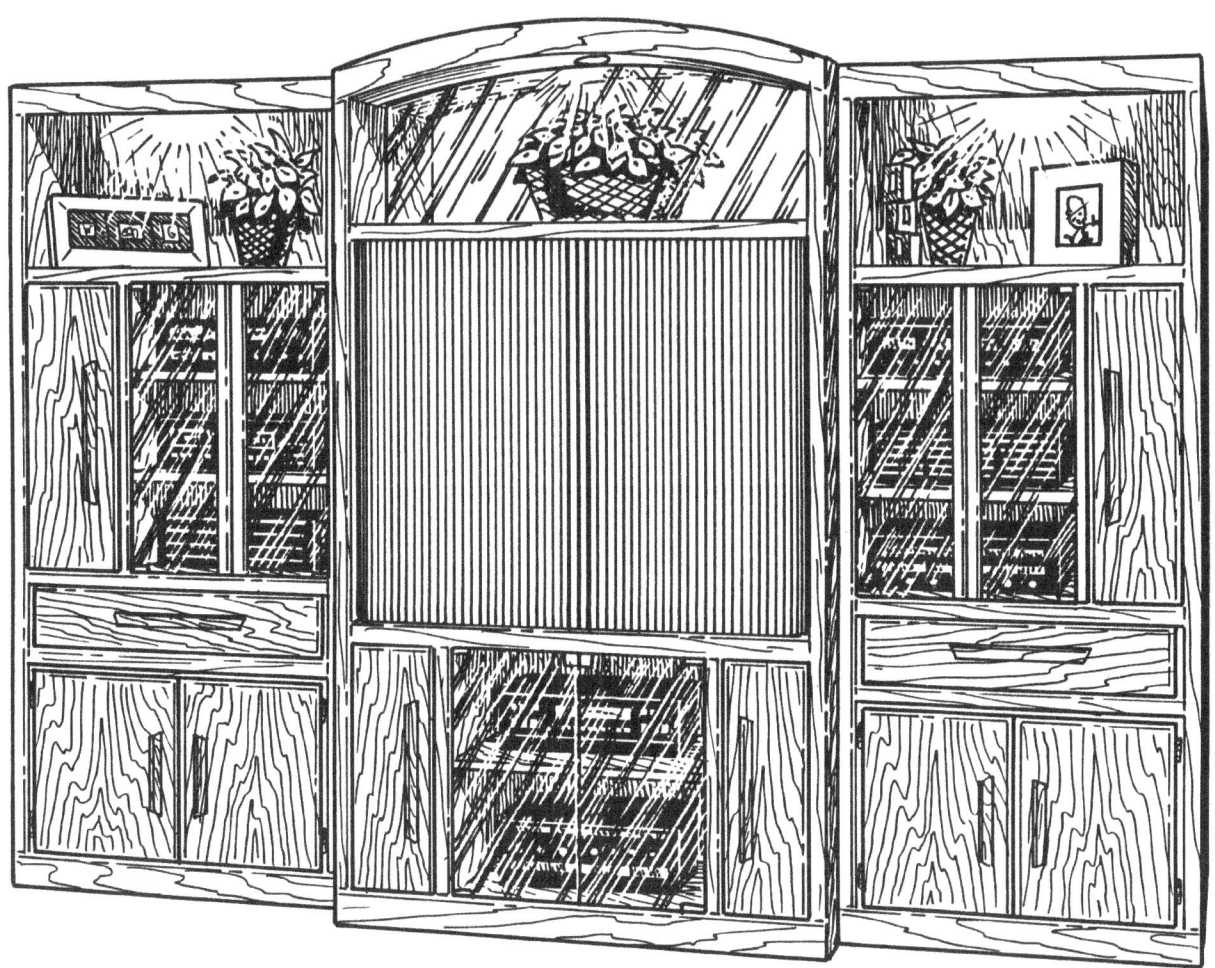

A two point perspective with the image placed closer to the right side pin. If you look at the right side of the image you will see that it is almost on top of the area of where the pin would be. Pen.

ings it was limited because I could not use my sliding parallel blade. I did not need it for two point perspectives but it was handy for single or center point perspectives and for setting my triangle on for the vertical lines.

So I decided to do a third version and I might have went over board with the last version. I completely rebuilt the drawing table from scratch using oak. The top is 36" x 44" and it adjusts from perfectly flat to 85°, which is almost vertical. This time for the perspective guide I got an aluminum one inch square tube that was six feet long. I fastened this tube to the underside of the top on the ledger bars and made sure it was perfectly in line with the sliding parallel blade. I added sections of wood to the exposed part of the tube to be flush with the surface of the top. Then I drilled a series of holes again for the pop rivet locating pins. I then used an aluminum 'T' stock, 48" long with a small hole in each corner of the same side

which fits over the pins and is my straight edge for ruling perspective lines. The 'T' shape was easier to grab. Now I had a full sized, adjustable, clean smooth surface, a new parallel blade, and a perspective guide that could be used for any application.

Now to the visualizing aspect. If I ever needed to be using my mind's eye it was for these furniture illustrations. All I was given was a Polaroid snap shot and the overall dimensions. The drawings were to be used for newspaper ads and black and white catalogs for distributors. After I would do a rough initial sketch, I could position the paper where I felt it would match up to corresponding points then set up vertical and horizontal scaled guides for the dimensions.

The *visualizing* extremes I went through for the final drawing table and perspective guide should give you an idea of how many of these furniture illustrations I did over the years.

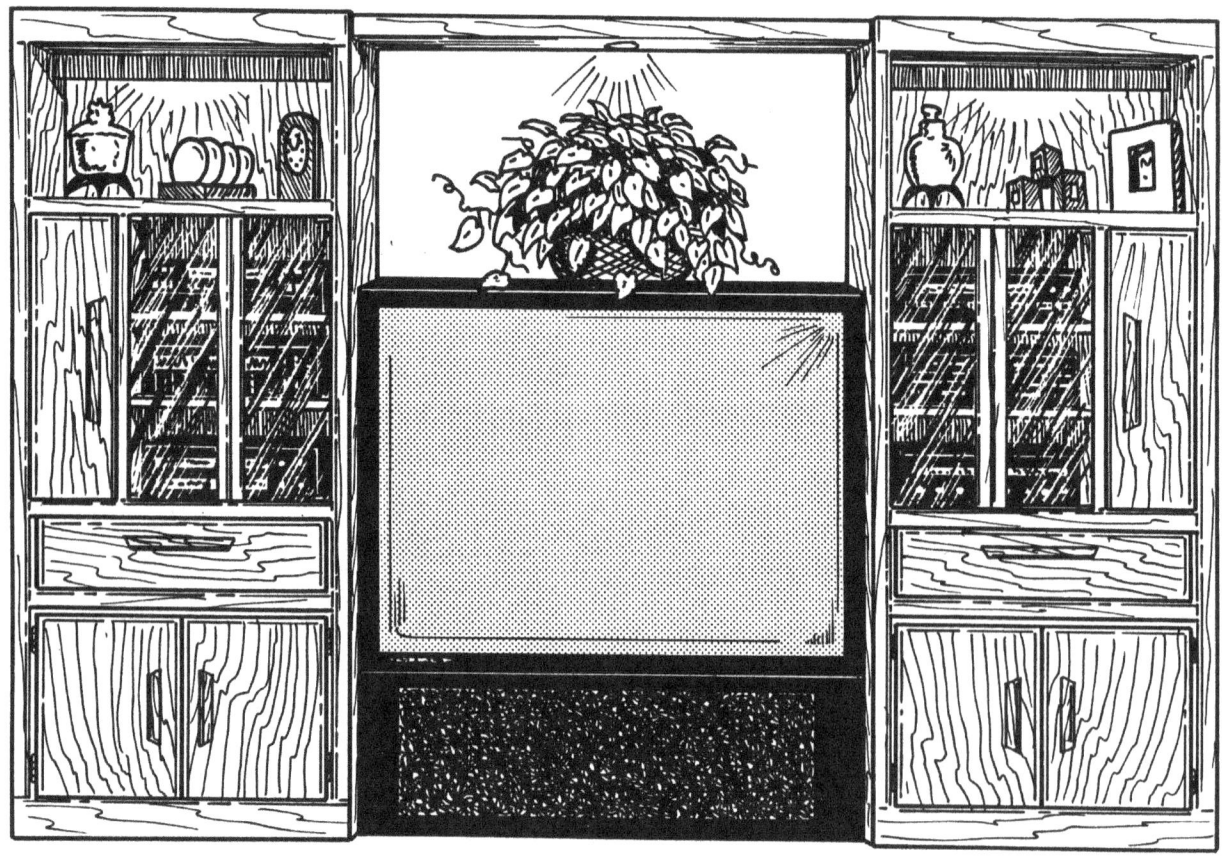

This is a version of a single or center point perspective which is in the center of the image about three quarters of the way up. I almost always tried to put the perspective points on eye level (about five and a half feet) whether it was for a center point perspective or for a two point perspective. Pen, brush and transfer screen.

Visualizing with pencil and ink. Spontaneous technique number two.

Sometimes it is easy to see what will come from the initial spontaneous sketch. I had only just started this doodling when the squiggle lines in the center brought the image in my mind of a serpent's comb down the center of its back. I'm not sure why that image popped into my head but it was so instant that I had to go with it. That also happens sometimes when I start a painting. I will sometimes not want to do the initial image that comes to mind so I will start over, only to have the same image appear again in the second sketch. That has happened to me three times in a row once when I was doing a painting. It was weird.

The initial pencil doodling.

After I got the penciling to the point of where I knew how to proceed with ink, I attached a coated sheet of paper over the penciling. I used a drawing pen to then outline the entire image in with the layers in proper order. I then did all the scales with the same pen, which was easier to hold then holding a brush to a point for that amount of lines. Once that was done I switched to a brush for all the shadows, the heavier lines, and the depth effect for some of the scales that are opposite of an imaginary upper right light source. As I proceed with ink, I will basically just keep rendering until it is obvious that I should stop before it gets too overdone.

I chose to do the egg in a type of pointillism with both the pen and the brush. I figured I was already cross eyed from doing the scales so what the heck. Some people call that therapy.

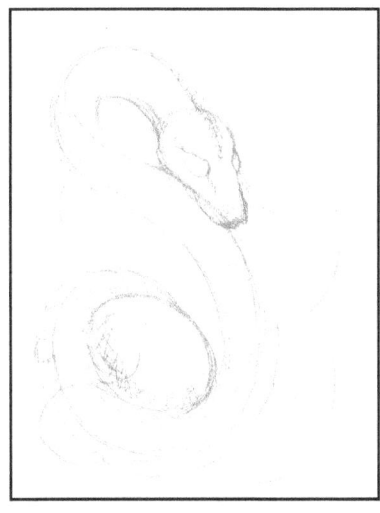

The second phase where I saw the image in the sketch and began the development.

This image has very little background (almost none). I believe that is why my unconscious continued with the amount of detail in the scales. If I had included a background then the entire piece would of been too busy or confusing. The main image fills the picture plane anyhow.

In the samples following this technique I show a similar piece that has no background as well. After the drawing was copied and used what it was for, I added a background for my own interest.

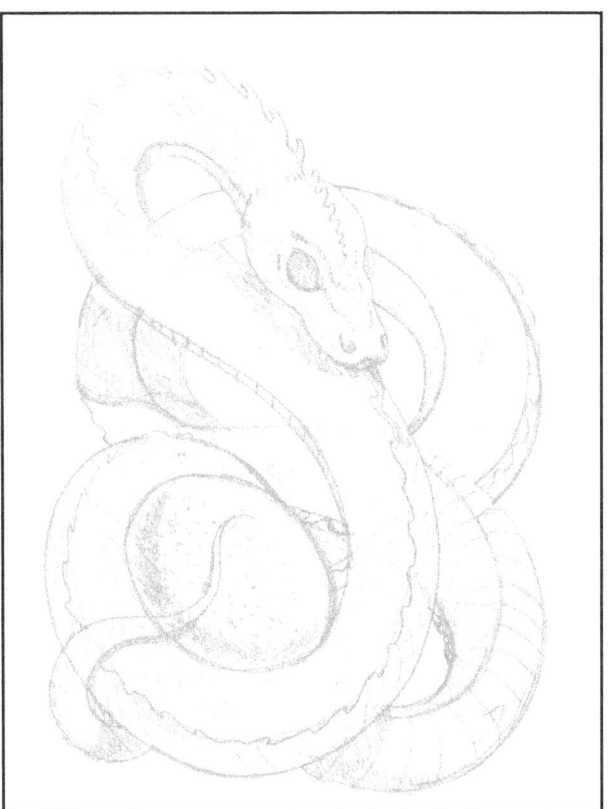

The third phase with the pencil sketch brought to a reasonable finish.

23

"Mother"

The finished inking complete with detail and shading.
Pen and brush.

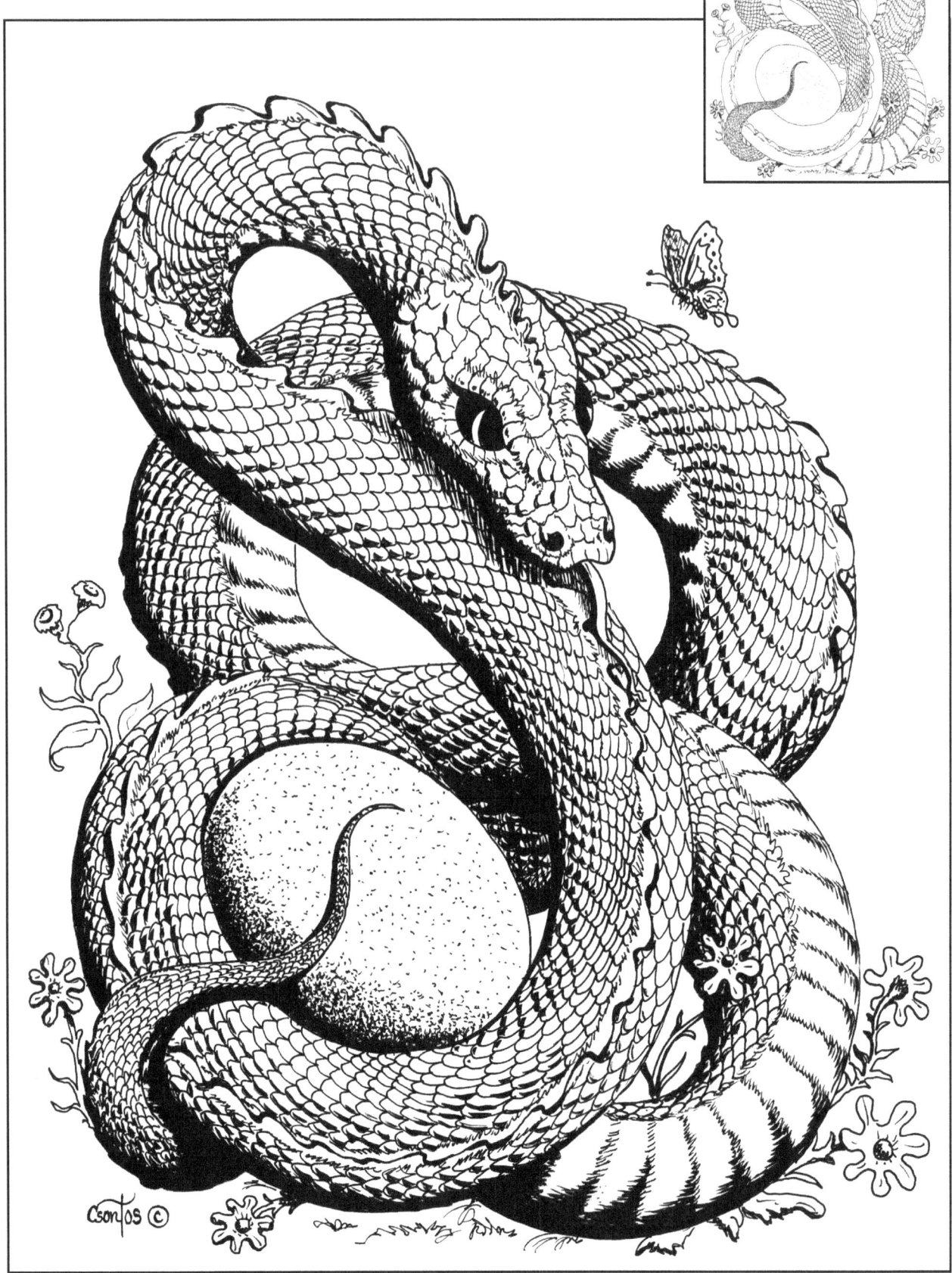

csontos ©

More spontaneous illustration samples with limited backgrounds.

These samples are similar to the preceding one to give you an idea of my approach with limited backgrounds. An exception is the last image on page 29 and 30, which is shown with and without a background. All these images are finished in ink. The first six are also studies in ink techniques.

I decided not to show the original sketches because if you squint at the finished works you can usually get the idea of what the sketch looked like. Besides, the imagery that I come up with will be entirely different then what you may come up with.

The key is to not picture anything at first. Just relax and let the pencil do its thing. It will seem like the image just magically appears in the doodling. If you try to force an image it just doesn't seem to work. Just let it flow. If it doesn't, then start over.

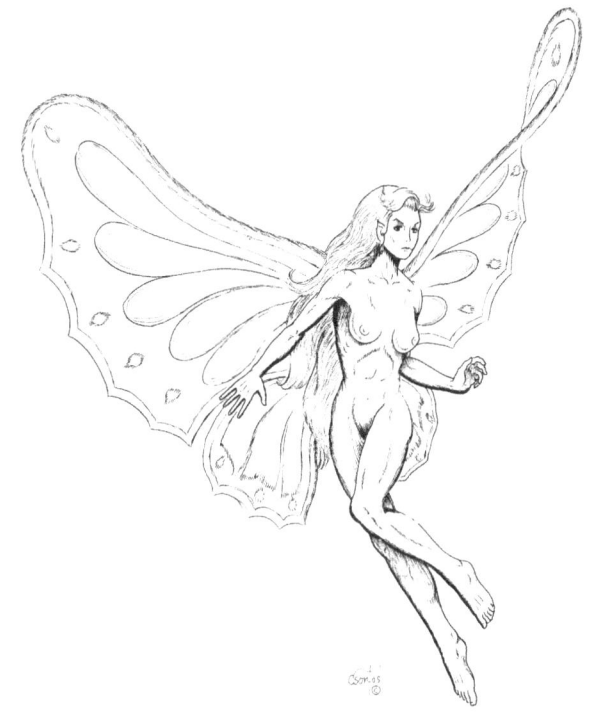

"Fairy"
Drawing pen.

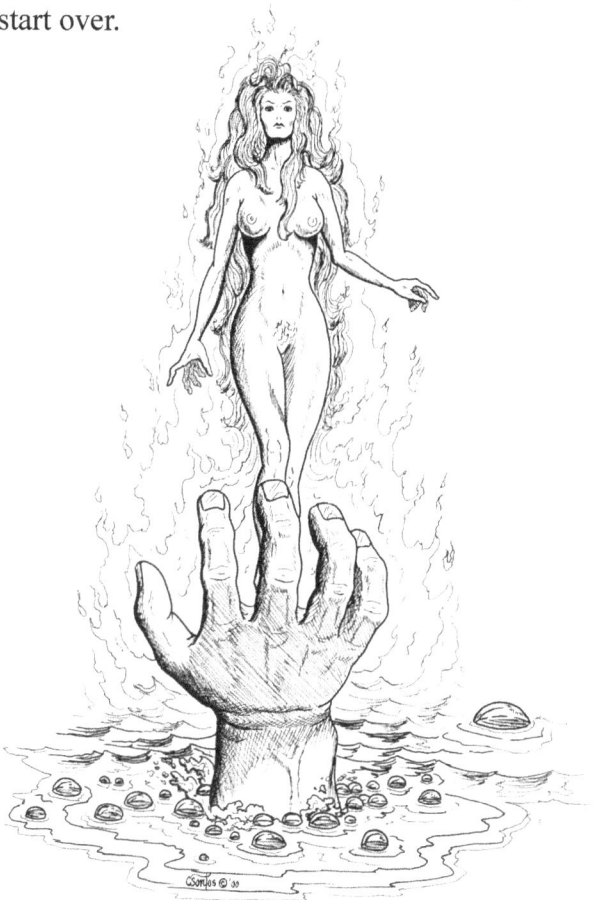

"Lady of the Lake"
Drawing pens.

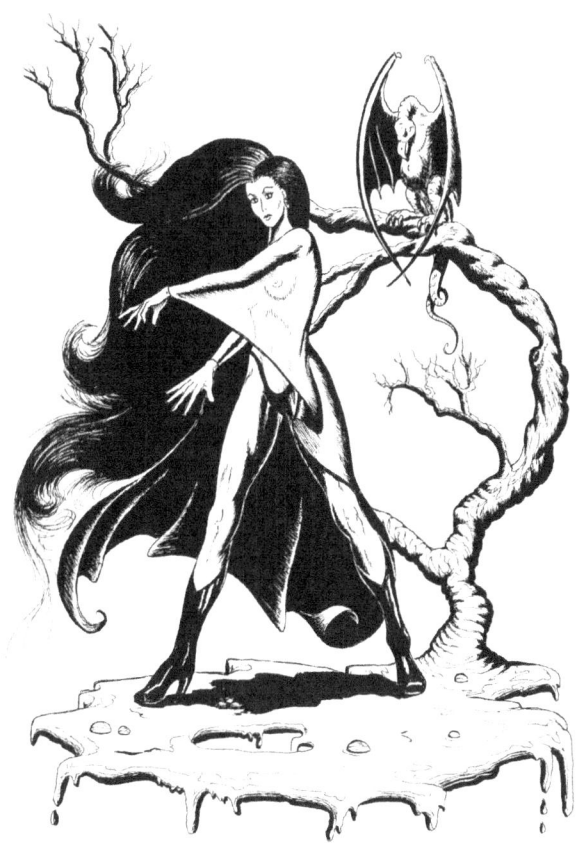

"Keeper of Spells"
Brush.

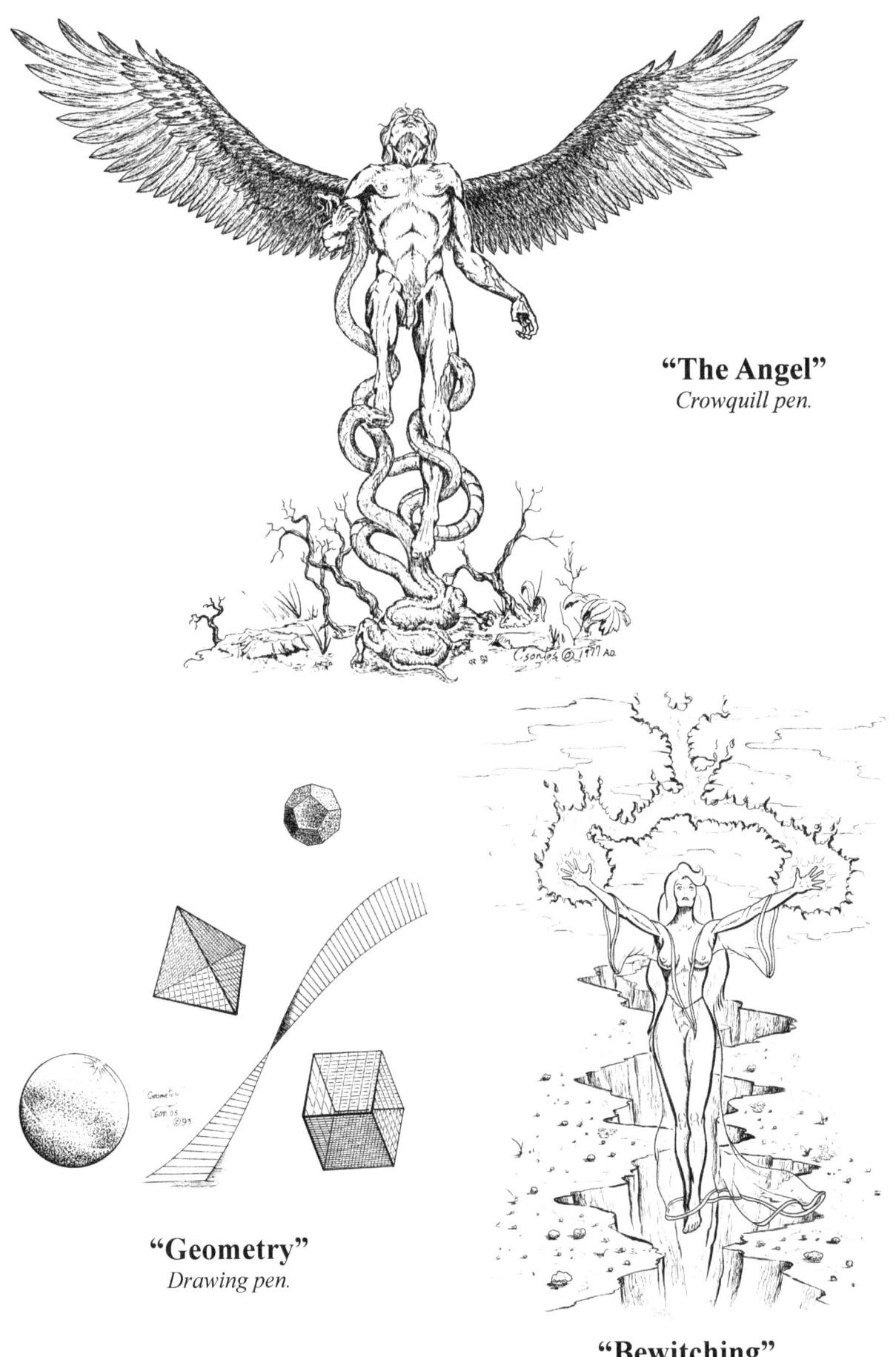

"The Angel"
Crowquill pen.

"Geometry"
Drawing pen.

"Bewitching"
Brush.

26

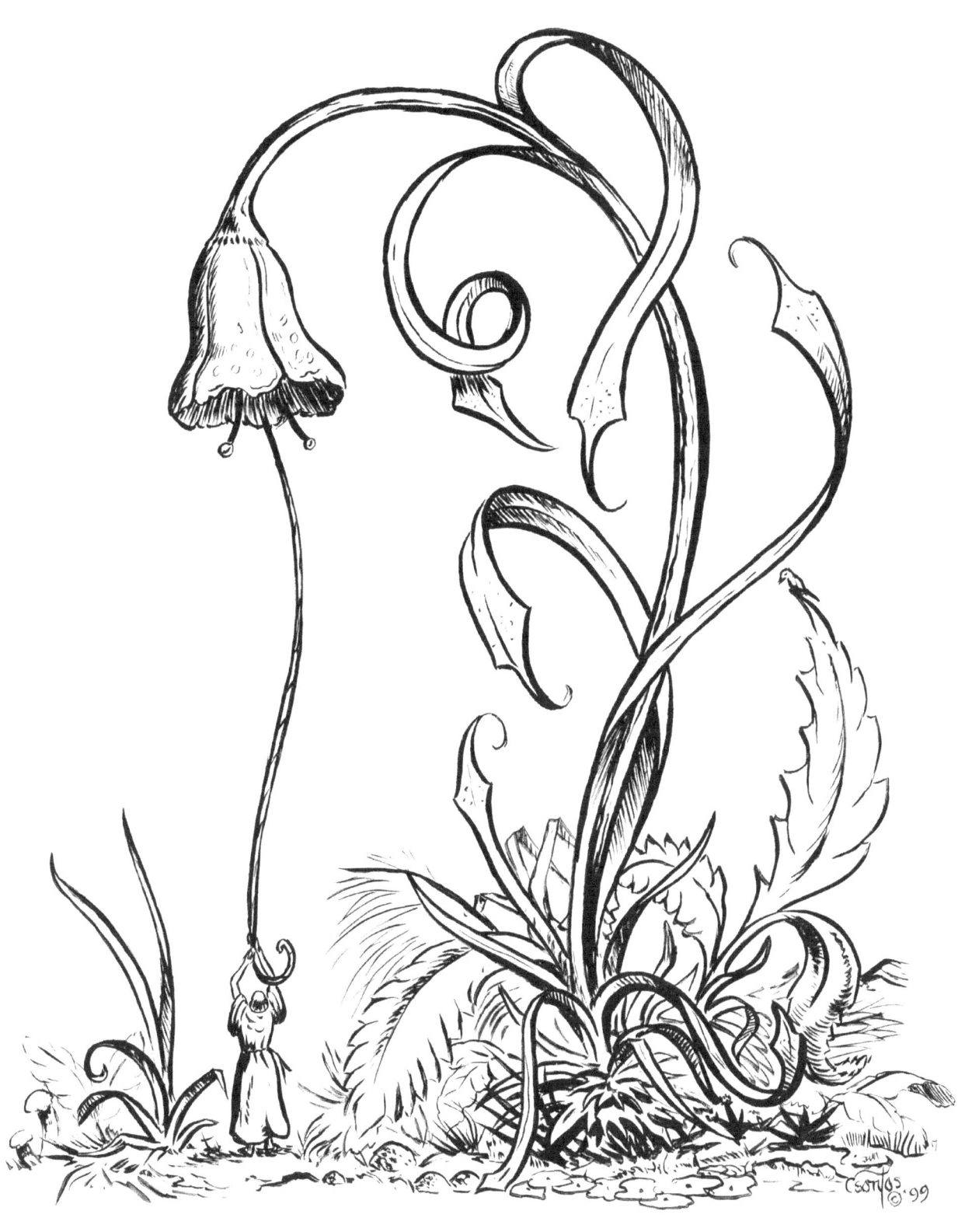

"The Bell Tower"

I believe images like this come from my hobby of photographing plants close up at the ground level.
Brush.

27

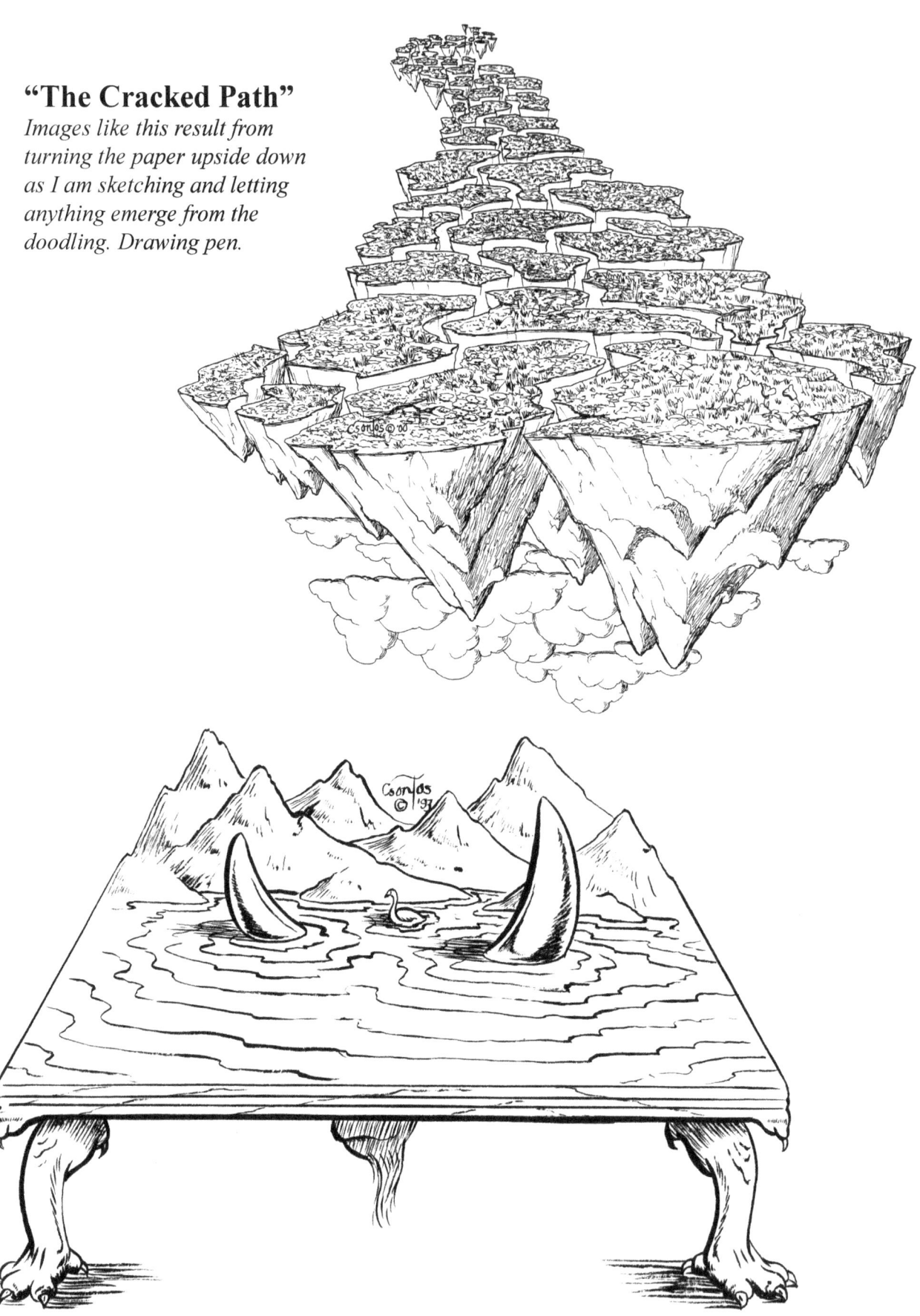

"The Cracked Path"

Images like this result from turning the paper upside down as I am sketching and letting anything emerge from the doodling. Drawing pen.

"Medieval Table"

This is most likely the result of my other hobby of occasionally making furniture. A psychologist would probably have a field day with what goes on inside my head. Brush.

28

I went into this camera store to pick up my prints. The owner having seen some of my images in the photos asked me to do a drawing to deter shoplifting. He said, "Anything you want. I like your style." I came up with the drawing directly below. Not sure why or how it came about. No one mentioned any dragons. I added the lettering on an acetate overlay and made several copies for his store.

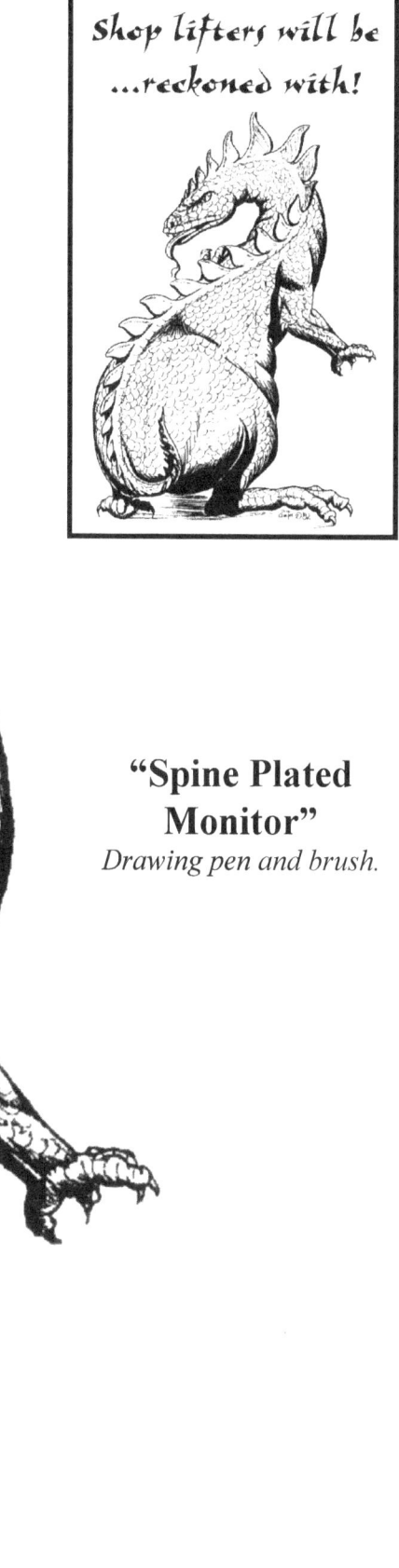

"Spine Plated Monitor"
Drawing pen and brush.

When I finished putting the copies into frames
for the store owner, I took the original and re-
made it to create the background below.
Ink - pen and brush on illustration board.

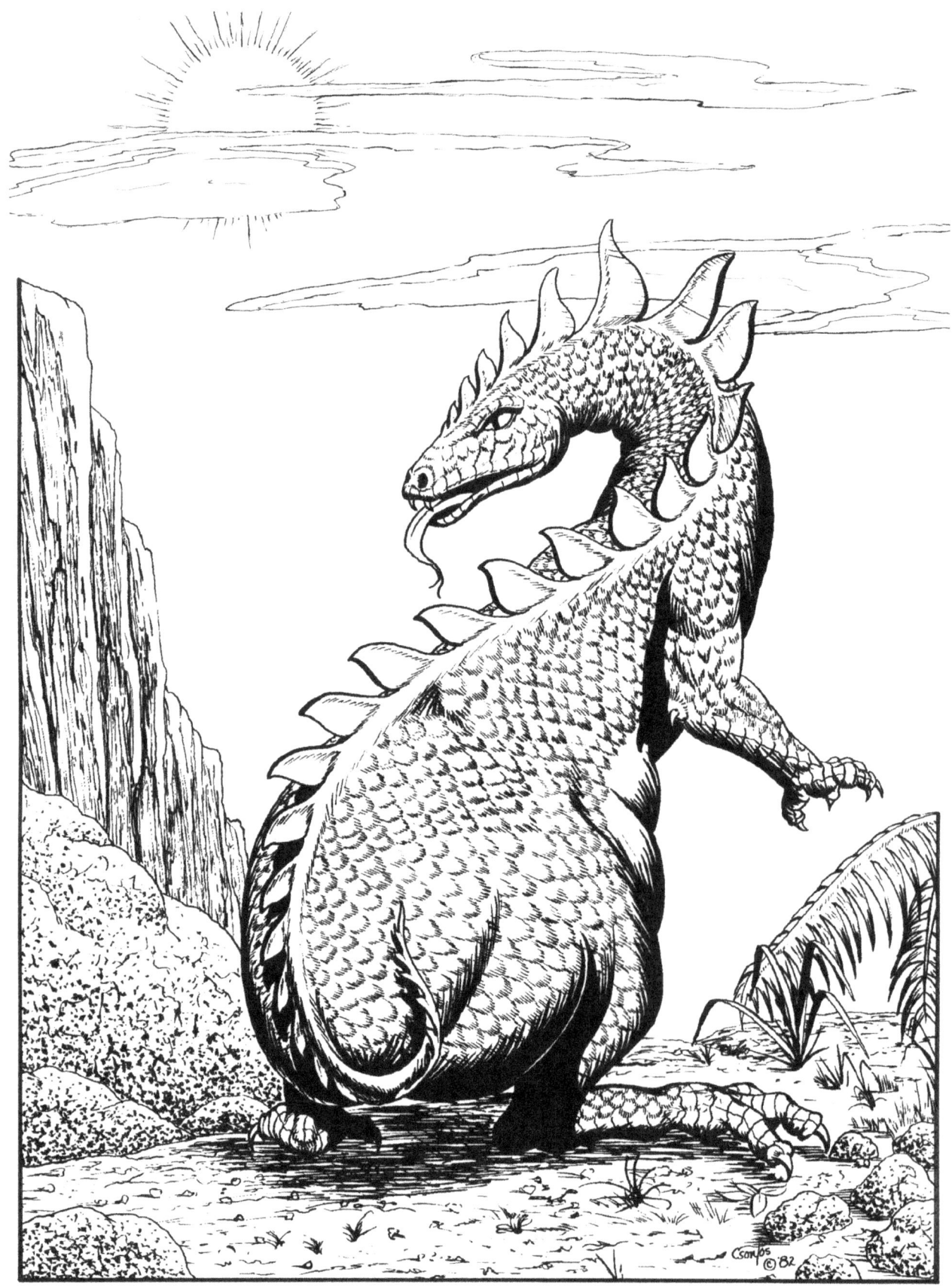

Visualizing black and white t-shirt designs and themes.

I have to admit that these types of projects do not seem like real work. My only regret is that I did not get copies or some facsimile of a reproduction of all the t-shirts I have done. Sometimes the jobs came in and went back out in as little as 24 hours. I always seem to get those deadline jobs.

The ideas for these particular t-shirts came from the restaurant owner, his wife, myself and a few other restaurant regulars brain storming about ideas. All of the concepts for the shirts had to be centered around a buffalo theme because they had their own pet buffaloes. All the ideas came before any sketching. The visualizing was already done

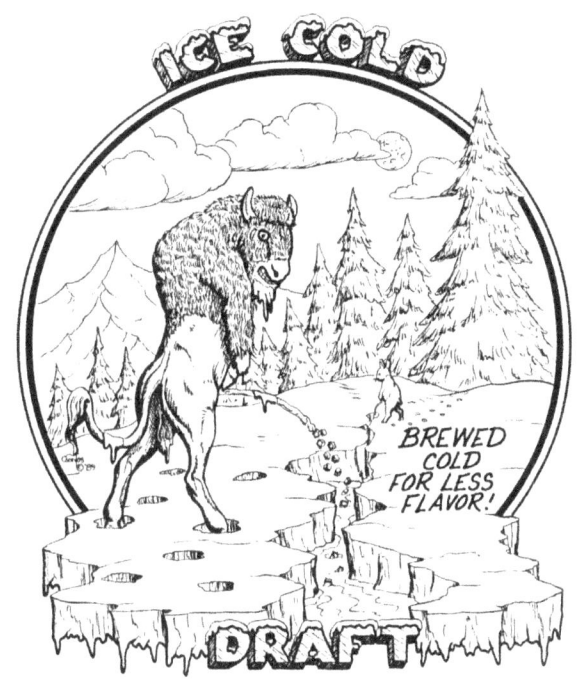

Ink - pen and brush.

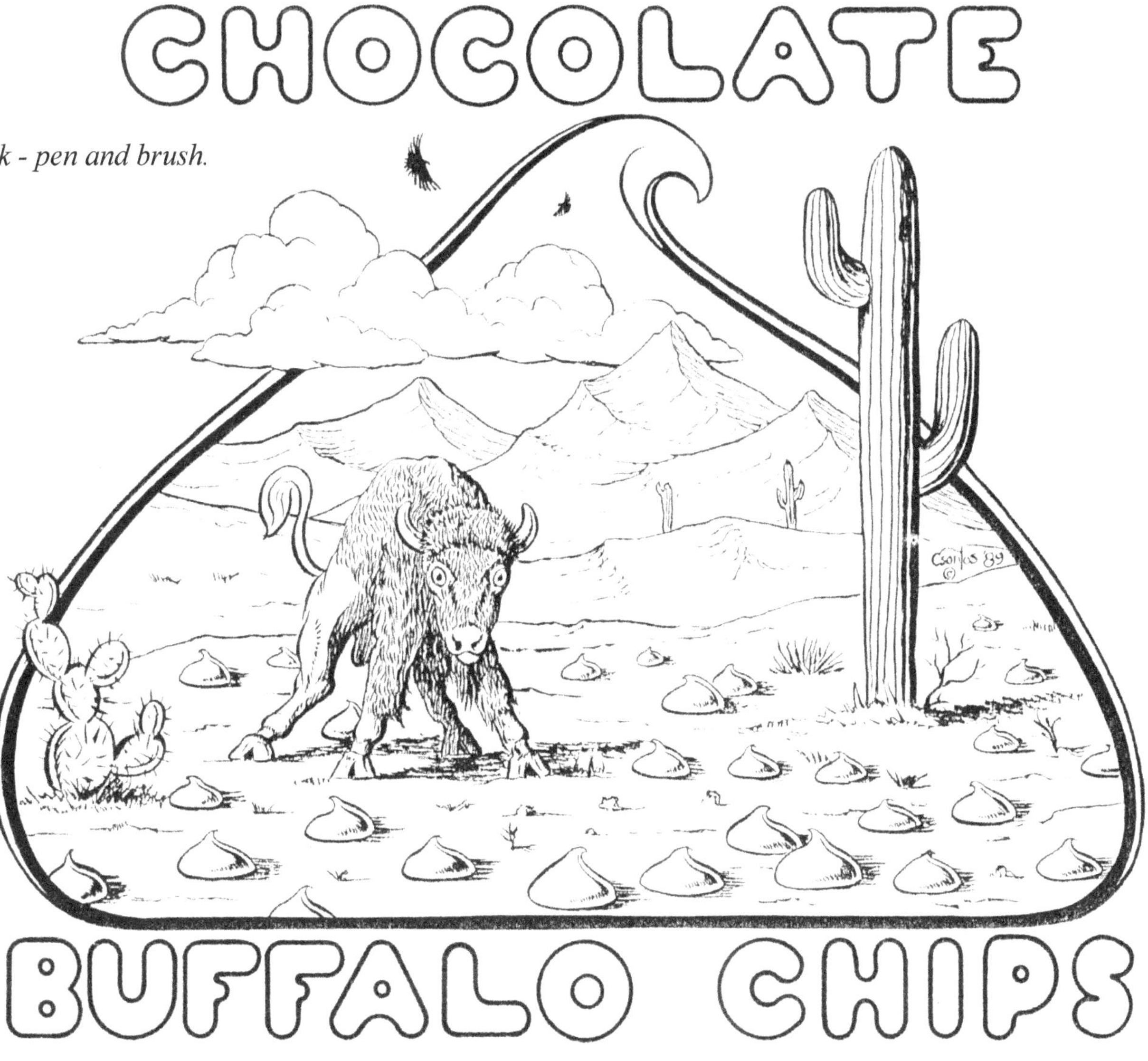

Ink - pen and brush.

31

so now all I had to do was bring the drawn image to the level of the mental image. None of the t-shirt designs had to be critiqued. The idea for the shirts came about after I had finally mastered the anatomy of the main buffalo for the menu cover which I show last in this section.

The challenge behind these layouts was not really the idea but the characterizations of one or more buffaloes. Once I had the anatomy down for the main male buffalo (his name was Teddy) it was just a matter of morphing the animal anatomy to mimic either other animals or humans. I also had to position the pose of the buffaloes to coincide with the comment on the illustration.

All these illustrations were done on illustration board. I did not overstate the contrast or

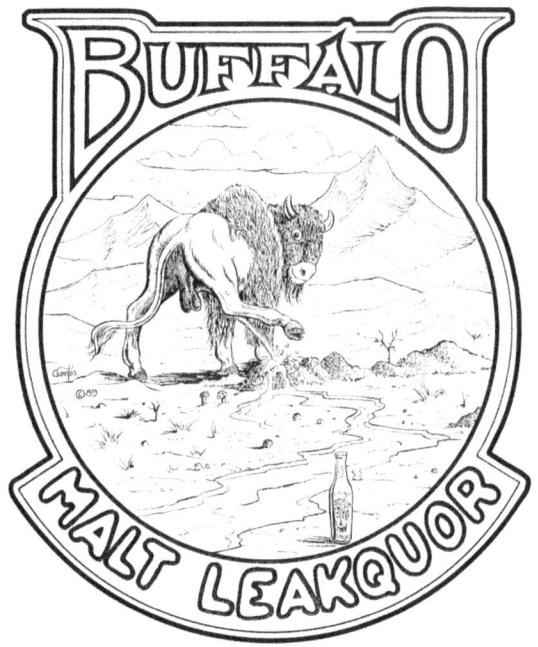

Ink - pen and brush.

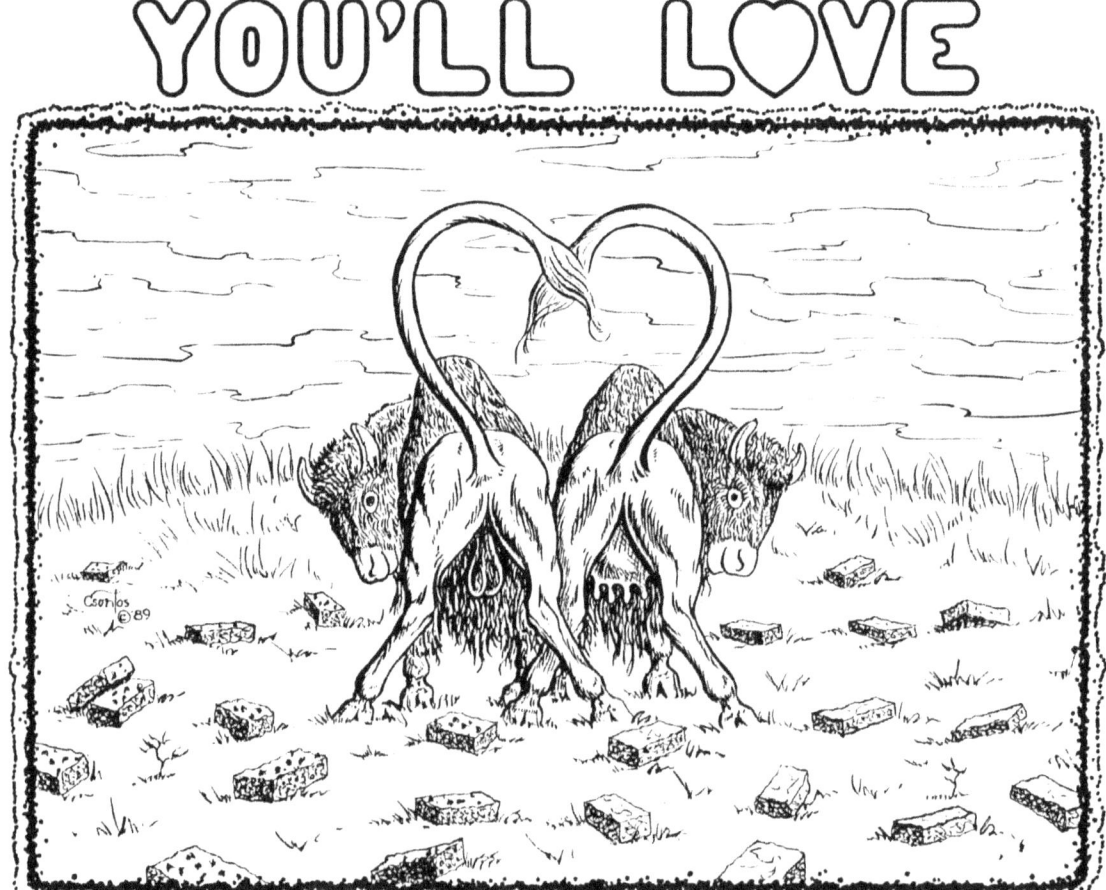

Ink - pen and brush.

get heavy on the shadow sides because there was talk of adding color at the silk screen shop. If I was footing the bill for these designs I would have left them as only black and white and deepened the contrast or continued with more rendering for screen printing on white t-shirts.

The only drawback to using illustration board is that if I mess up with the ink I have to use a type of white-out that will be easy to go over with the ink corrections. I have tried them all and the ones that specify being opaque watercolors seem to be acceptable. White acrylic paint also works well but not when using crowquill pens.

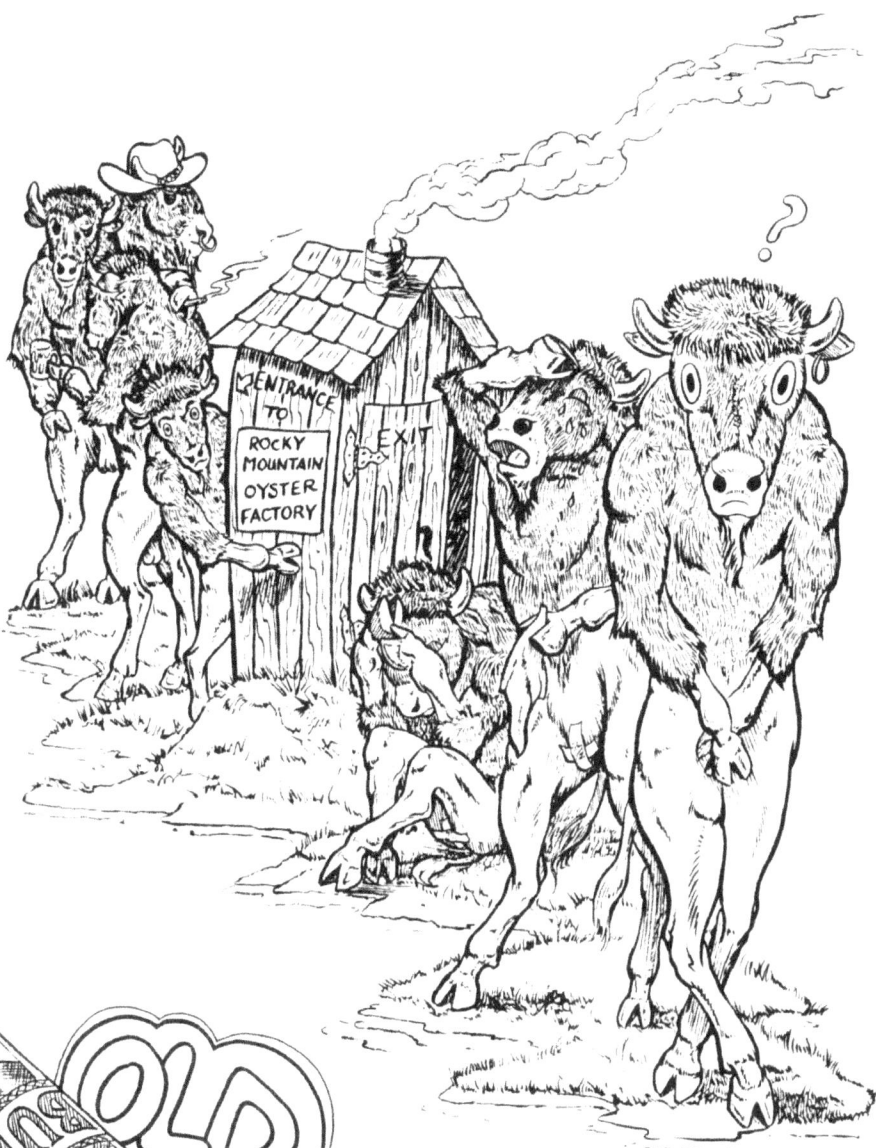

Ink - brush.

THE GOOD OLD BOYS

And DAMN PROUD OF IT!

This was a t-shirt design for a rowdy bunch of fellows that loved to drink, party and gamble. They did not have any plans to add color so as you can see I did add more contrast and rendering then I did for the buffalo ideas.
Ink - pen and brush.

33

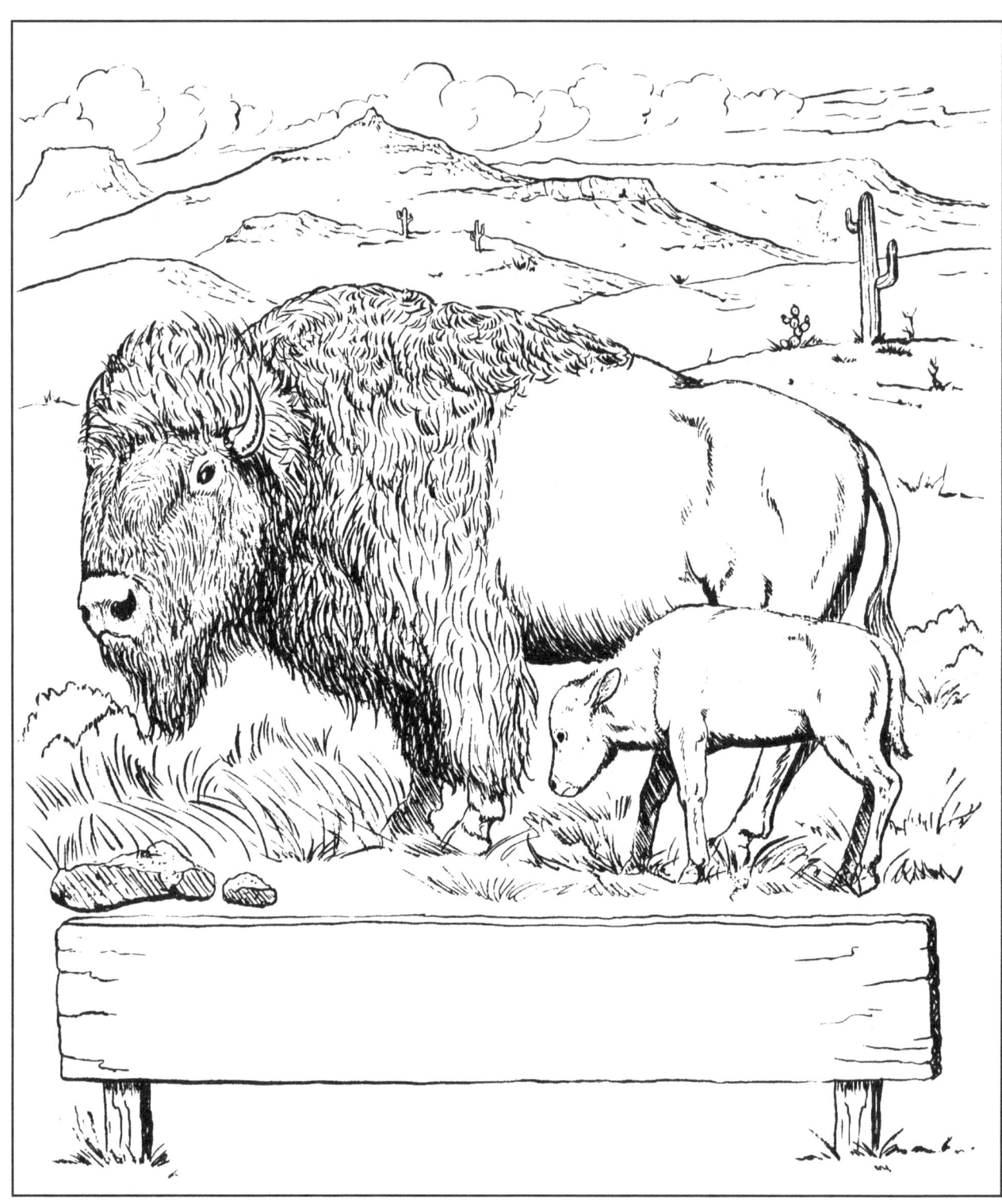

This is Teddy and his son on the cover of the menu. Believe me the scale of his head in relation to his body is no exaggeration. The restaurant owner said I finally got it perfect after numerous attempts. Even though I took photographs, I just couldn't believe the size of his head. To give you an idea of how big Teddy was: When his girlfriend was giving birth to twins the veterinarian wanted to help her out as she was having problems but Teddy would not let anyone in the corral area. They shot him twice with tranquilizing darts so the vet could get in there. The darts had no effect and they did not want to use a third dart. One of the twins died as a result. I am sure the though I had in my mind as I drew Teddy was, 'Do **not** mess with me'. Ink - brush.

Visualizing book illustrations in black and white.

These book illustrations (for the science fiction novel "One Sided Doors") had to coincide with the descriptions in the text exactly. As I sketched the ideas for each character or situation I could see in my mind how it would look finished with ink. So when I had each penciling ready to ink I would scan the pencil work and send it by email to the author. Unfortunately the author did not realize that inking would accent the illustrations. I did not care to ink every illustration before having him critique them as that would be numerous redundant work on my part if he objected to any of the sketches.

The author actually did find fault with a few but considering there was sixteen of them it was not all that bad. I also had a problem with the scanned pencil images. Pencil does not scan perfectly well (especially sketching). The scanner sees all the faint lines as well as the darker ones but it shows them up as all faint lines. So when you adjust the contrast to show the darker control lines the faint sketching lines darken up as well. Sometimes the adjusted scans looked like sloppy inked sketches. We ended up having lunch together every time I had a few of them penciled out to solve the email communication problem.

I kept all the illustrations on a vertical format so they were consistent with the book layout and page size.

I started to realize this was one of the harder projects I've done. Probably because the author has a mental image of exactly how his characters look whether or not he specifies all the

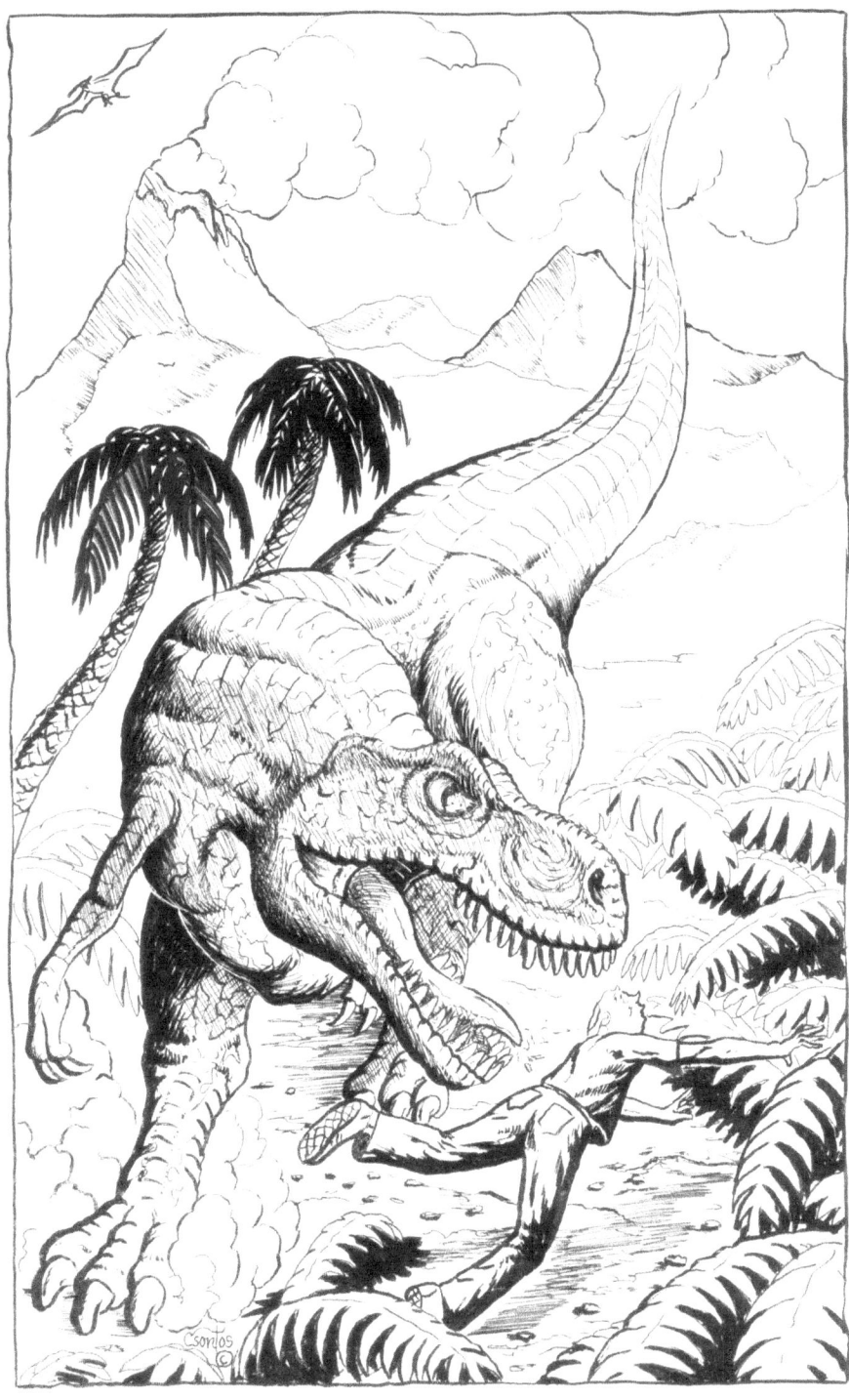

Tom, the story's hero, gives a tyrannosaurus rex a lesson in the laws of physics, as he dodges to the right to avoid the giant lizard's lunge. Brush.

attributes in the text. The artist on the other hand starts to build up a mental image of his own as to the way he sees the characters. These different interpretations are most likely the result of stylized writing. In other words, the author's visualizing was different from mine because he originally created the images.

Sool, the scary dominator medicine man with bad intentions. Brush.

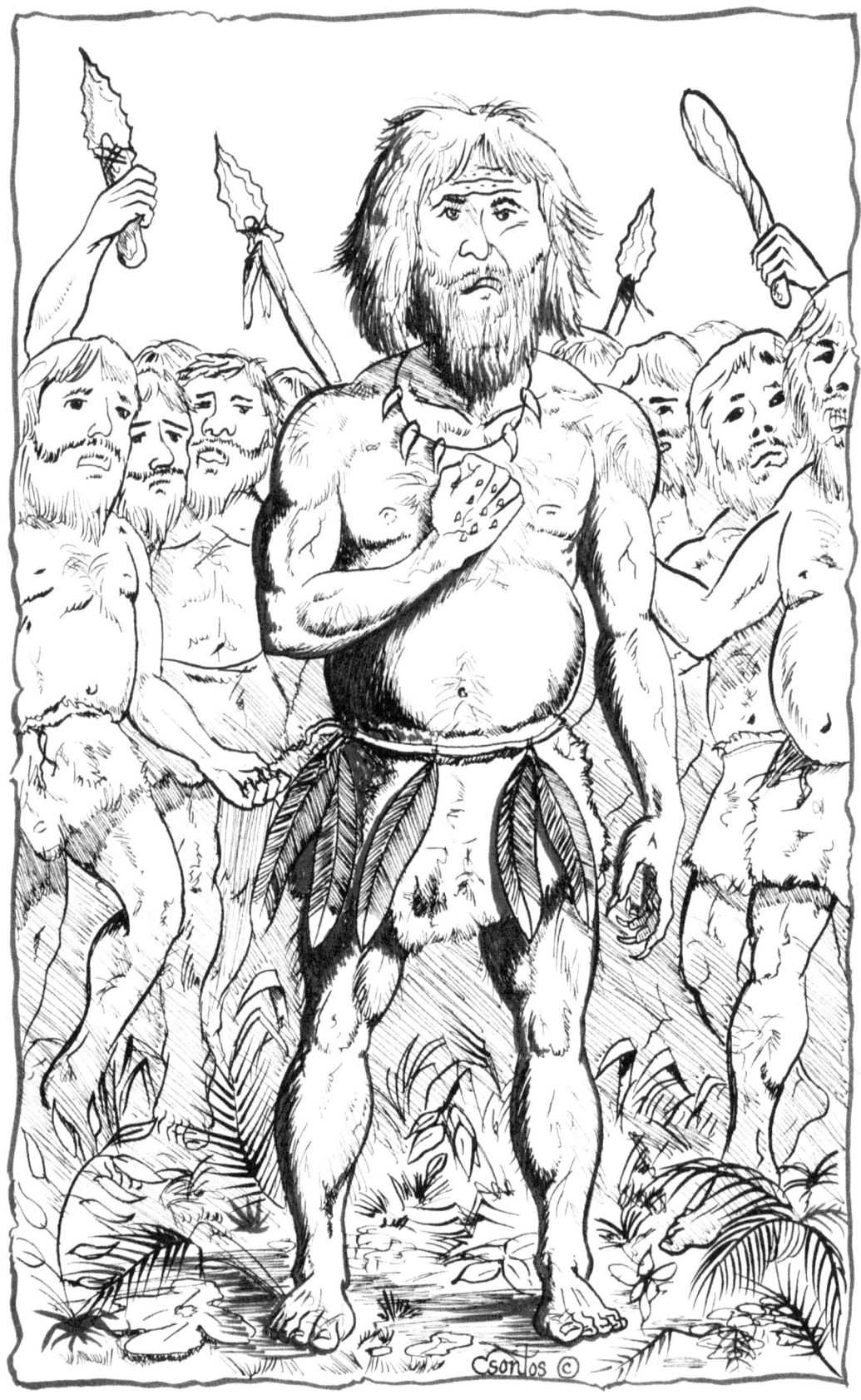

36

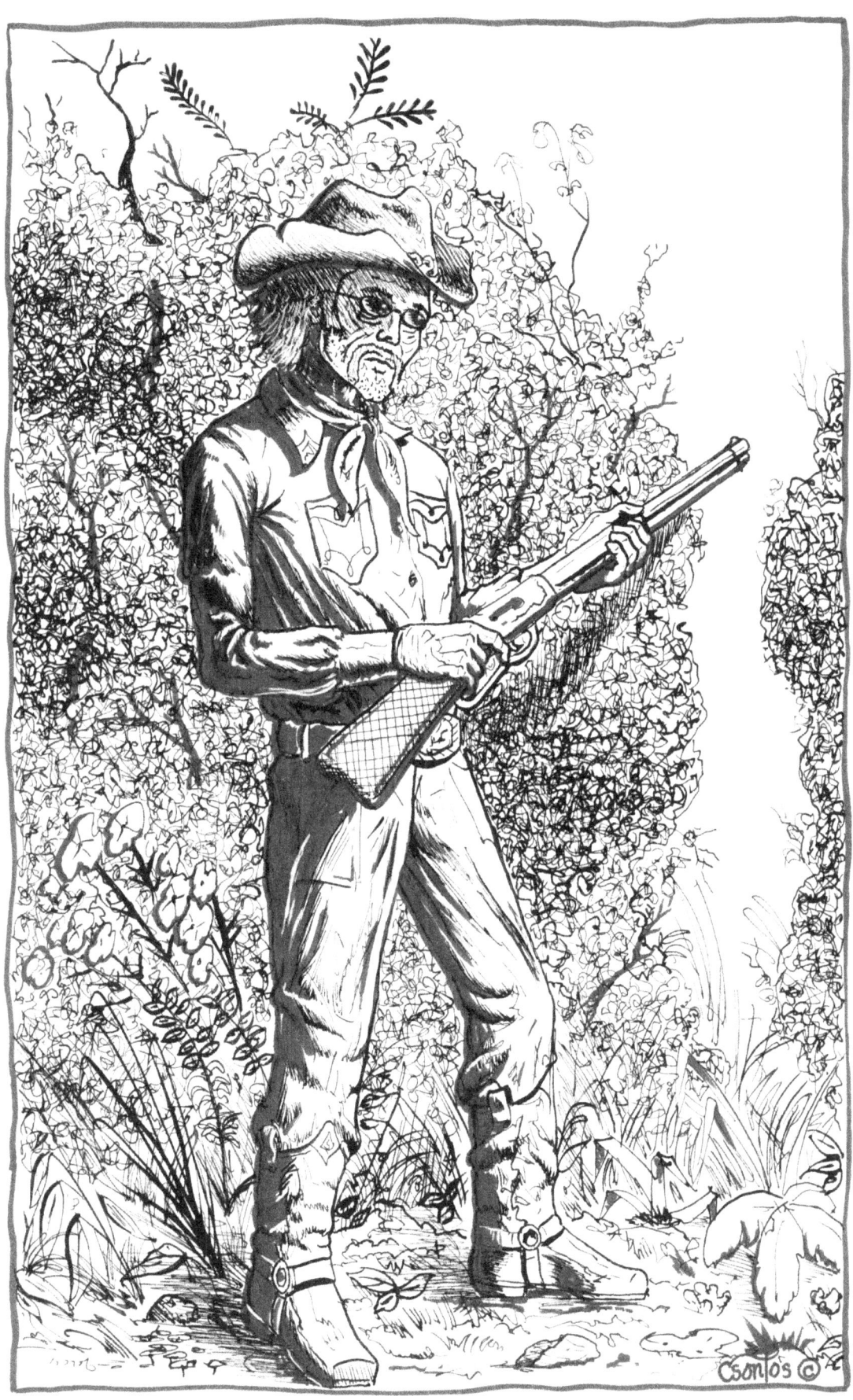

Jake, the gentleman cowboy who is just a little leery of the gov'ment. Pen and brush.

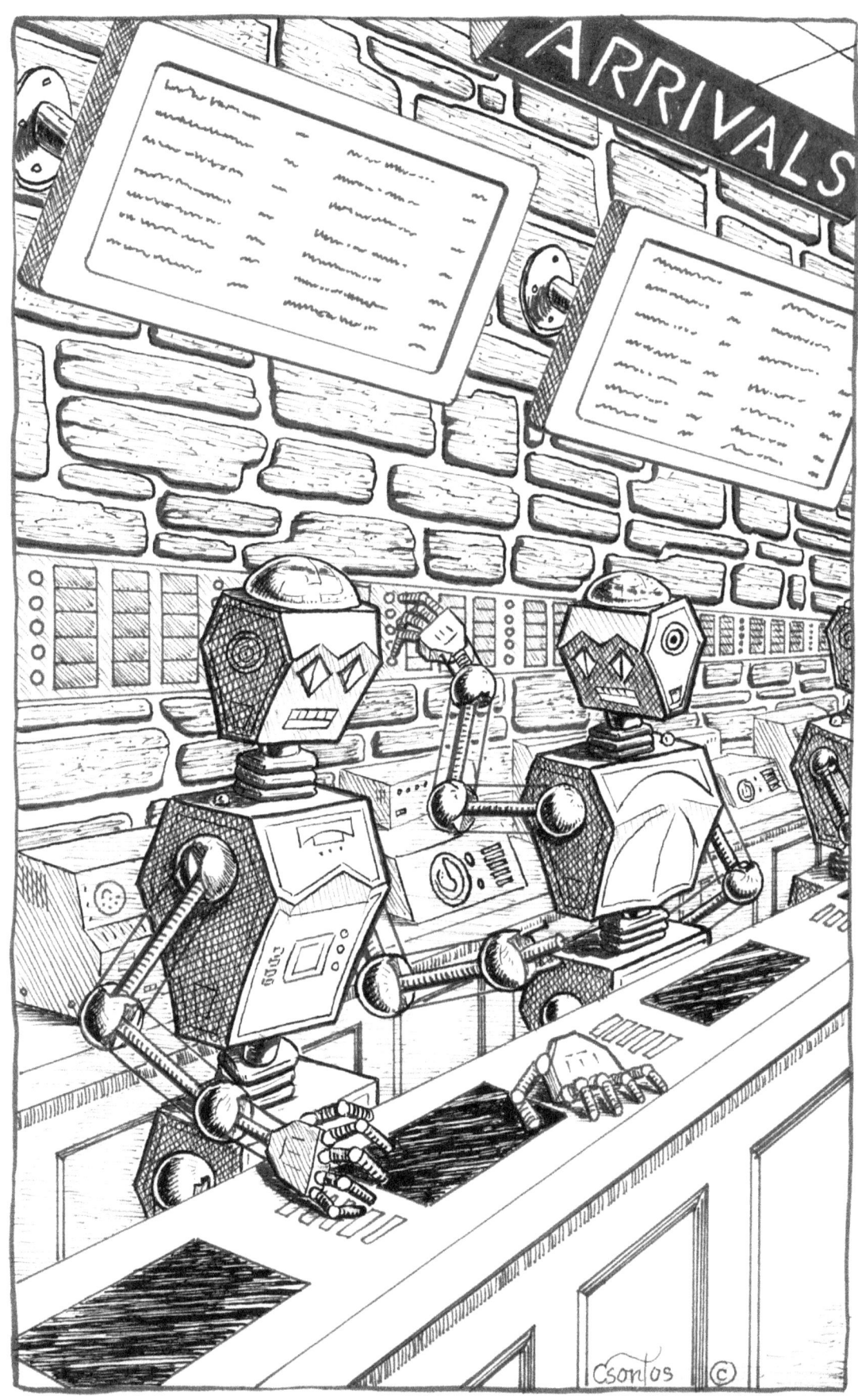

Even an automaton can have an off day. A robot with mechanical problems.
This one is my favorite illustration for the book probably because of the humor. Drawing pens.

Visualizing spontaneous images with backgrounds

The last two sections have dealt with images with backgrounds, so following that format, here are some more samples with backgrounds. As I compose the imagery (after the initial theme has come out of the sketching) the background develops as a result of the main focus. There are some exceptions and I will explain them. It's that my mind's eye sees two different methods of images with backgrounds. One is where the background is a type of filler to the main focus and the other is where the background and the foreground are part of the same area of focus utilizing continuity. In other words there are some images where the main focus could stand alone without a background. The other type is where the background is a necessity.

This type of background formatting can be used for both a spontaneous or a preconceived approach, as you've seen so far in this book. Once again, I believe it quite often depends on the 'feel' one gets as the image develops.

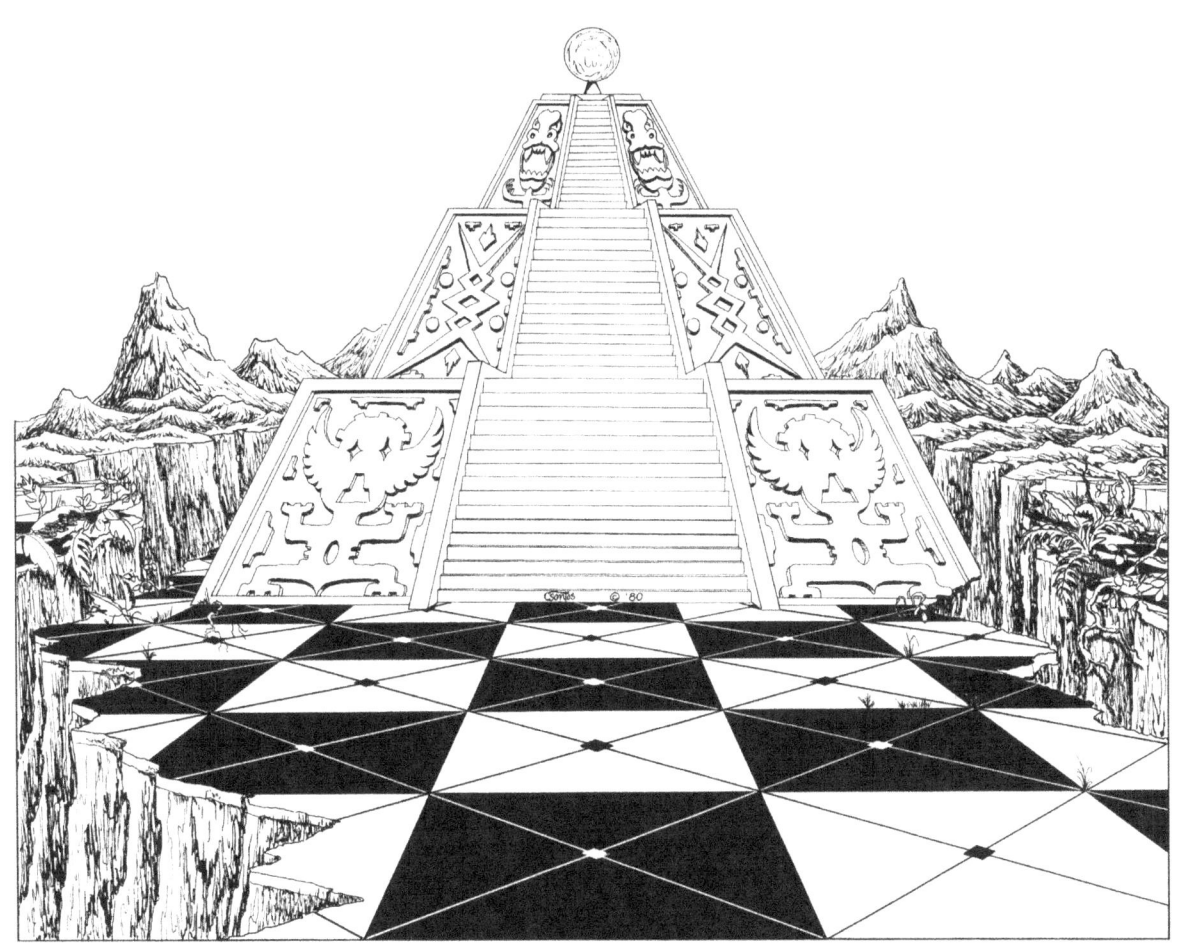

"Pyramid Power"
Ink - drawing pens with very little brush work.

I have shown this image first to indicate that the sky area can be left blank. I grew up in New York state where you rarely ever see a completely clear sky. But I have lived in Arizona for over 35 years now and a clear sky happens almost too often. All it would take to change this piece to having a sky background as well would be a few brush stokes to simulate wispy clouds or even cumulus clouds. The background hills and cliff edge in this piece were secondary to the main pyramid image. So I could have left them out but they added continuity because of the cliff edge in the foreground.

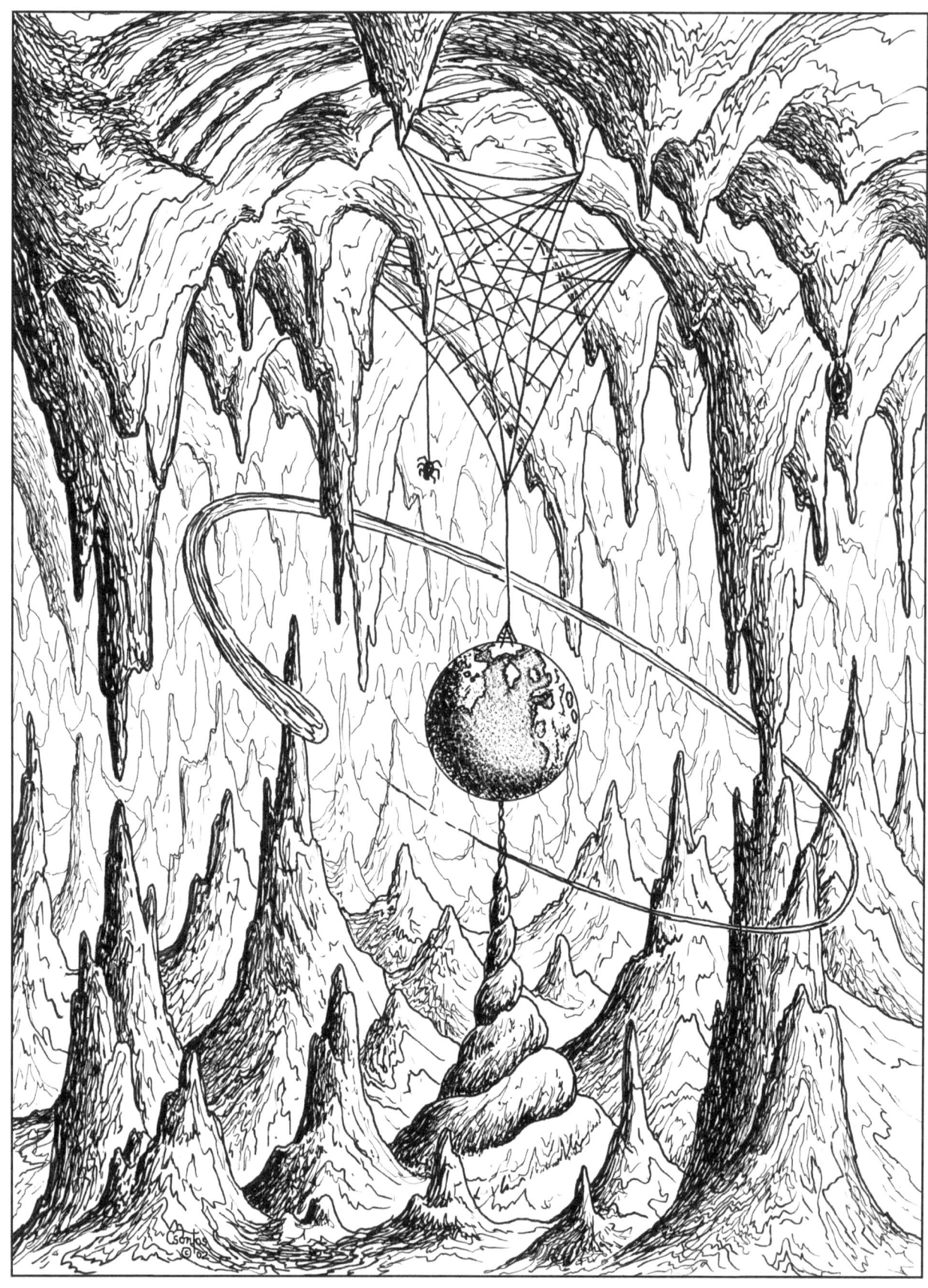

"Quantum Suspension"

Ink - drawing pens.

This is an image where I believe the background is integrated with the foreground and middle ground. I get confused trying to figure where the different boundaries are actually located.

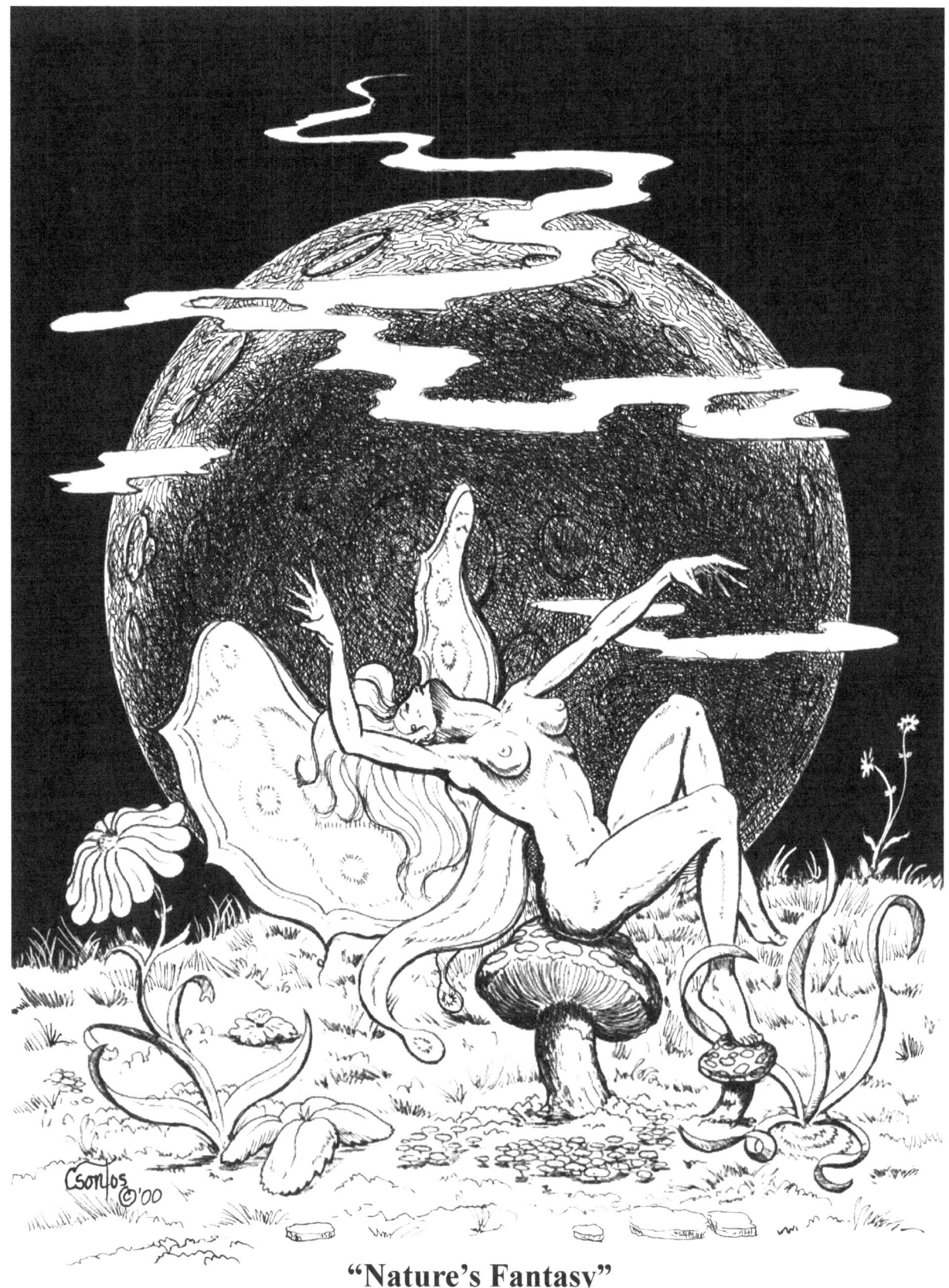

"Nature's Fantasy"

Ink - drawing pens and brush.

This piece was originally drawn without the background at all. I did the foreground and middle ground originally and made copies for my portfolios. About a year later I was going through the portfolio and the image of the moon and the cloud wisps popped into my head so I reworked it. The moon is probably my ultimate test of crosshatching.

41

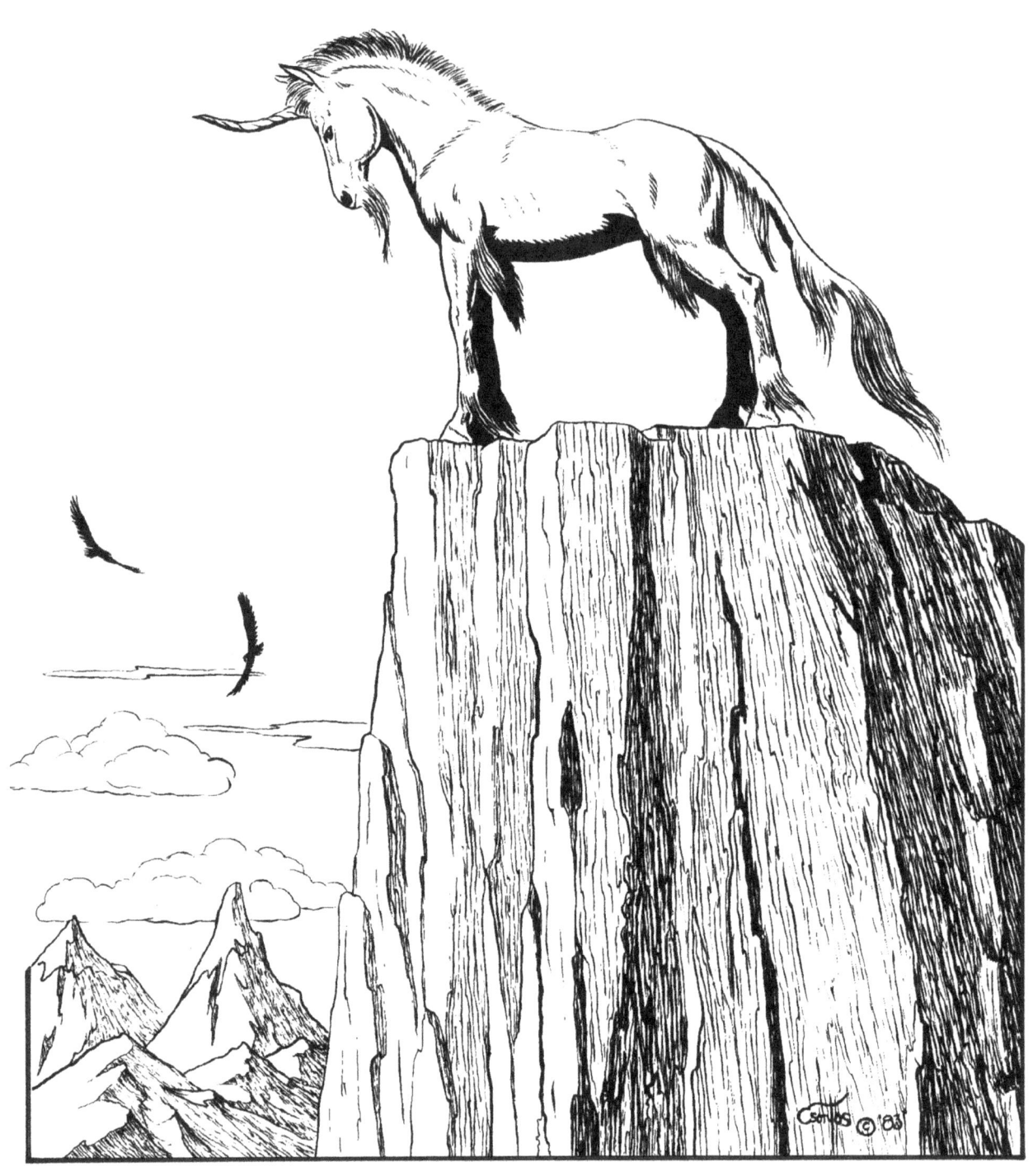

"Atop the World"
Ink - drawing pens and brush.

The background imagery in this piece adds to the lofty feeling of the foreground. The placement and size of the background imagery is the key.

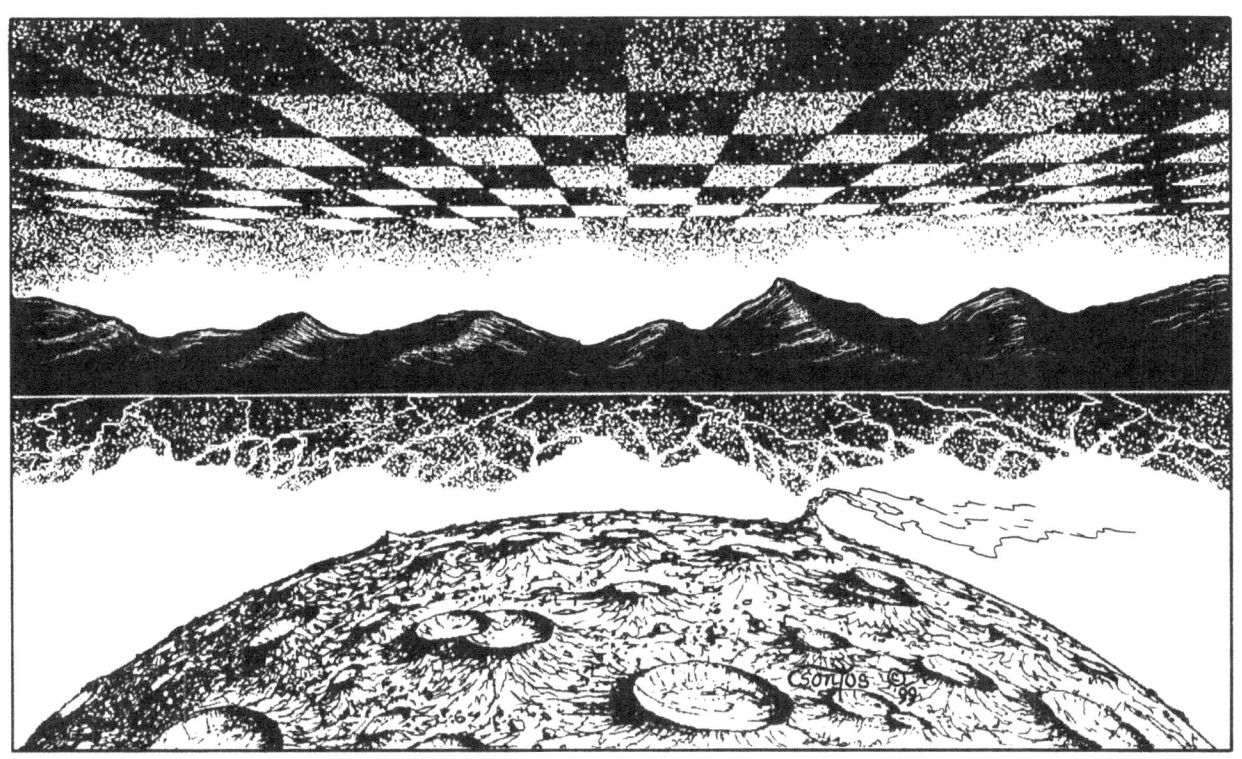

"The Game of Chess"

Ink - pens and brush. The background is the main focus because of the intense light and dark contrast.

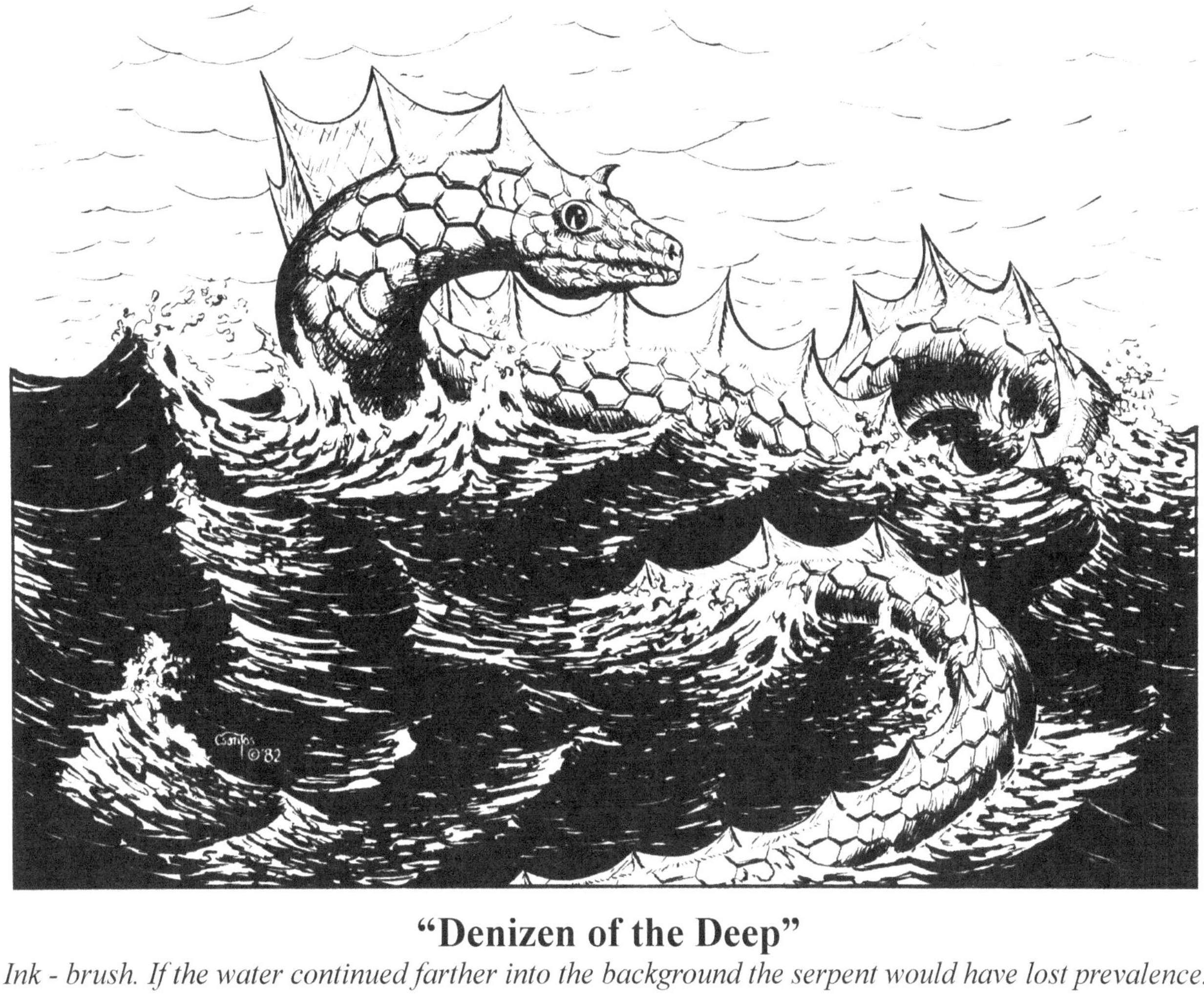

"Denizen of the Deep"

Ink - brush. If the water continued farther into the background the serpent would have lost prevalence.

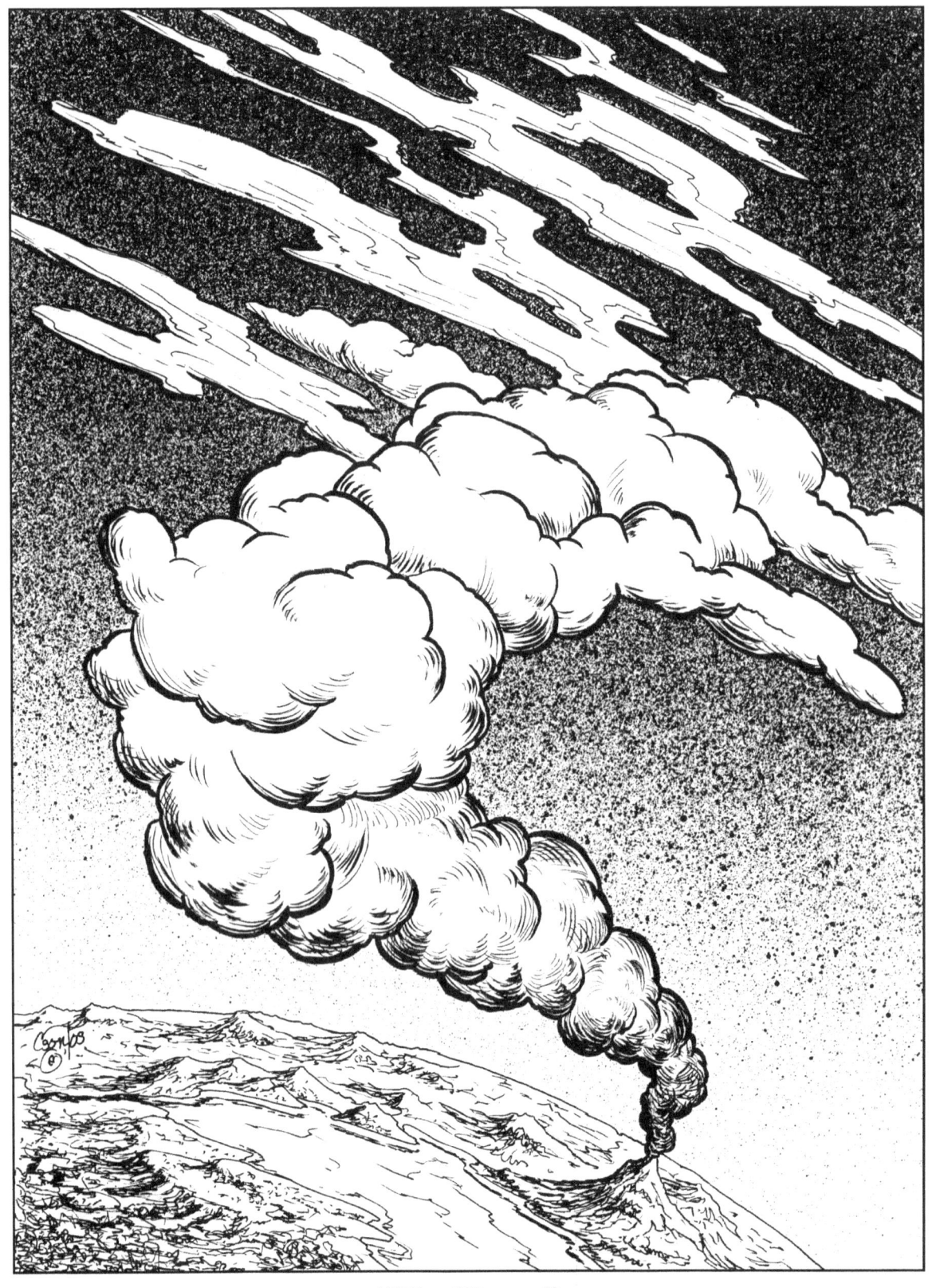

"The Plume"

Ink - drawing pens, brush, and airbrush with a stipple effect on illustration board.

This image was interesting. As I saw a cloud or smoke in the original sketch I remember thinking, "Well that looks kind of boring." But instead of abandoning the idea I went ahead and just tried to do something different with the handling of the ink. The background sky could be removed and the plume could be changed to almost completely dark, which would have reversed the effect but not the focal point.

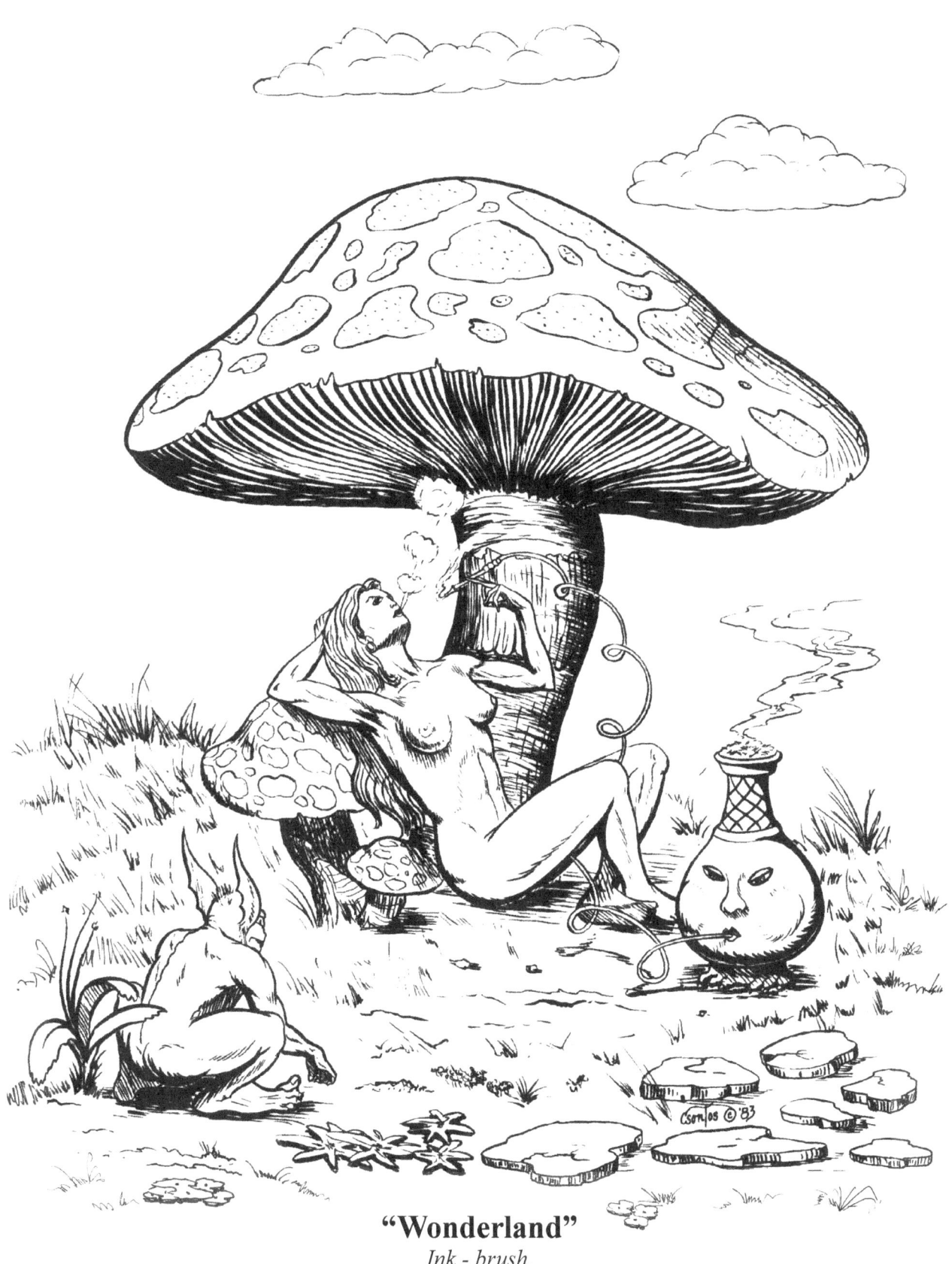

"Wonderland"

Ink - brush.

This is another sample of a background without a background. What I mean is that a few simple lines could establish distant mountains for the far background. I do not think it would add to the overall impact of the piece but it might have removed the illustration effect which sometimes gives a better rendition than a complete scene.

Visualizing two different approaches having the same style.

I wanted to put these two older images (1978) up together because they show a similarity in style, but they were conceived completely different. The other similarity was that they were both done at the same time period. One other aspect, is the similarity to the preceding samples, both of these images could eliminate the dark backgrounds if it became necessary.

I find it interesting that these two approaches (spontaneous and preconceived) go way back to when I had first started earning a living from my personal artwork. I originally thought that the only way to earn an income from drawing would be doing just what customers, editors, and art directors asked me to do.

I found out as the years went by that many people would appreciate and buy images from my unconscious (so to speak), as well as the images that represented objects and scenes of a more familiar nature. Whether it was selling prints at an art show or getting a commission.

There is no hard and fast rule which way to approach a project. Obviously if a customer wants an image that deals with a particular subject you have at least an inkling of the theme. It is extremely rare that a customer comes along and says, "Do anything you like, anyway you care to do it, and I'll buy it." I assume there are a few famous artists out there that have that luxury.

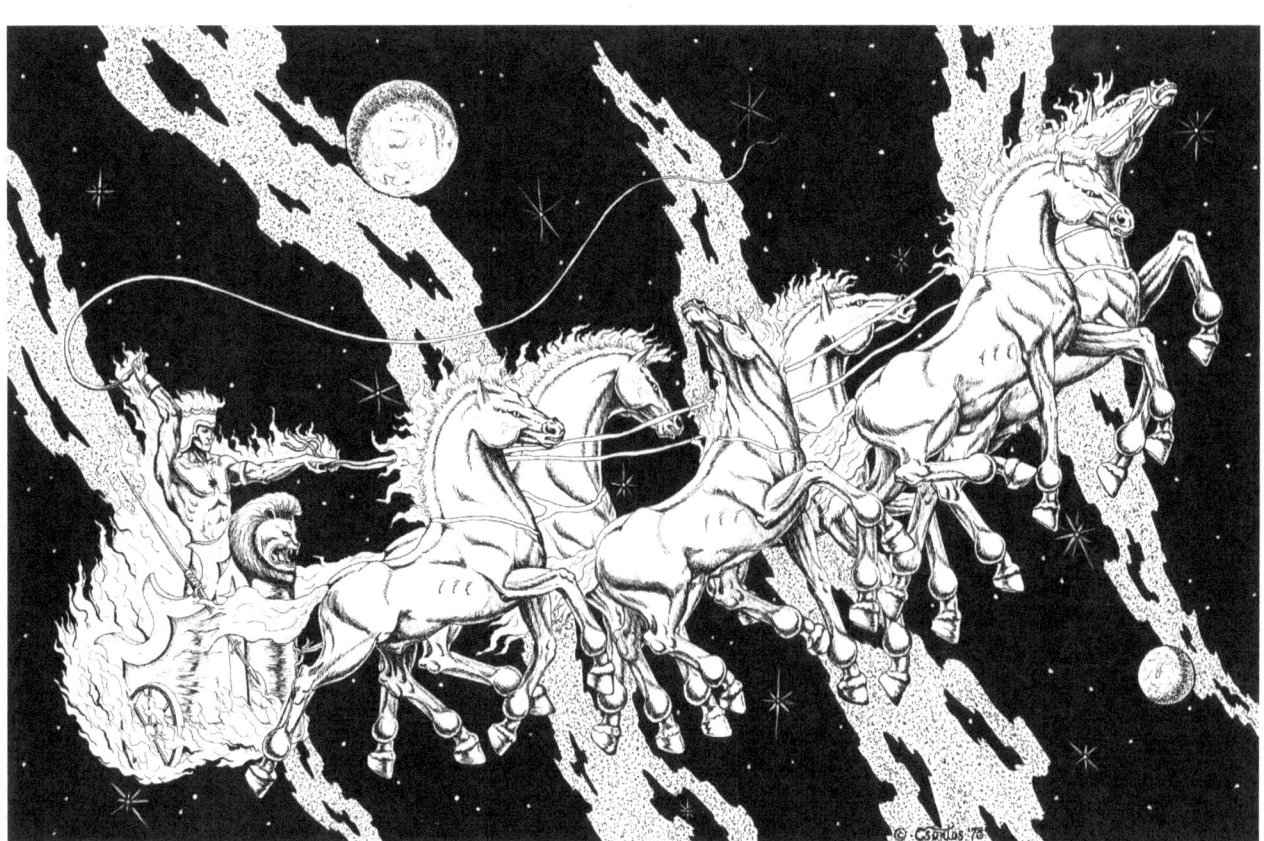

"The Flaming Chariot"
Ink - drawing pens and brush on illustration board.

This image seems like it was a spontaneous work. Actually it was a commission. I had no reference material other than basic mythological history to go by. It was not an idea or a phrase, just a single word, 'Apollo'. Eliminating the background in this image or even making it almost solid black might have made it stand out better but at the time (1978) I had to consider current printing methods because I also wanted to make prints.

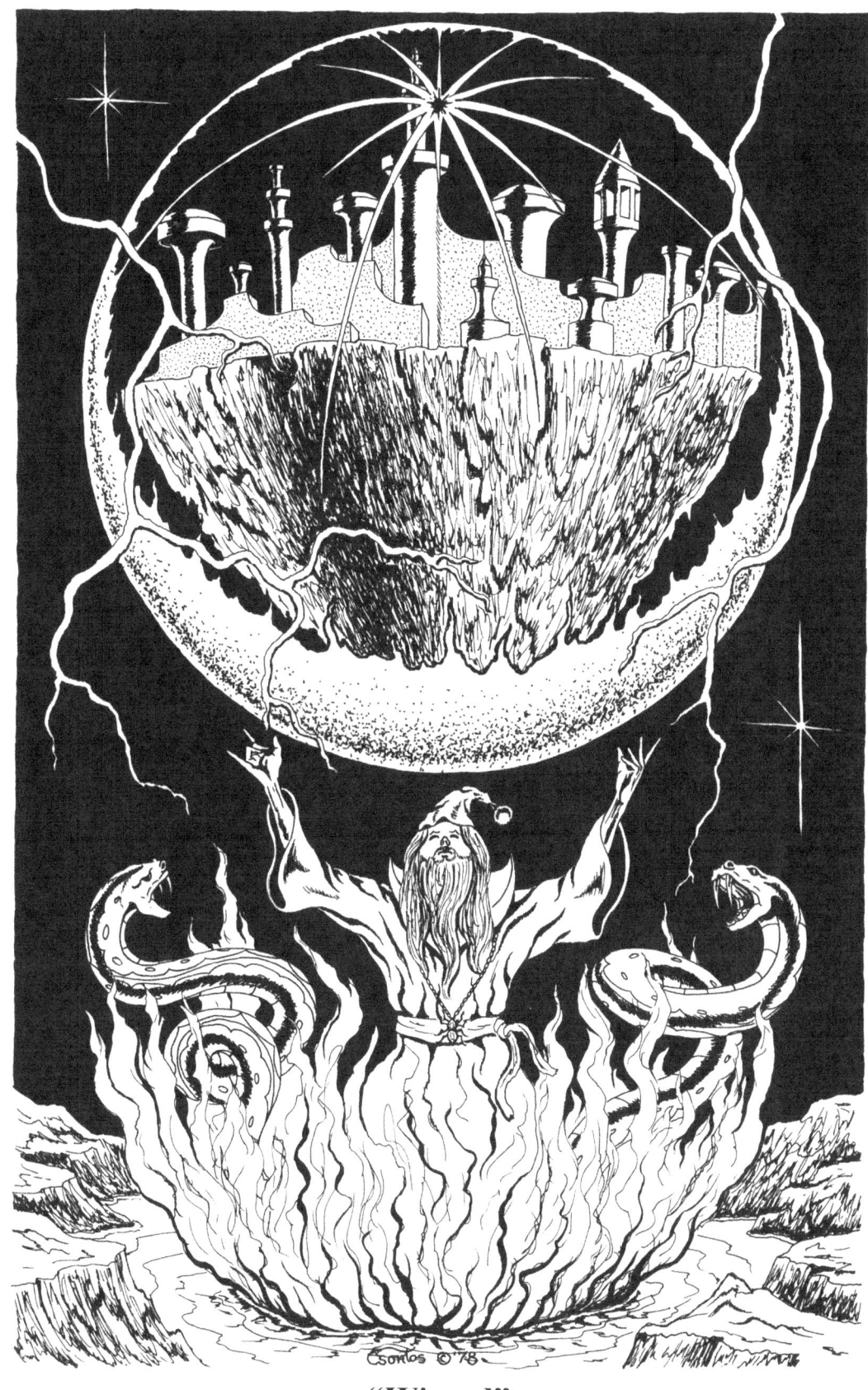

"Wizard"

Ink - pen and brush on illustration board.

I remember drawing a circle at the beginning of this piece. Then I saw that the circle was a bubble. Then inside the bubble a castle. I had done several spontaneous pieces even earlier then this time period but it took me until 1983 to realize that this is the way I wish to create my personal art.

Visualizing science fiction images in black and white.

Now that you've seen quite a few images with a dark background I'd like to show some more of the same. These works were for a speculative presentation to a magazine that did reviews on science fiction writing. I approached some of them in my traditional pen and brush method as well as with other techniques. Some I did with a pen and then finished them on the computer. And I did a few more strictly on the computer. As they progressed I found myself liking the di-vergent theme so I probably did quite a bit more then I normally would have. The editor asked for science fiction images. That was all he said. Apparently I associated only black backgrounds with the words 'science fiction'. If the editor had mentioned he did not want only black back-grounds I'm sure my brain would have come up with others. But since these were a break from my preferred style I used this opportunity to experiment with other techniques.

I still did spontaneous sketches to get the juices flowing. It seems that because of my particular approach to art I have to do that because that is the way I trained myself.

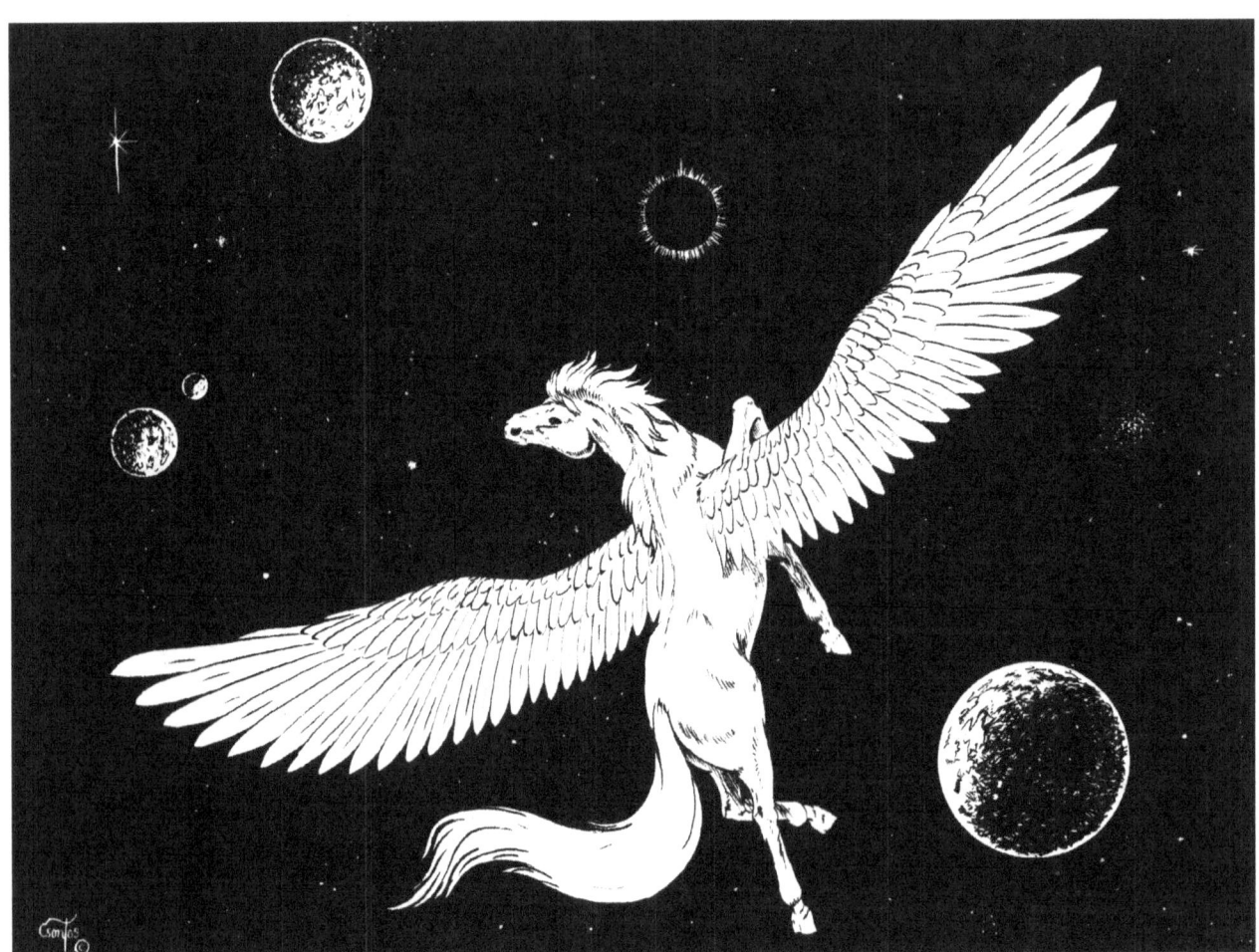

"Deep Flight"
Ink - pen and brush.

This was an image that I had already done, but I had included it in the presentation anyhow. As you can see I was probably assuming that fantasy also applied to science fiction. Pen and brush on il-lustration board.

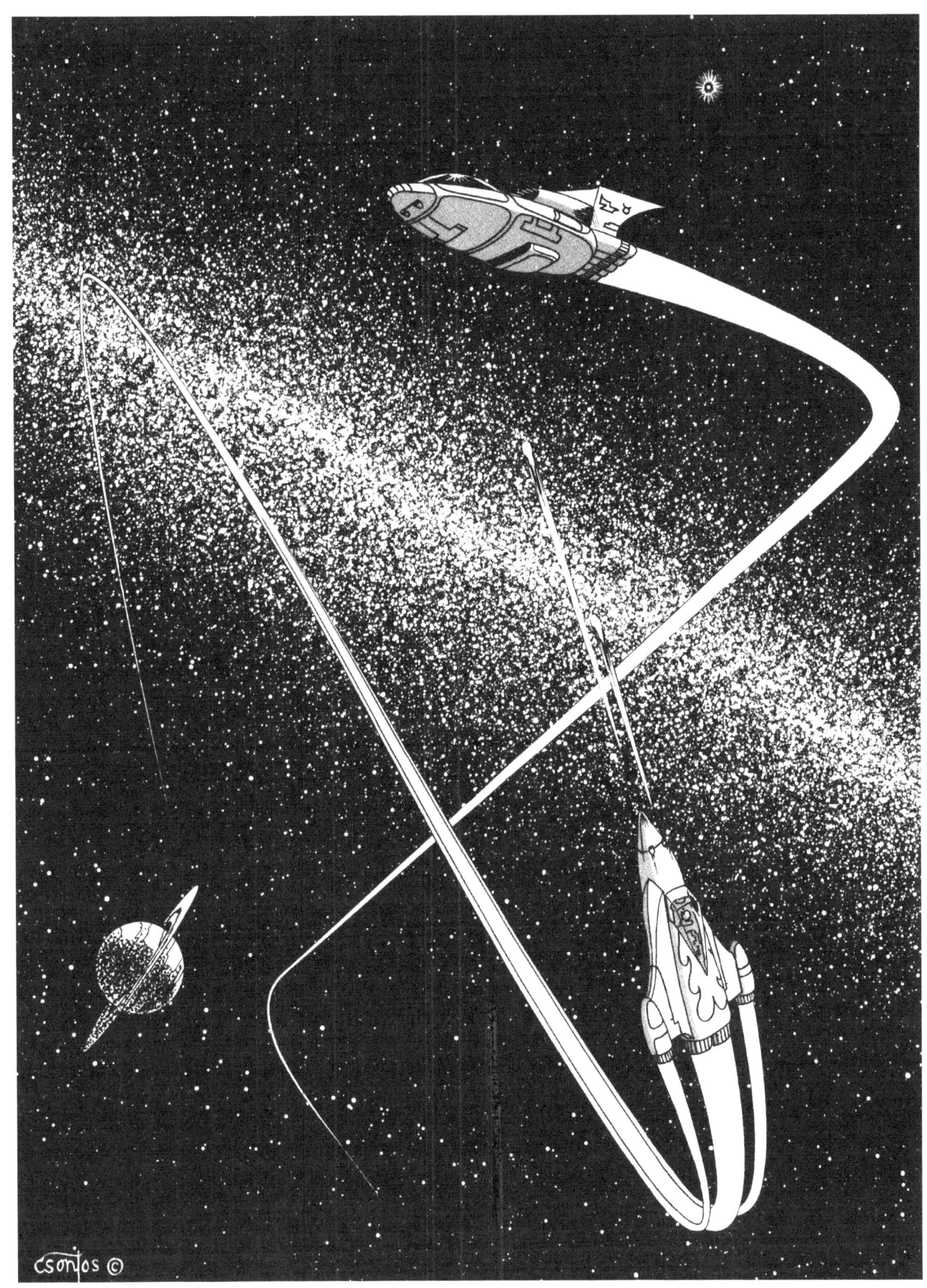

"At the Edge of the Galaxy"

Ink - pens and brush; transfer screens; and airbrush stippling with acrylic paint on illustration board.

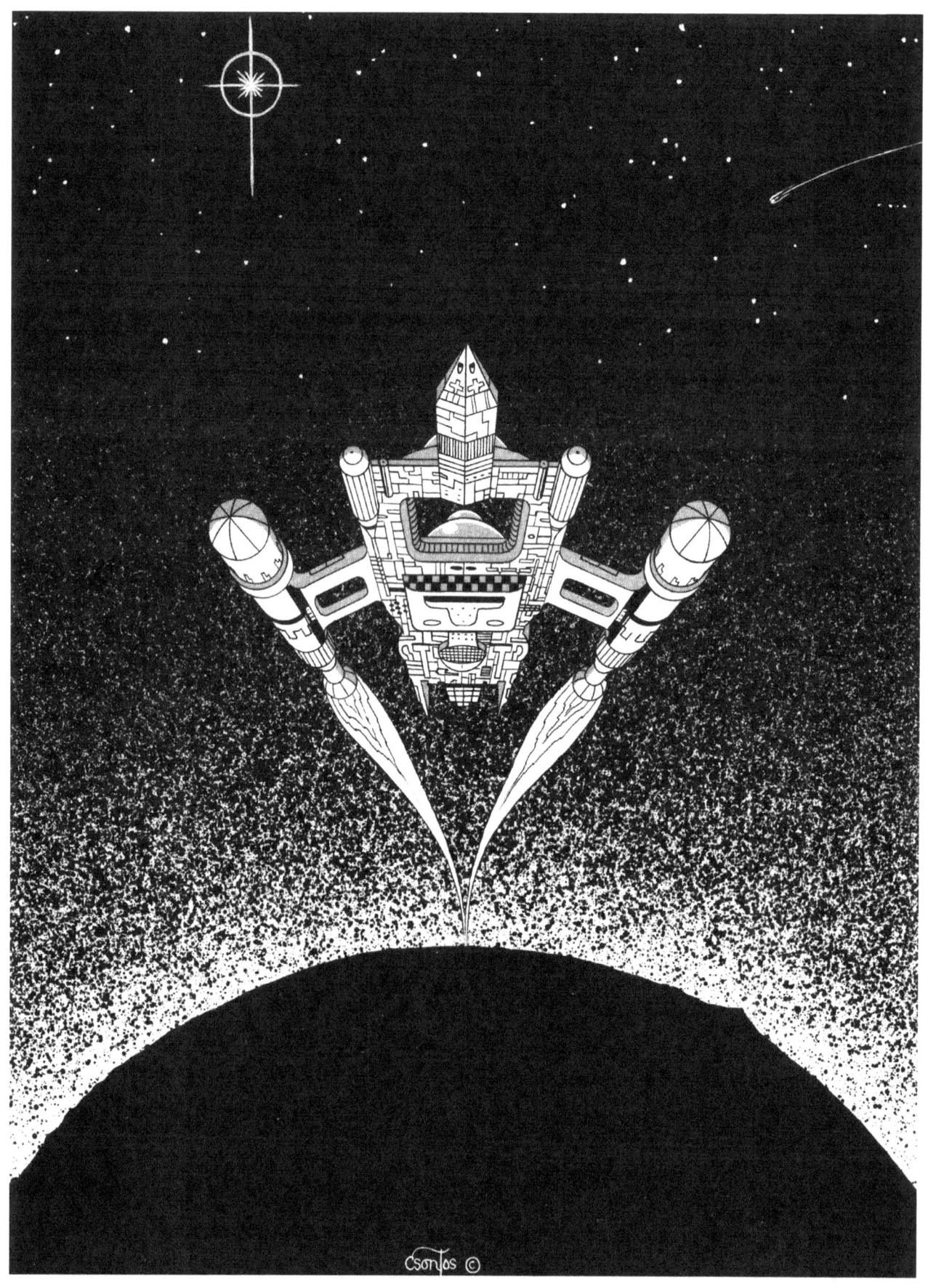

"Black Moon Rising"

Ink - pens, brush, and airbrush stippling; transfer screen; and acrylic paint on illustration board.

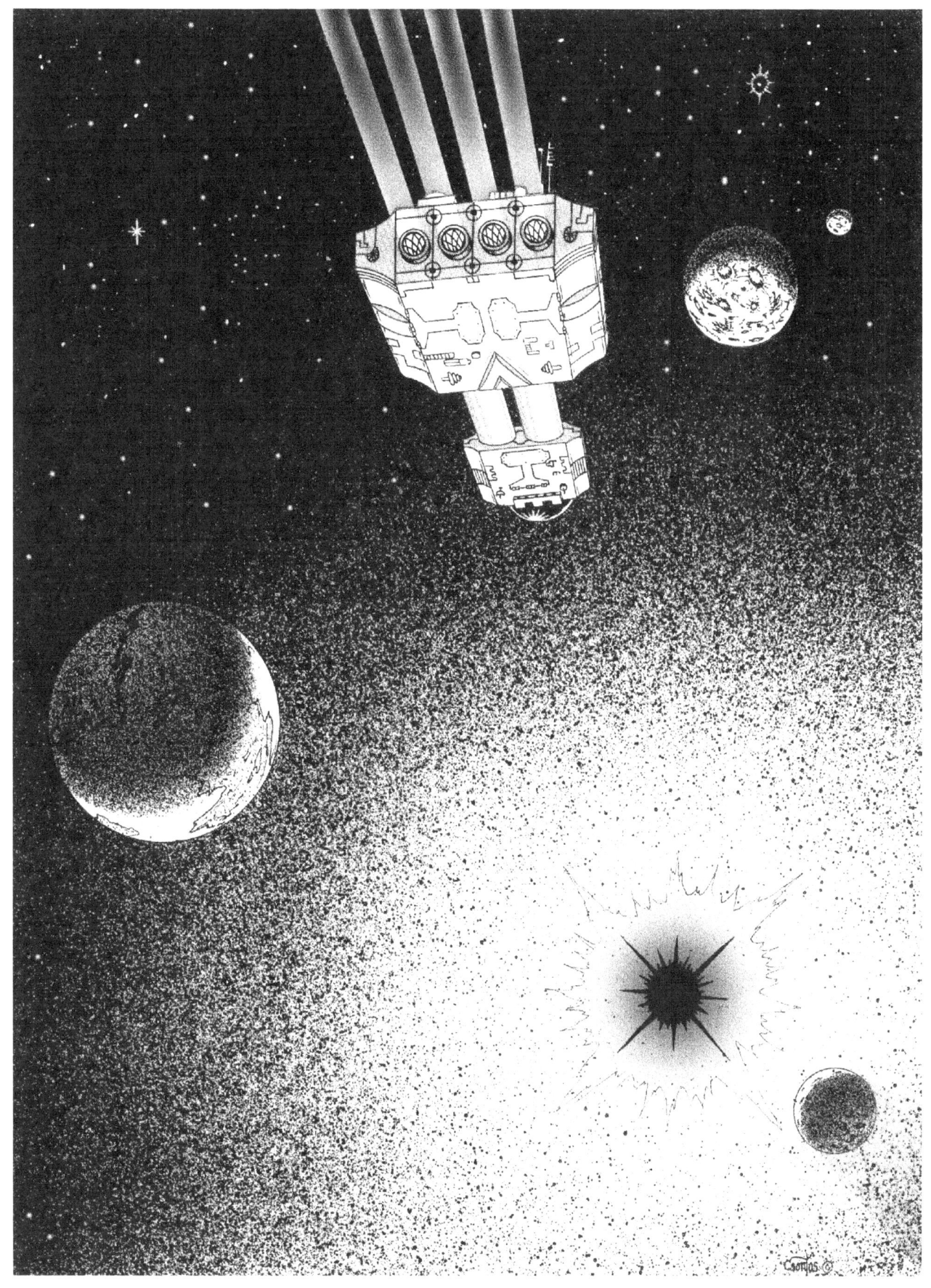

"Black Star"

Ink - pens, brush, and airbrush stippling; transfer screen; and acrylic paint on illustration board.

51

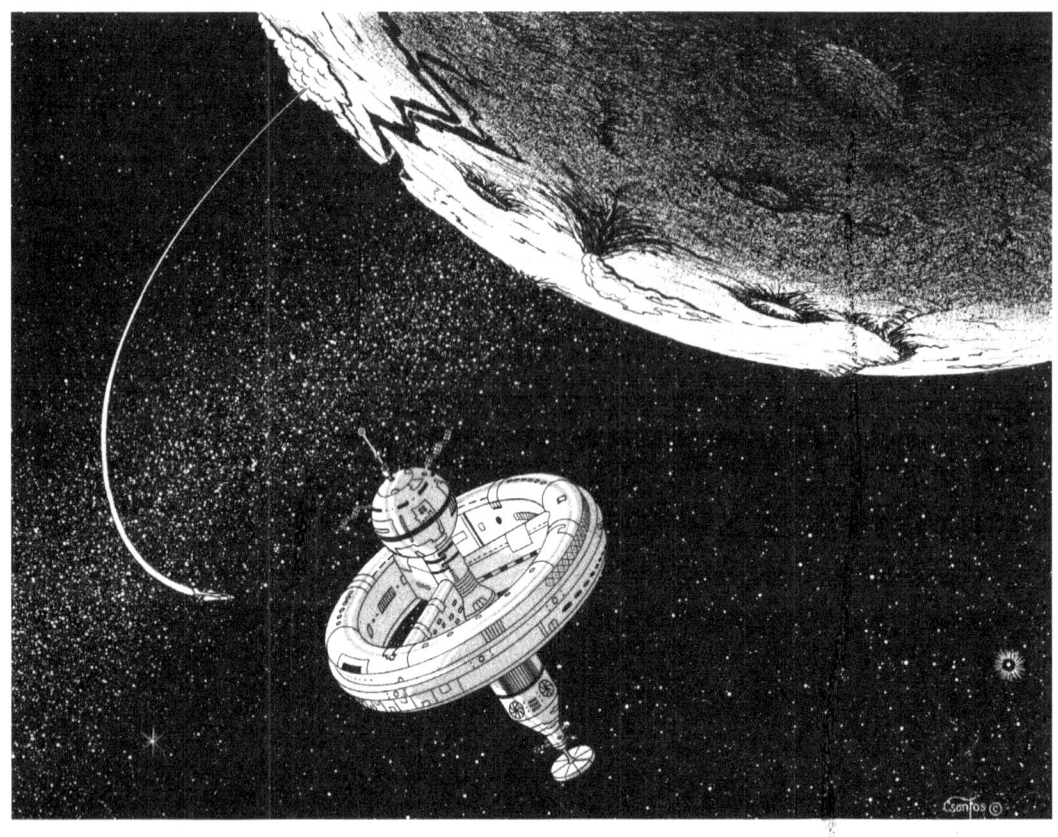

"Orbit"

Ink - pens, brush, and airbrush stippling; transfer screen; and acrylic paint on illustration board.

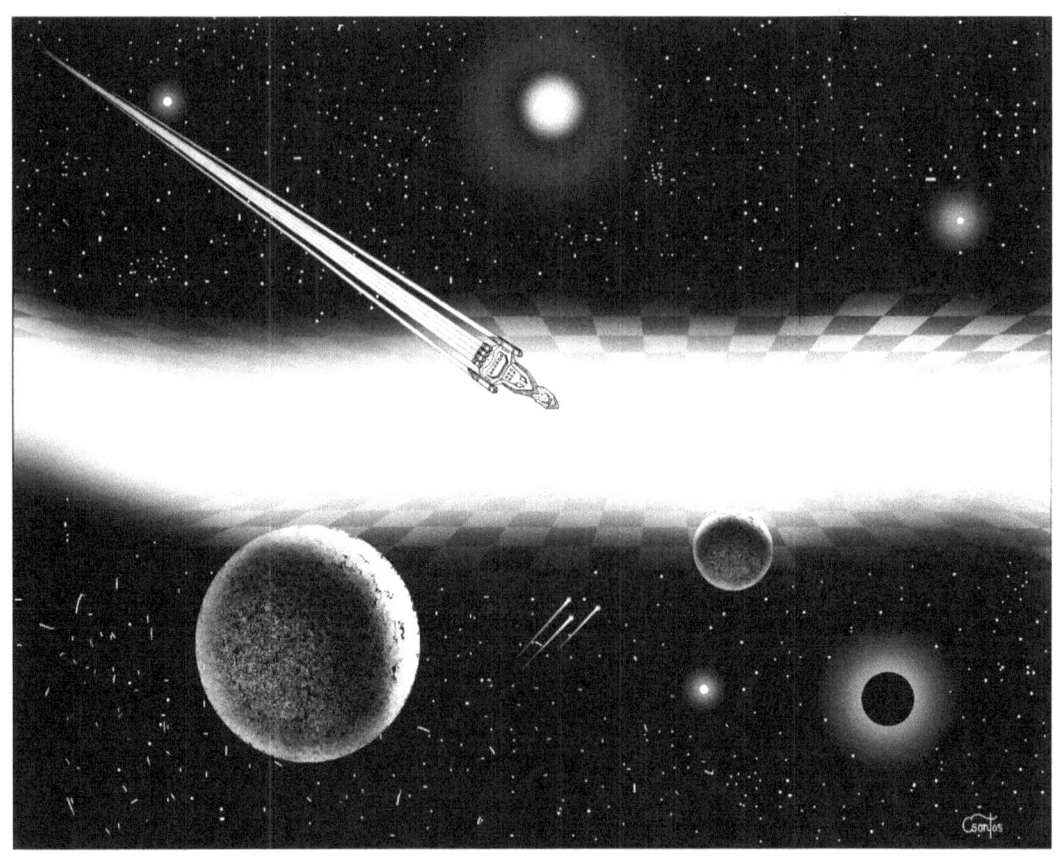

"Cosmic Aberration"

Ink drawing pens for the spaceship and then finished on the computer.

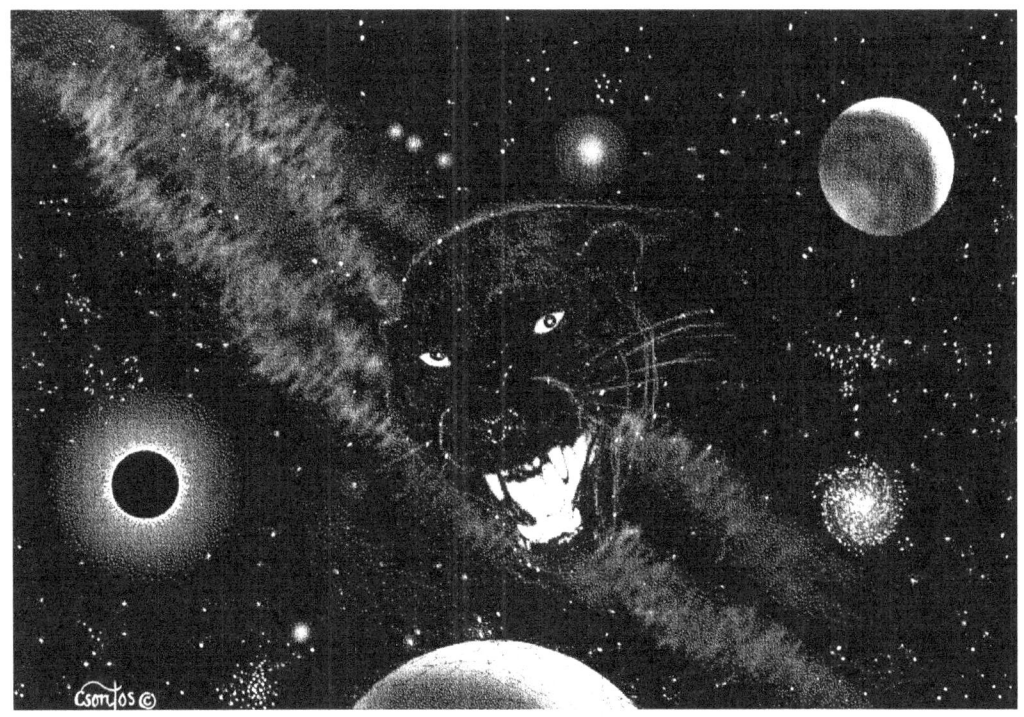

"Constellation of the Panther"
Drawing on the computer.

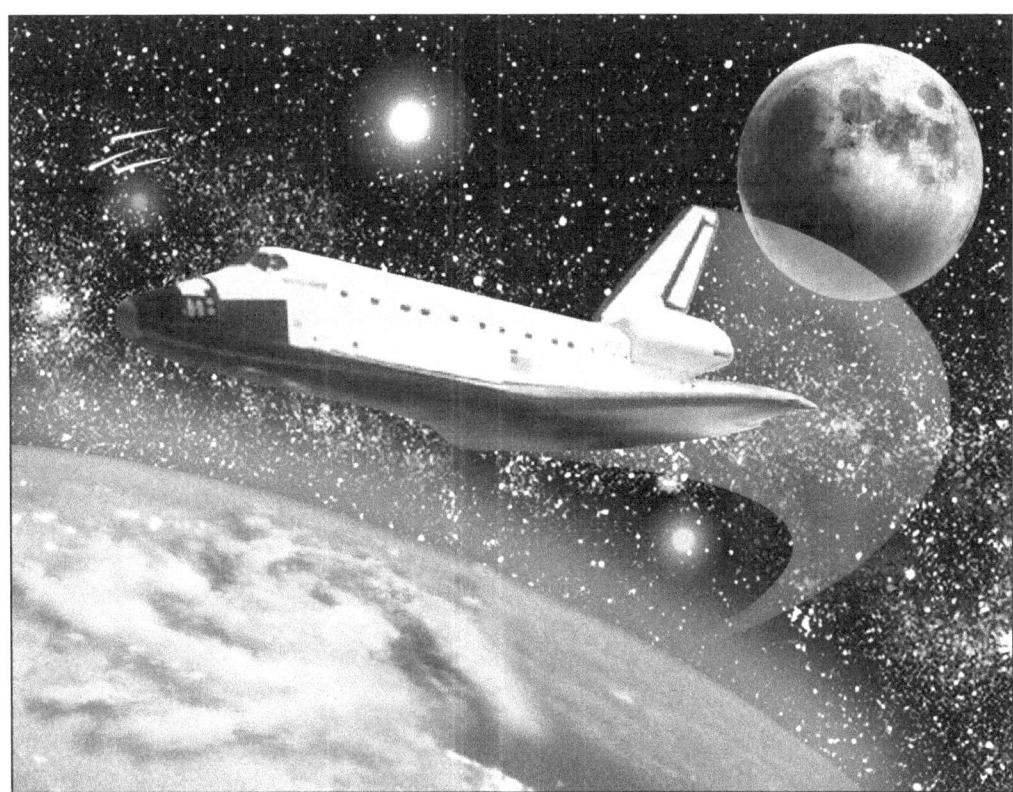

"Returning Home"
Photo manipulation on the computer.

This is the one image where I used photographs. I was fortunate enough to take pictures of the space shuttle mock-up when my son and I visited the Kennedy Space center in Florida. The one drawback with this style is that you are limited to photographs you have, Hubble telescope pictures or computer simulation. I do have a photograph collection from 35 years of picture taking but not of outer space.

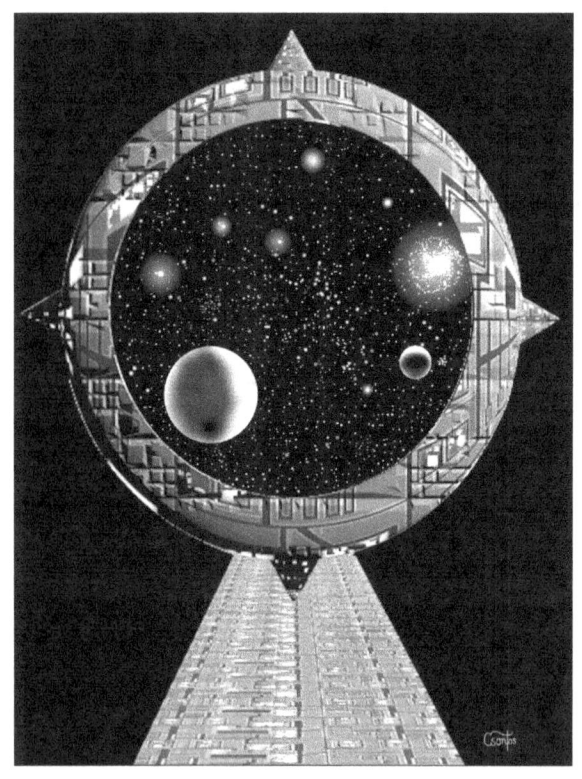

"Stargate"
Composed on the computer following a preliminary sketch. Bryce and Photoshop.

Spontaneous sketching was used for all of the images in this section but as you can see I am not as proficient with a variety of science fiction imagery as I am with surrealistic/fantasy imagery. I have no absolute reason as to why that is except maybe it is because the science fiction imagery is easily created by other artists where the surreal/fantasy imagery is totally my own. Plus we can only create what is in our hearts.

I used these two images last because they tie into the next section that deals with images done strictly on the computer.

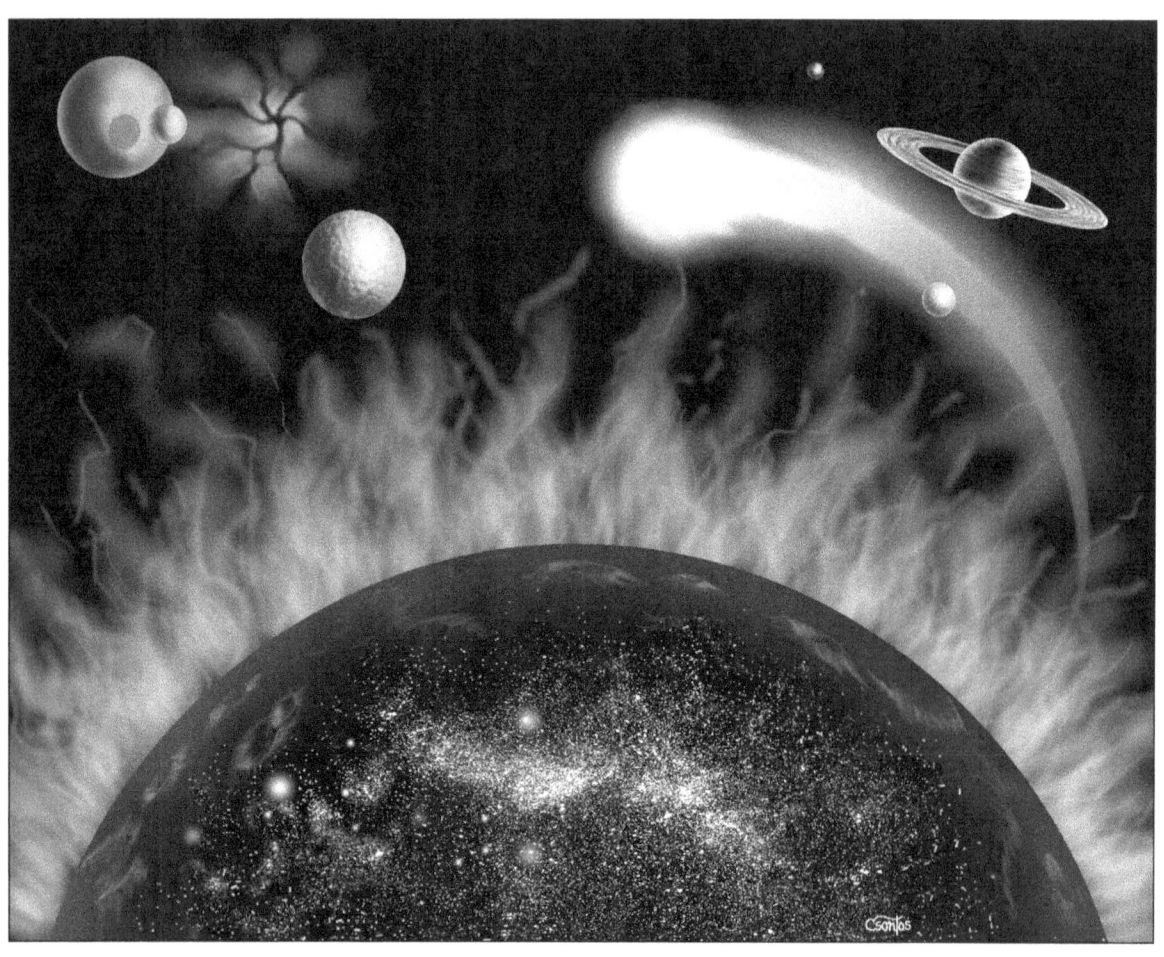

"Birth of the Stars"
Composed on the computer following a preliminary sketch. The stars were made by spritzing ink on a piece of paper with a toothbrush and scanning and reversing the ink spots in Photoshop.

54

Visualizing commercial black and white images using the computer.

These next samples were finished completely on the computer. It is my least favorite style because I have done thousands of this type of commercial illustrations (with and without the computer) which has made commercial artwork seem somewhat impersonal. I think it is also because the freedom of expression is limited to the customers request. However the computer is still perfect for commercial assignments and the challenge is still there. Sometimes I still get to insert a little bit of cleverness into the project. I also did initial pencil sketches for each project to get the creative juices flowing because nothing beats a pencil for spontaneous creativity. Especially if you are an incurable doodler.

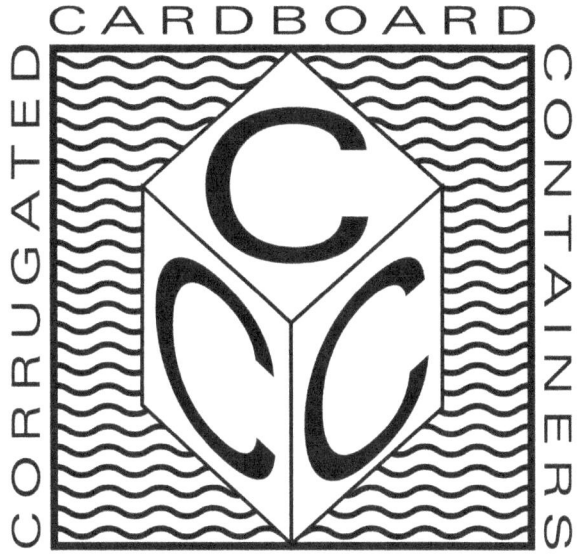

Logo for a cardboard box company. Illustrator.

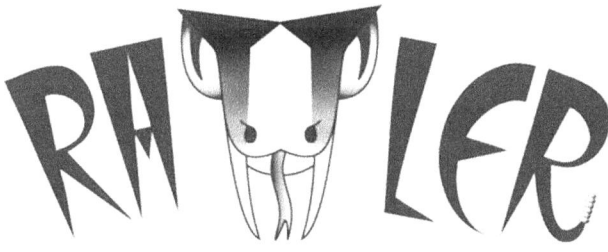

Sign for a hiking trail. The full verbiage was 'Rattler Country'. Illustrator and Photoshop.

A mediation group. A different approach to my usual drawing style. I tried to be in a corporate frame of mind. Illustrator.

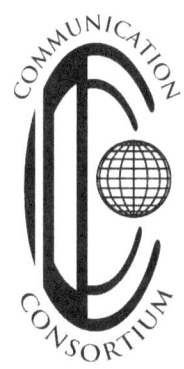

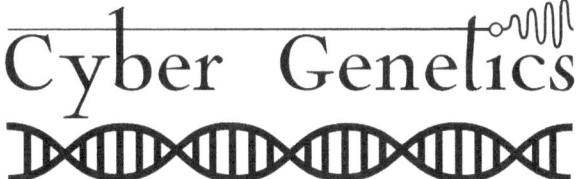

Illustrator.

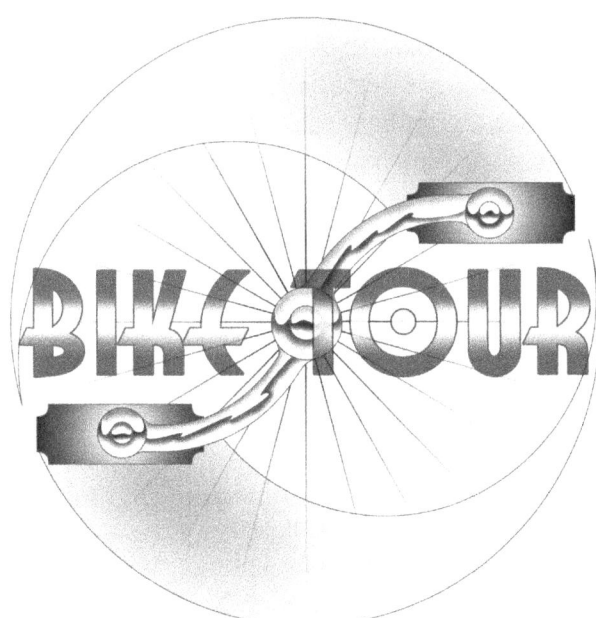

Image for a poster advertising an excursion on bicycles. Illustrator and Photoshop.

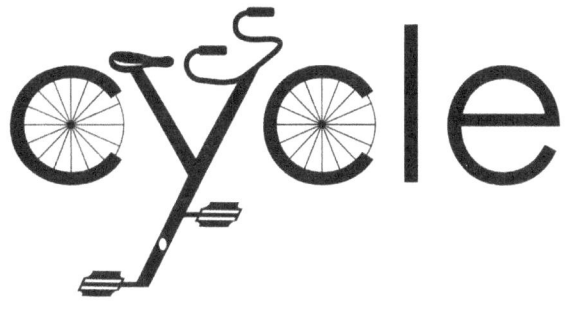

Bicycle shop logo. Illustrator

55

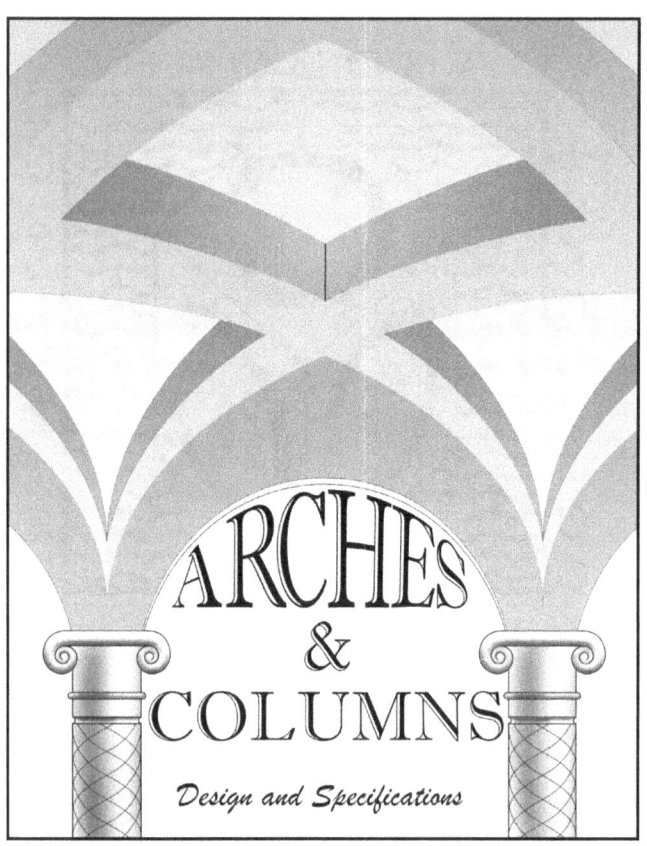

Book cover for timber frame construction and other aspects of post and beam support. Illustrator and Photoshop. I did linework on my drawing table first and then scanned the image and opened it in Illustrator where I redrew over the lines. Exported to Photoshop for toning.

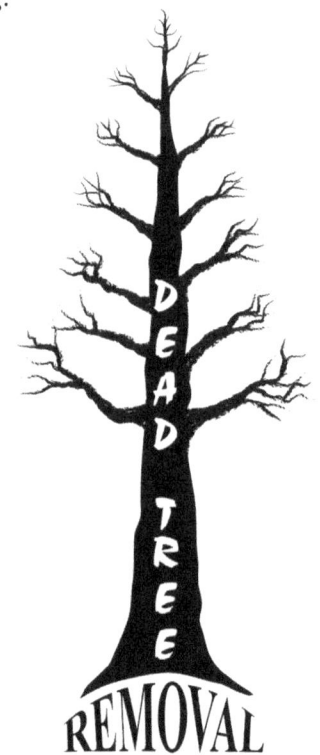

Sign layout for a crew that specialized in removing trees that died from the bark beetle infestation in our area. Illustrator.

The one drawback to doing commercial images with my style is that I have to recompose the idea on the computer each time the customer critiques it. Which also means re-sketching the idea with the requested changes for my own referencing.

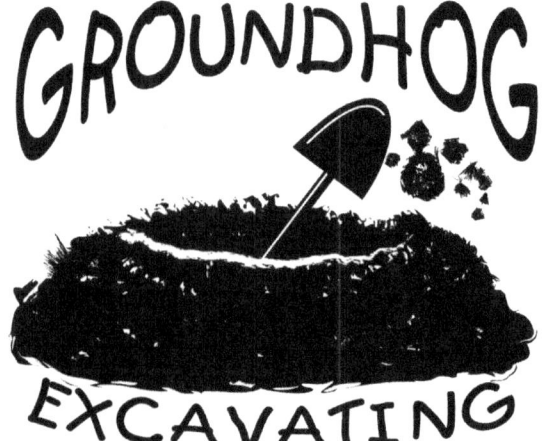

It was fun hearing the name of this business because my birthday is on groundhog's day. The concept was almost too easy because I was always digging holes as a kid. Illustrator.

Layout for an automotive painting business. I did a tight drawing by hand and then scanned and redrew in Illustrator.

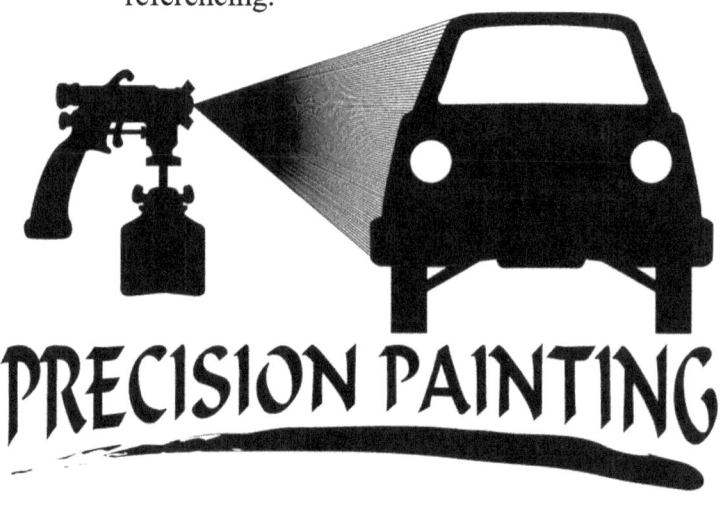

Technique of a hand drawn image toned and painted on the computer.

Now we get back to good old hand illustrations, which is my favorite method of representation. This one came about as a result of me posting a photo composite at the local college of a castle in the clouds. After someone had seen it they inquired about using it for a CD album cover. I could not allow it because the castle was from clip art. I could however, make this image from scratch, with no third party copyright issues.

I have only done a few of my personal works which combined hand drawn images and the computer. The computer seems to work well with the toning and even better with coloring but as far as the linework goes I would rather stick to a pen and brush. I have followed up with other images that were redrawn in Illustrator as well as drawn by hand with a very fine tip pen. The linework tends to be very similar in size, just a little more natural looking when drawn by hand. Once again, it depends on the 'feeling'. I keep it a very fine line so it almost disappears after the toning is laid in.

Considering how well some of the hand drawn images come out after being toned in Photoshop, I will probably end up doing more, as it is easier than using an airbrush and masking.

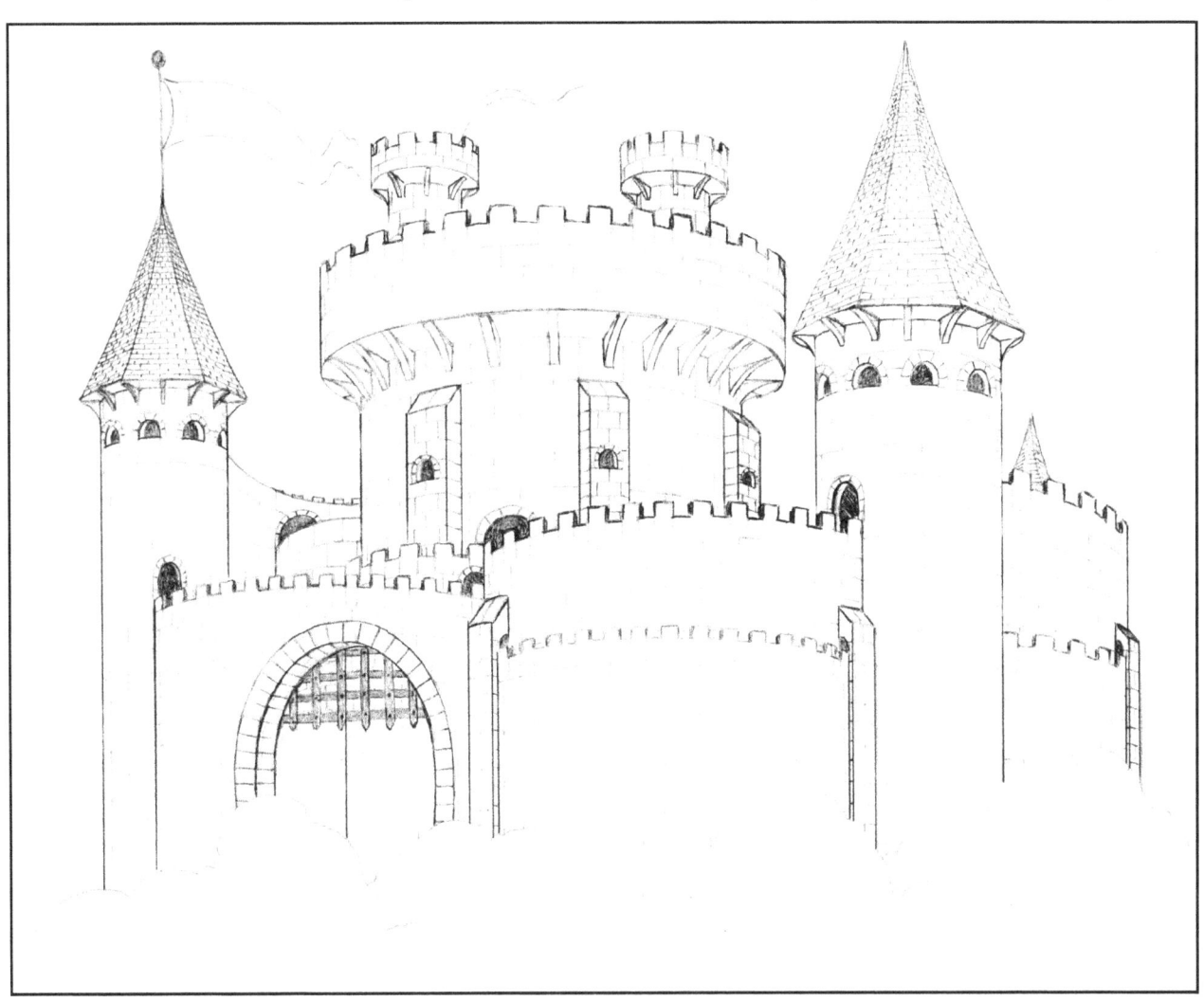

This is the original pencil drawing I did on my drawing table. I kept it rather tight because I had thoughts of using it to overlay the toning I would do on the computer. I have to admit I was not exactly sure of how to proceed after this point. I knew I did not want to redraw every single line on the computer because past experience had shown that technique does not always look natural. I decided to scan the image into Photoshop and tone the piece section by section.

This is the image with the toning underway. There are well over 50 separate selected sections that were individually toned on several different layers. I also used the brush in Photoshop to add a light source edge to every single stone. I guess I was in the zone. In the original I had posted at the college, I used a photo of a cloud I took during the monsoon season in Arizona. For this image I just used the brush tool on a separate layer and kept adding and subtracting cloud puffs.

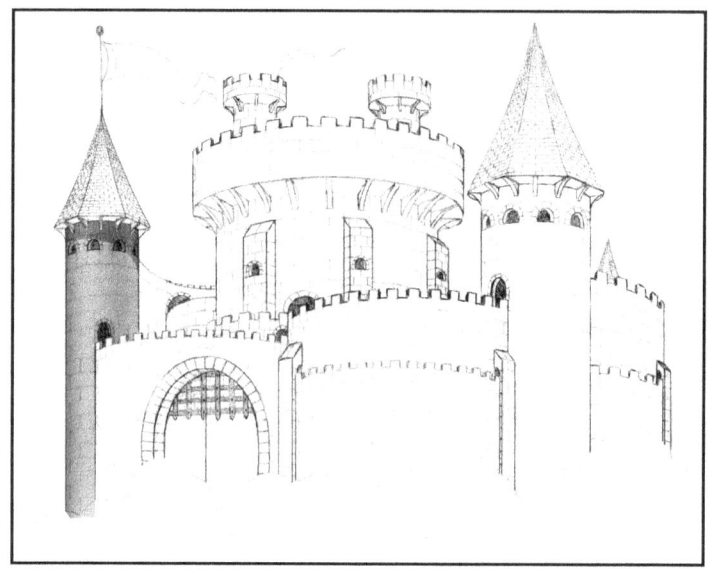

Since I've been using the computer to tone images like this I can't even remember the last time I used my airbrushes. But before the advent of computers and Photoshop I used them all the time.

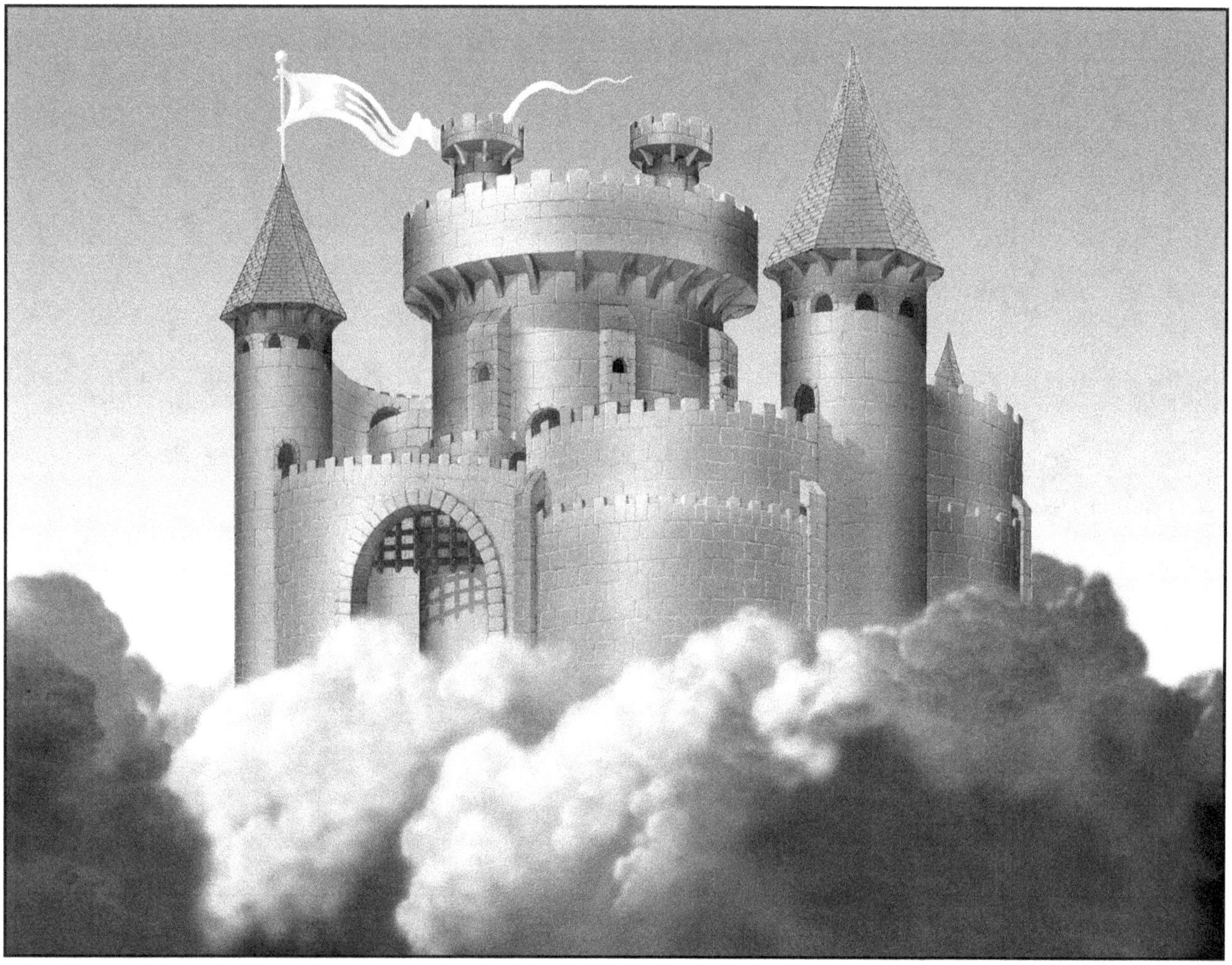

The finished image with all the layers merged together including the scanned pencil image which is being used as the joints between the stones. I especially liked the cast shadows. The only other way I could have gotten this effect would have been with an airbrush and masking on illustration board.

Technique of a hand drawn and inked image, toned and painted on the computer - number two.

This image has been inked on a separate coated sheet over the penciling using a light table. I used a very fine drawing pen tip. If I needed a larger line after I brought the image into Photoshop I could always select just the lines and expand them or draw over them. As I select the individual sections I can also expand that area. Then as I fill the section with toning it automatically covers the pen lines, which sometimes I do want, as in the clouds.

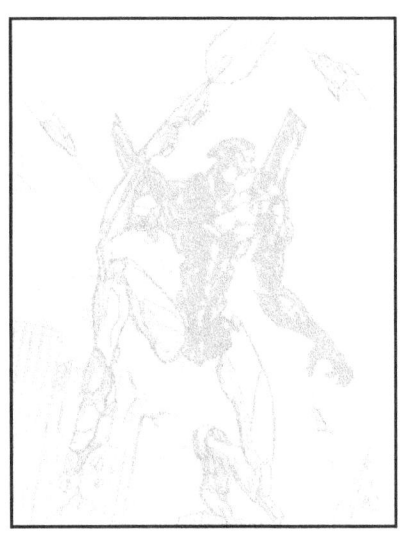

The original pencil sketch (above) drawn on just regular copy paper with an HB pencil.

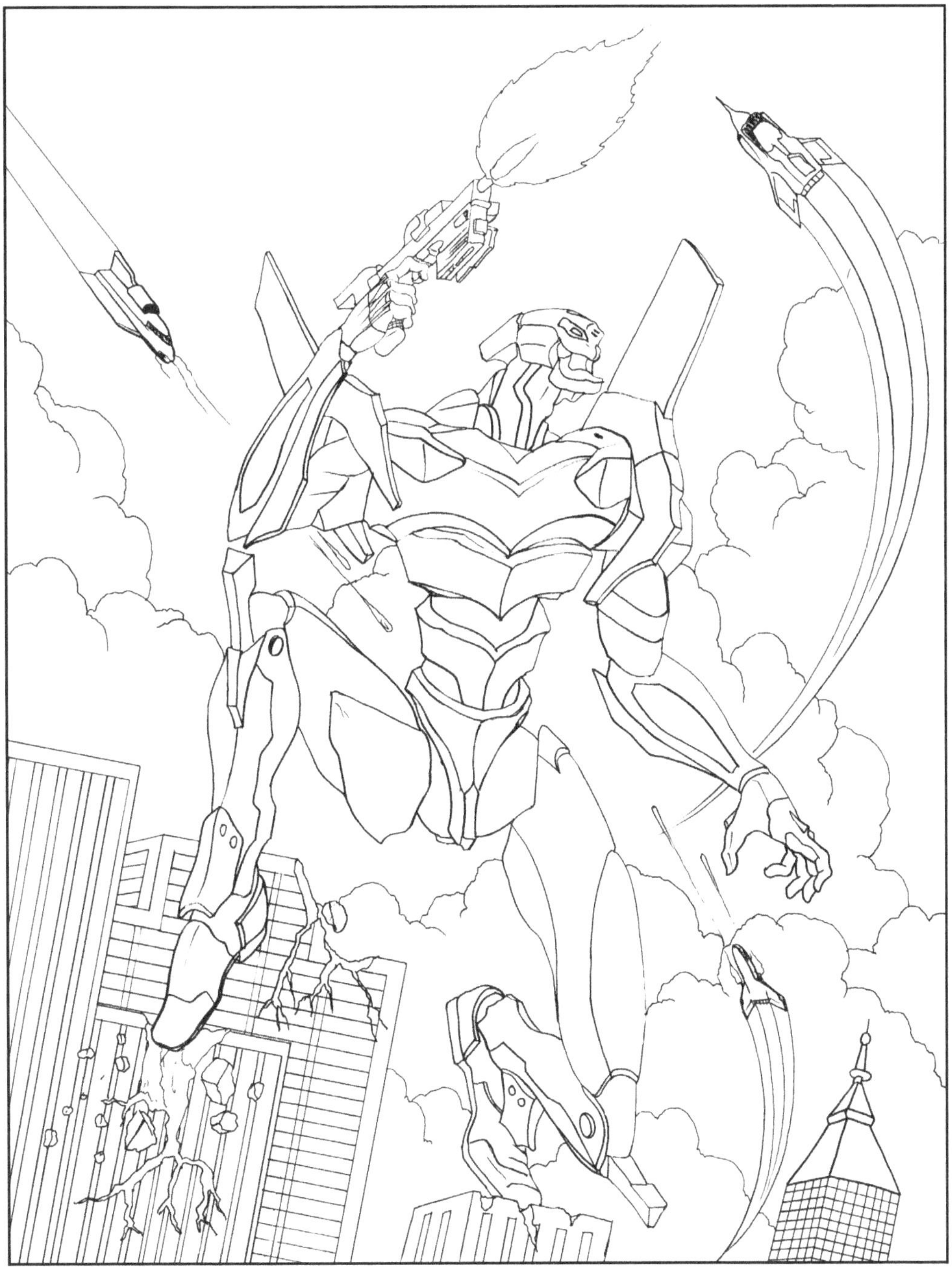

The finished inking (left) done on a coated sheet using the light table. After I scan it into Photoshop this linework is often duplicated so that I have a control layer which can be used with the magic wand. Just in case something goes wrong with the linework layer at the bottom.

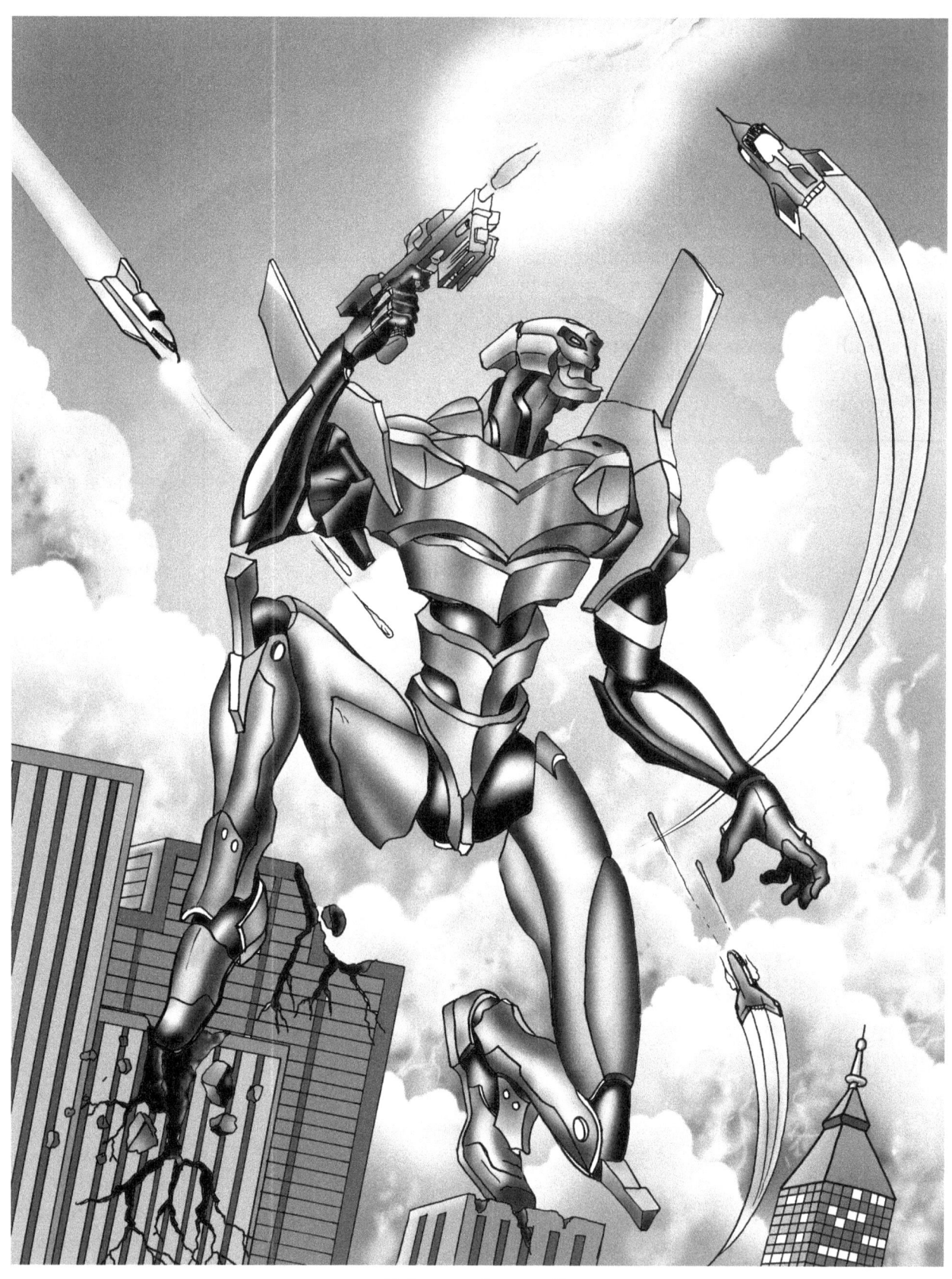

"Apocalypse"

The image finished in Photoshop. You can tell where I chose to expand the individual sections to cover the lines with toning (as in the clouds or smoke) and where I decided to leave the lines to give an illustrated effect. I now see I should have eliminated the linework in the trails behind the ships. Another instance where visualizing takes place even after you think the piece is done.

A computer drawn image toned and painted on the computer.

This image was spontaneously and completely sketched out in pencil and then scanned and brought into Illustrator. I then completely redrew everything with Illustrator's pen and pencil tools on another layer to create a vector based image of all linework. Then I imported the vector linework into Photoshop, which automatically makes any background areas transparent. I duplicate the layer for a top and a bottom layer. One for a selecting control and one for a final outline control, usually the top one (if needed). I then use the magic wand to select the different areas and tone and/or paint them with Photoshop's brush and gradient tools. Making a different layer for each area just in case I mess up.

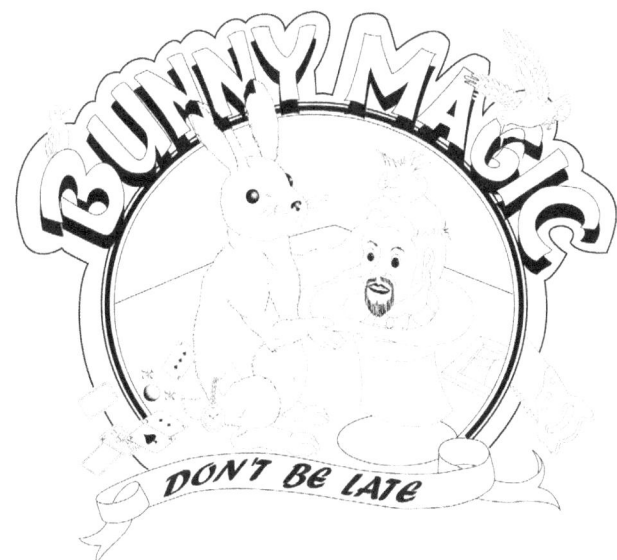

Starting to tone and fill areas in the exported linework in Photoshop.

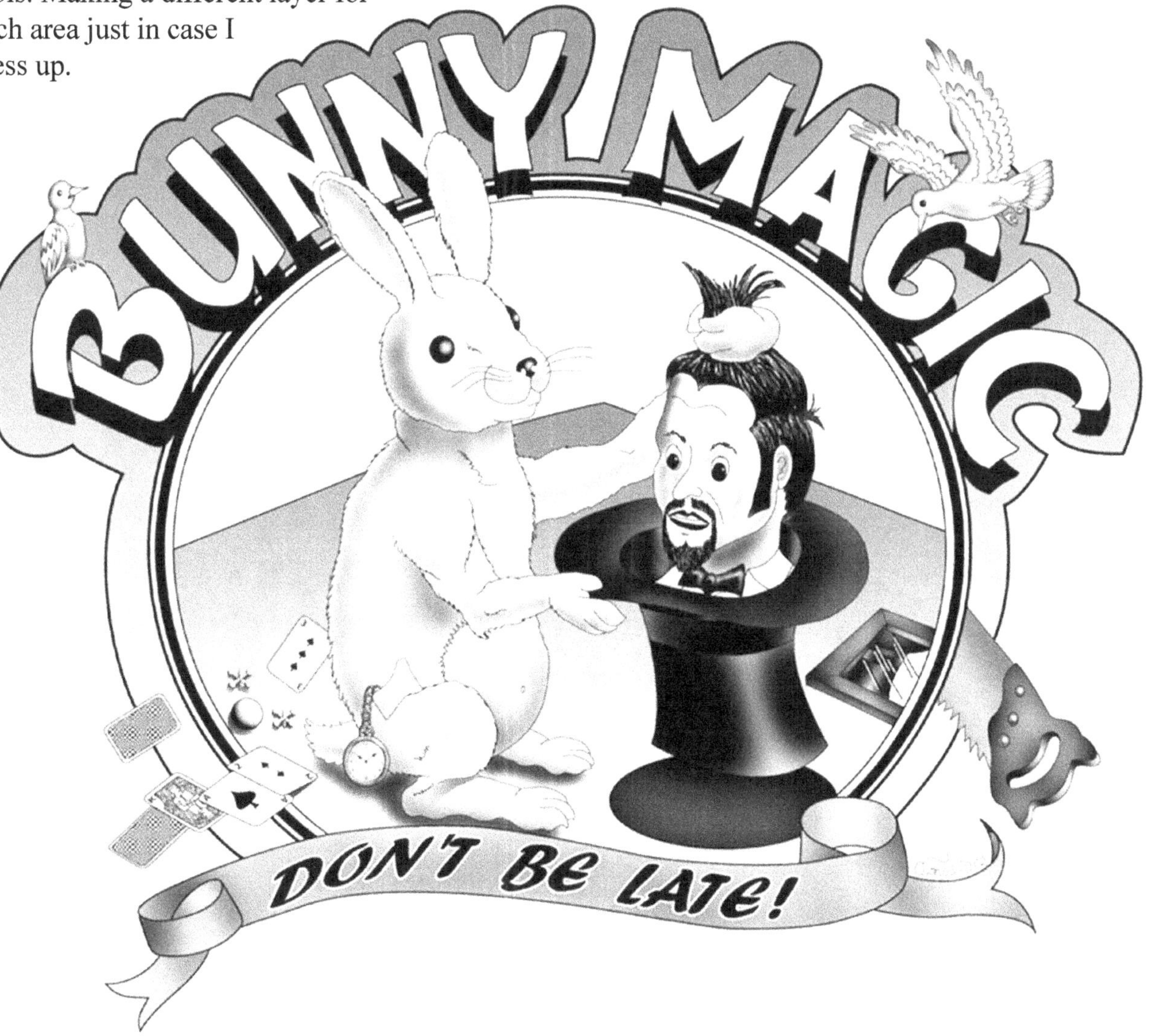

The finished image after being toned and painted in Photoshop. The magic wand tool works great as long as there are no open breaks between the lines.

61

Samples of hand drawn and computer drawn images finished on the computer.

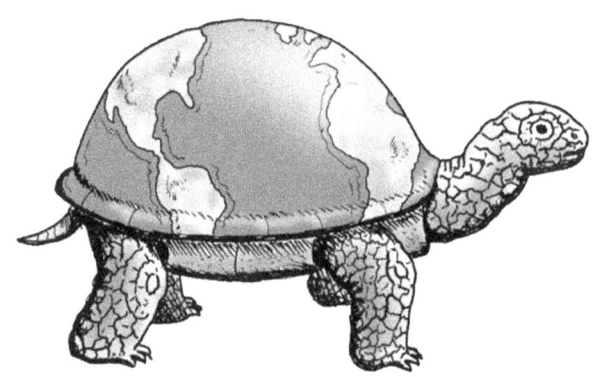

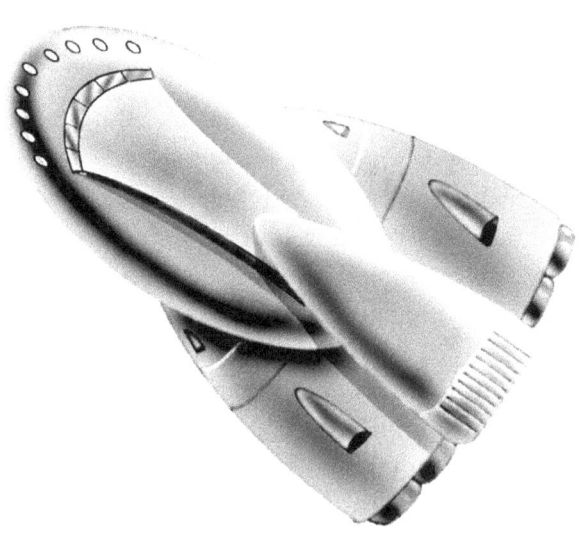

Drawn with pen and then scanned into Photoshop for toning.

Sketched in pencil, scanned into Illustrator, redrawn with the pen tool, exported into Photoshop for toning. Was to be used with the sci-fi presentation but I thought of it too late.

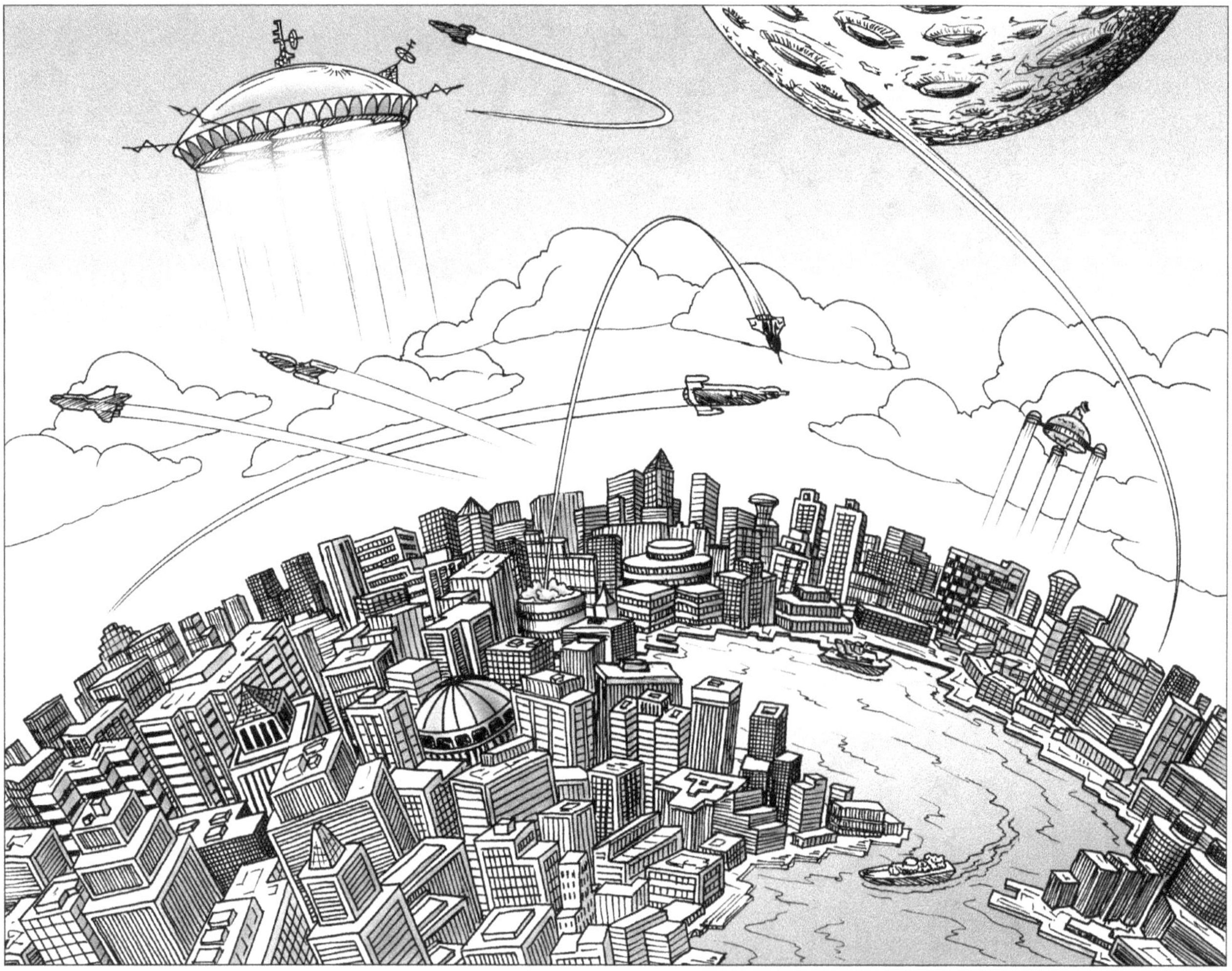

"Overpopulation"

Drawn with pens and then scanned into Photoshop for toning. Over 100 individual area selections. I thought of this image after I had already submitted the sci-fi presentation. Once again too late.

Visualizing spontaneous images in pencil.

Pencil is an easy media to use. Instead of stopping when you get to a certain point, you just continue rendering (and erasing).

The pros of using pencil are; the gradients for going from a light source side to a shadow side are easy to do; mistakes are easily corrected (I use a kneadable eraser); it is capable of having almost as dense of a contrast as ink; and it can resemble (with practice) a finish similar to black and white painting on the computer, an inking or even an airbrushing, (for example, the space ship on the preceding page could of been done with a pencil and looked almost exactly the same); areas of lighter values are a breeze to do; using a pencil on different paper textures can produce a variety of textured effects.

The cons of using a pencil are; smudging is a problem, especially with my style; dark contrasts are only available with hard pressure or pencils at the 4B range or softer (which smudges even easier); reproduction methods do not seem to provide the same level of values without adjustments (or even with adjustments); it is not capable of a super crisp a line as a pen; using a pencil on different paper textures can produce unwanted results for areas not suited for that type of texture.

That being said, once I have an idea pulled from a doodling I could draw that idea out and refine it to a degree where it would be similar to an outline with a fine tip pen and then use the pencil to tone and texture the image to a finish. More often than not though, I tend to add toning right off the get go which makes a clean finish not always the norm. I should study Burne Hogarth and Paul Calle more often because in my opinion they are absolute masters with the pencil.

Several examples of pencil works follow.

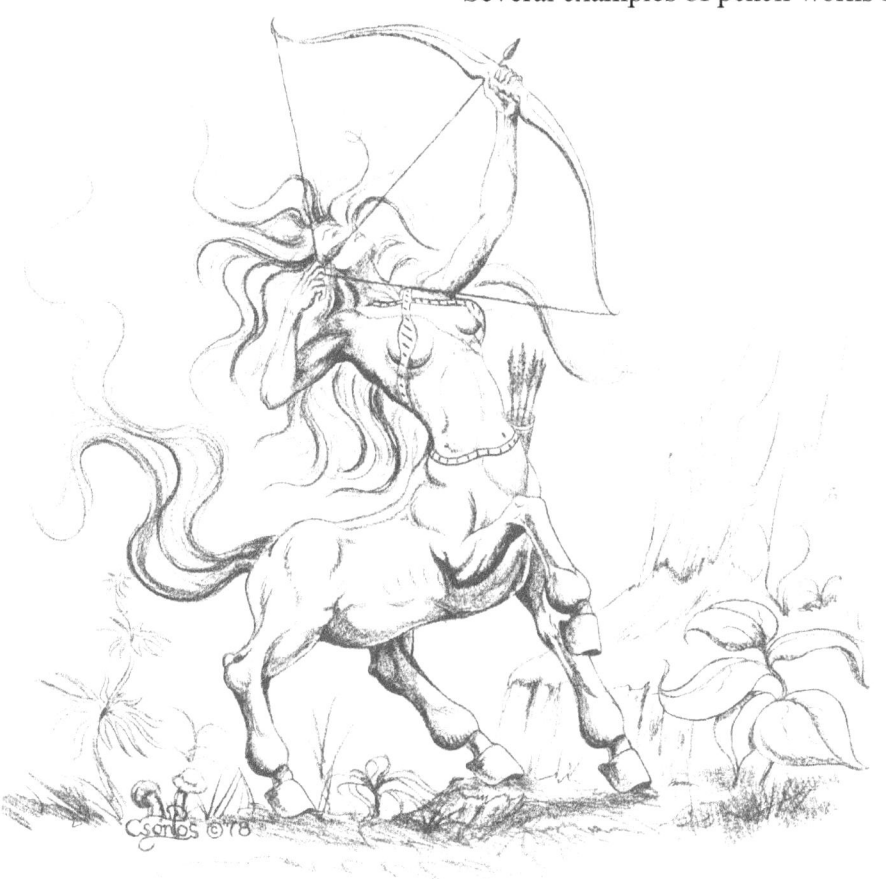

"Huntress"
A 30 minute sketch while waiting for the laundry. HB pencil in a sketch book.

63

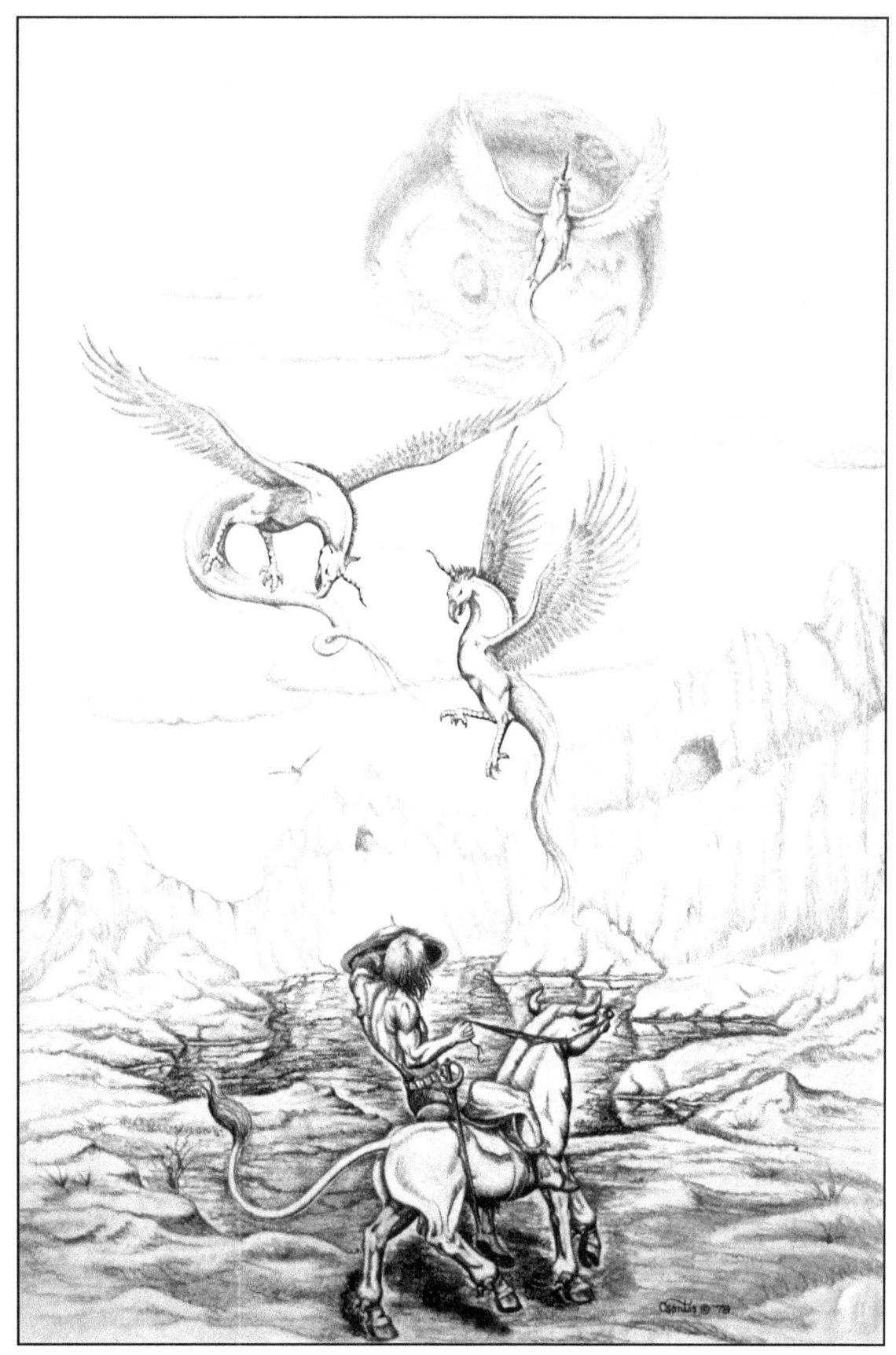

"Admonition"

HB and 2B pencils on cold press illustration board. Hot press board is almost non-textured and does not lend itself as well to smooth blends. This image came about after finding abandoned turquoise mines in the desert.

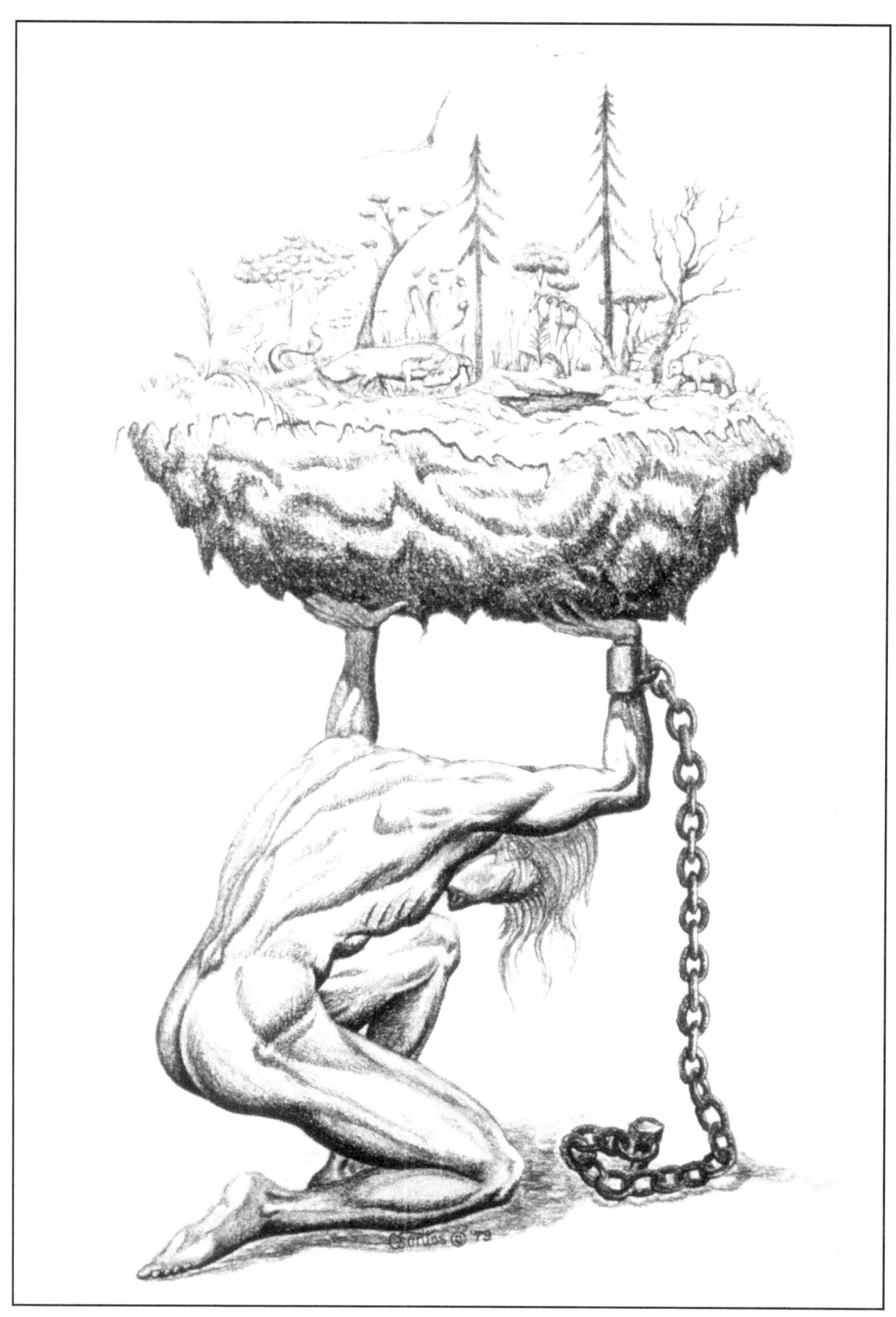

"Continent of Atlas"
Numbers HB and 2B pencils on sketch paper. This paper and illustration effect worked well together.

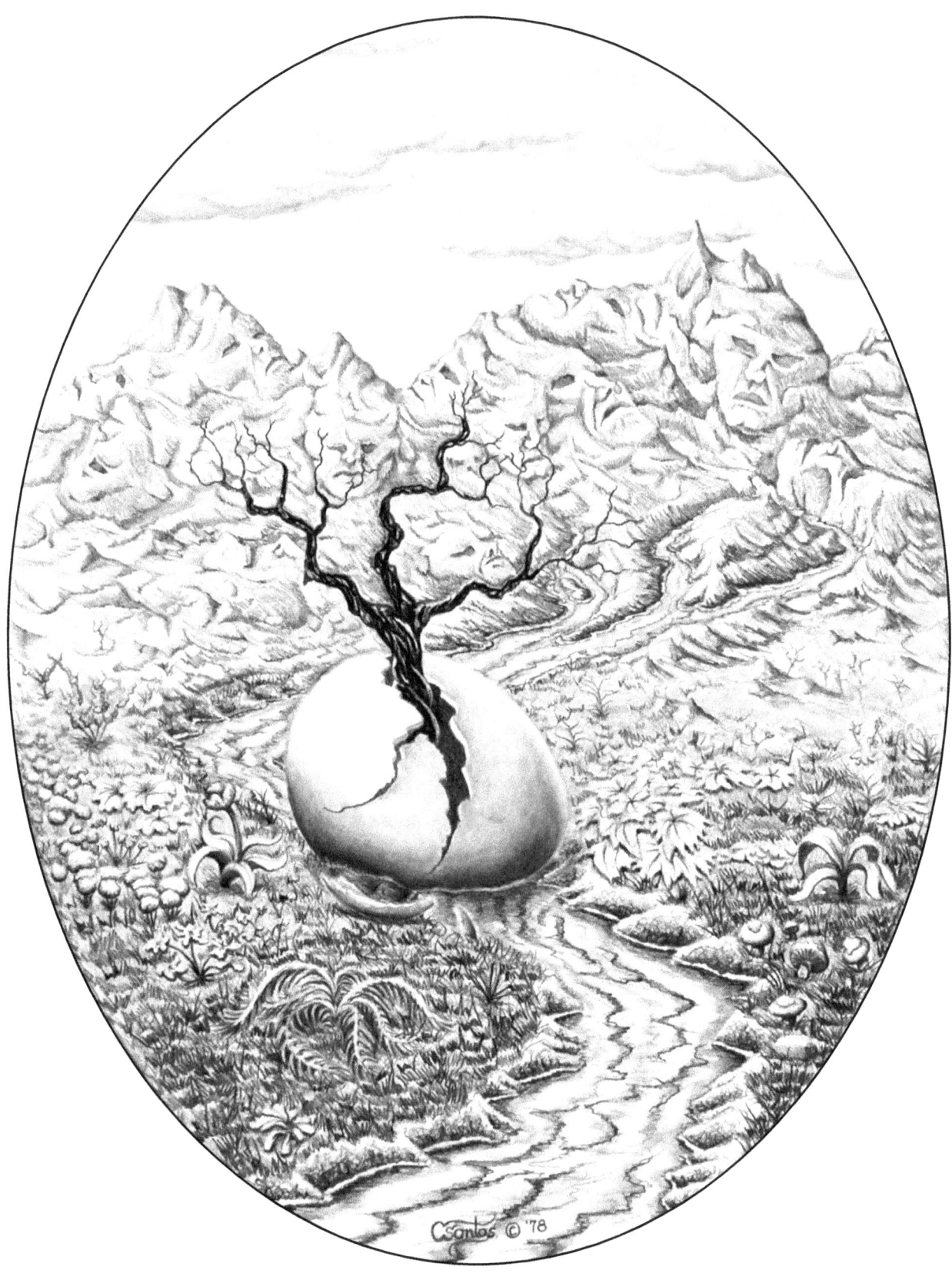

"Evolution"

HB pencil on drawing paper
I had just moved to this area where the view outside the back door was the Estrella Mountain range
with the Gila River flowing by it. As the morning sun rose it cast shadows on the mountains which,
(you guessed it) looked like faces. I drew this piece sitting on the back porch.

66

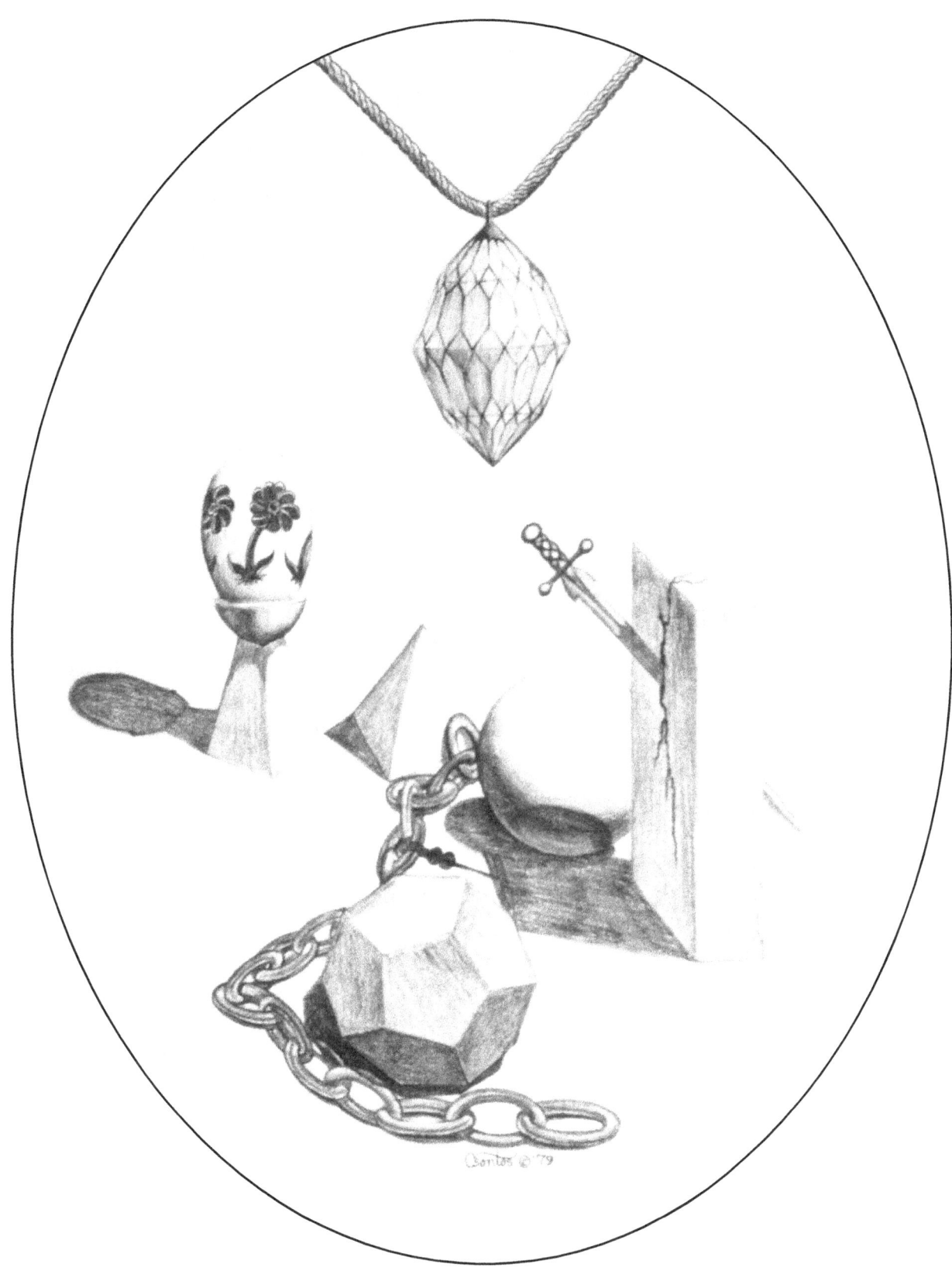

"Still Life"

HB pencil on sketch paper.

I was at an art show when I started this piece. From where I was sitting, the artist in front of me had a water color painting of some chickens. I remember seeing the egg in the sketching first. I'm not sure where the rest of the imagery came from.

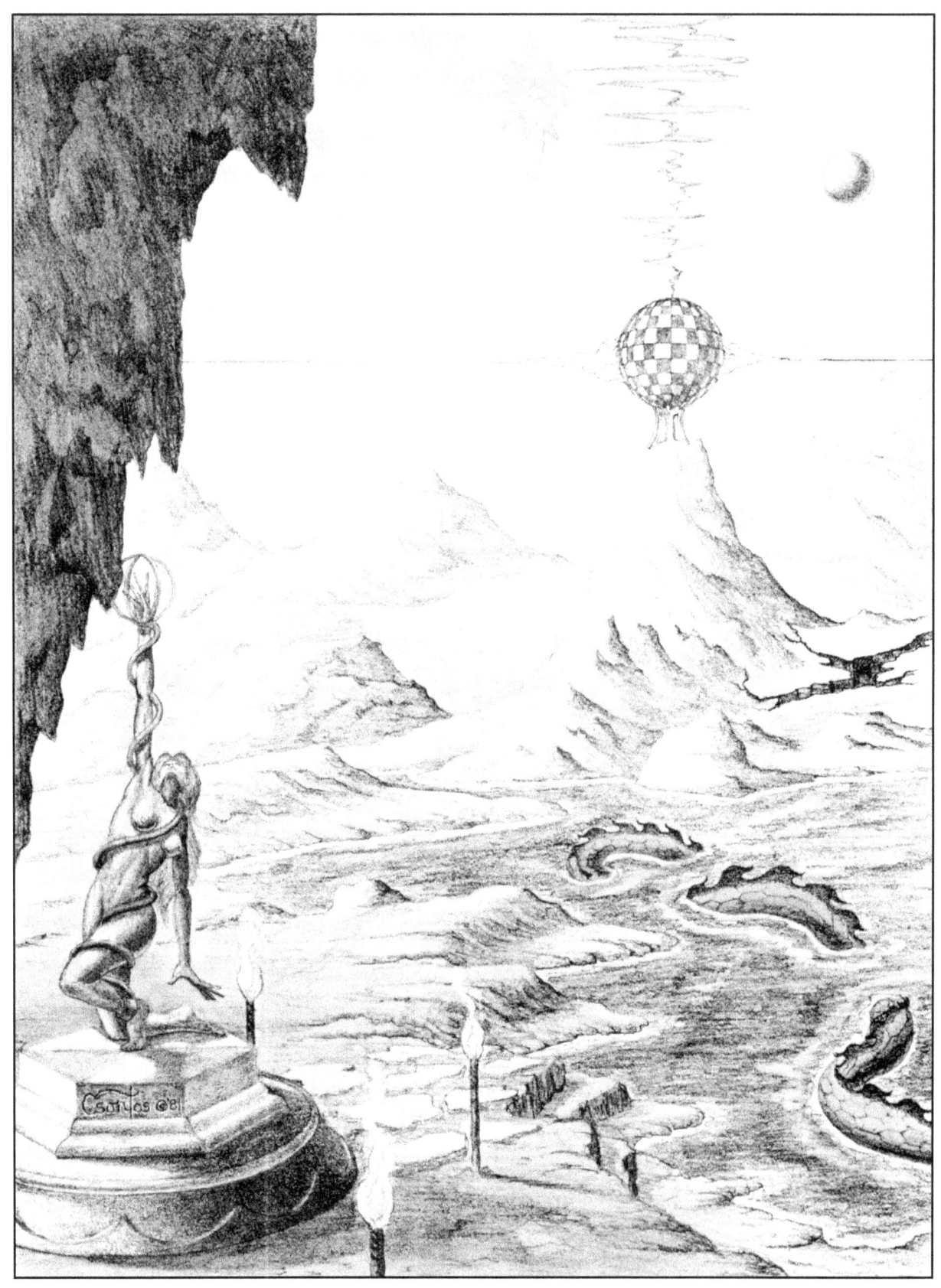

"Cosmographical Terrain"

HB and 2B pencils on sketch paper.

Sometimes just random images come into my mind as I start doodling. I then try to put them together as a scene. If I'm successful the piece comes across as a decent attempt at drawing and usually gets sold. This one was actually stolen. I wonder what that means?

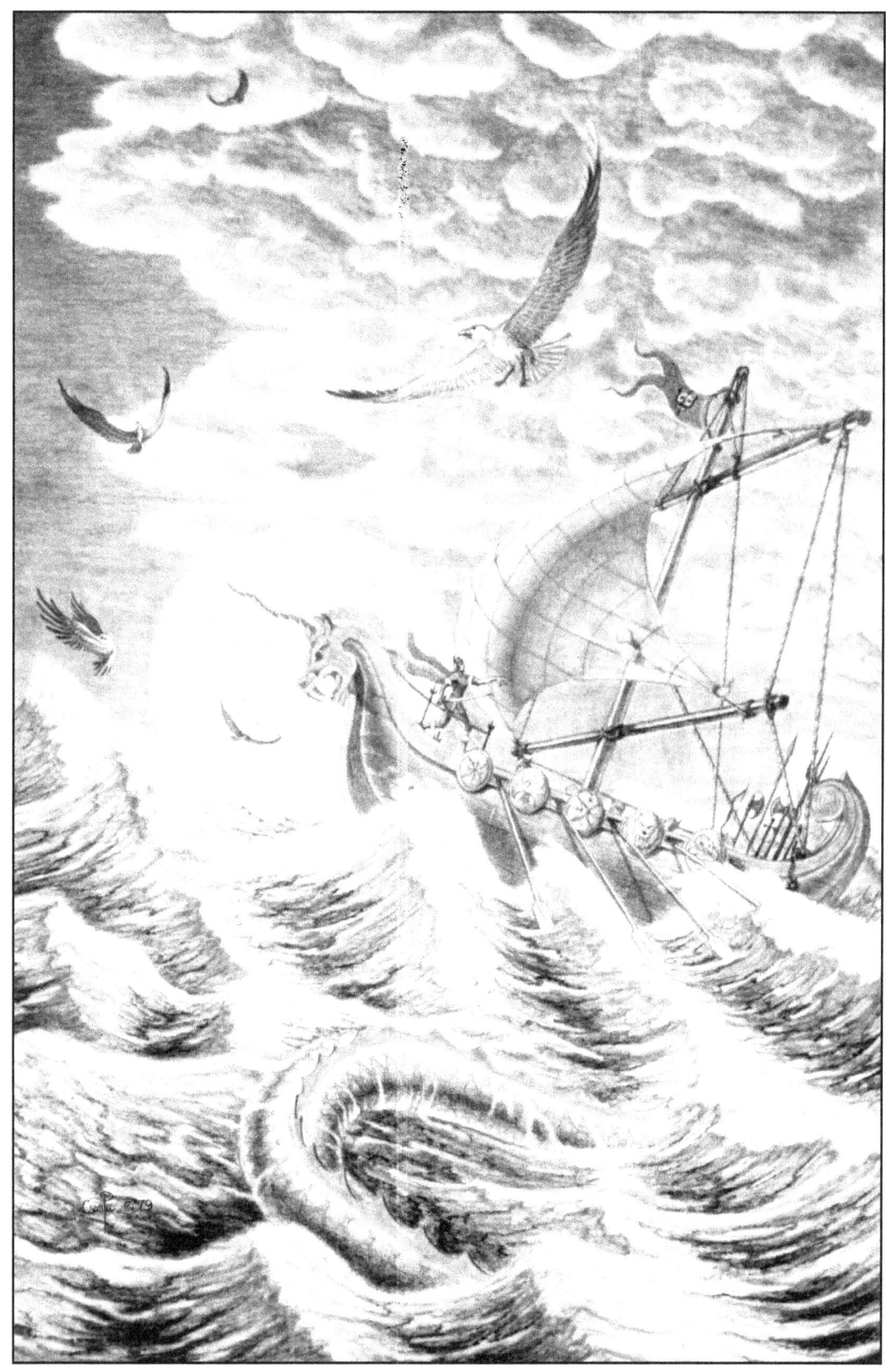

"Nightwind"

HB and 2B pencils on cold press illustration board.
This was my first high dollar sale of a work in pencil. I was at an art show in Fountain Hills, Arizona. The show was over and I was loading up my work and display. This lady came running up to me, asking if I still had it. I said yes and pulled it back out of the car. She then bought it and made my day. It was 20" x 30".

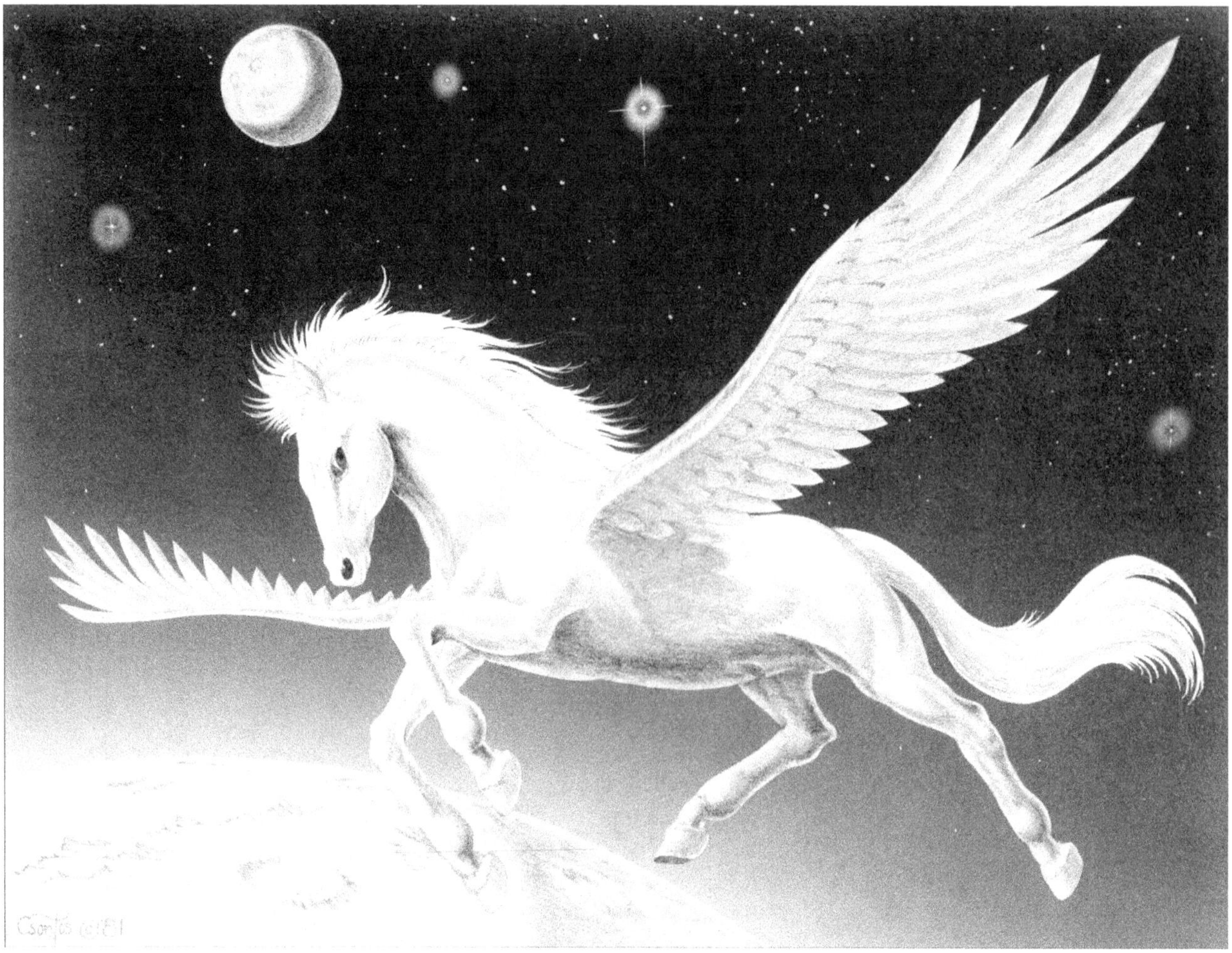

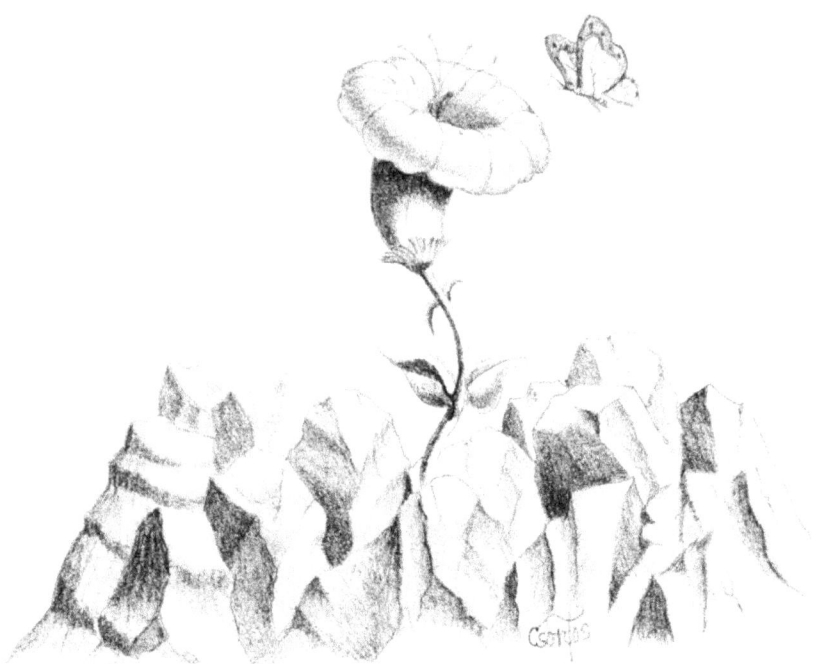

"Pegasus"

HB pencil, airbrush and white acrylic paint on hot press illustration board. This piece of artwork made me realize that pencil work which is meant to be brought to a finish should best be done on a surface with a slight texture such as cold press. I had to continually erase and use a smudge stick to get the smooth blends I wanted on the horse body.

"Hard & Soft"

HB pencil on sketch paper. I was thinking about building a new outdoor fireplace out of rocks. Apparently inspiration comes from just about anything.

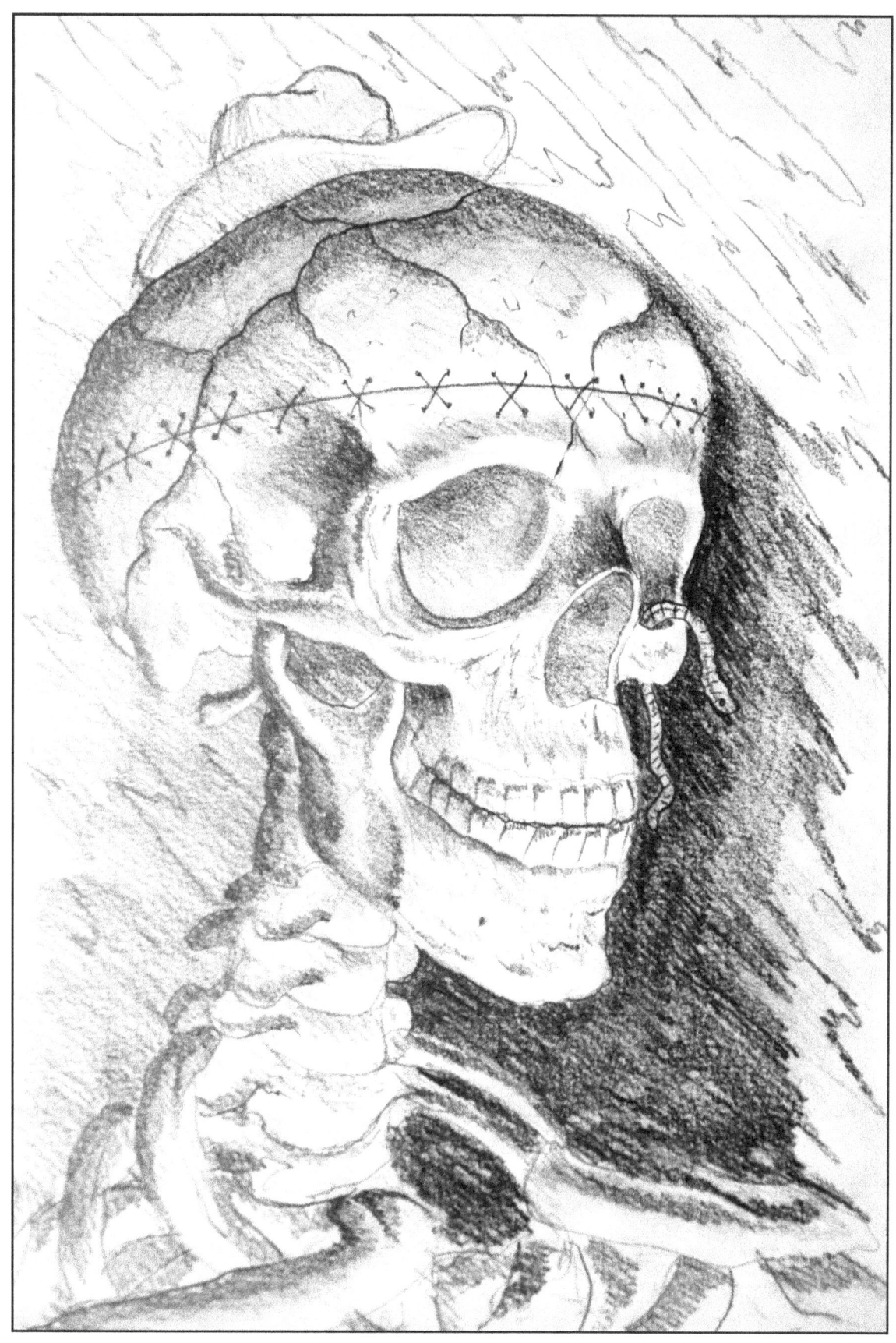

"Cowboy Bones"
4B pencil sketch on drawing paper.
It was a very hot day and I remember musing about cowboys in the old west crossing very dry
deserts. Not sure where the stitches in the brain area came from.

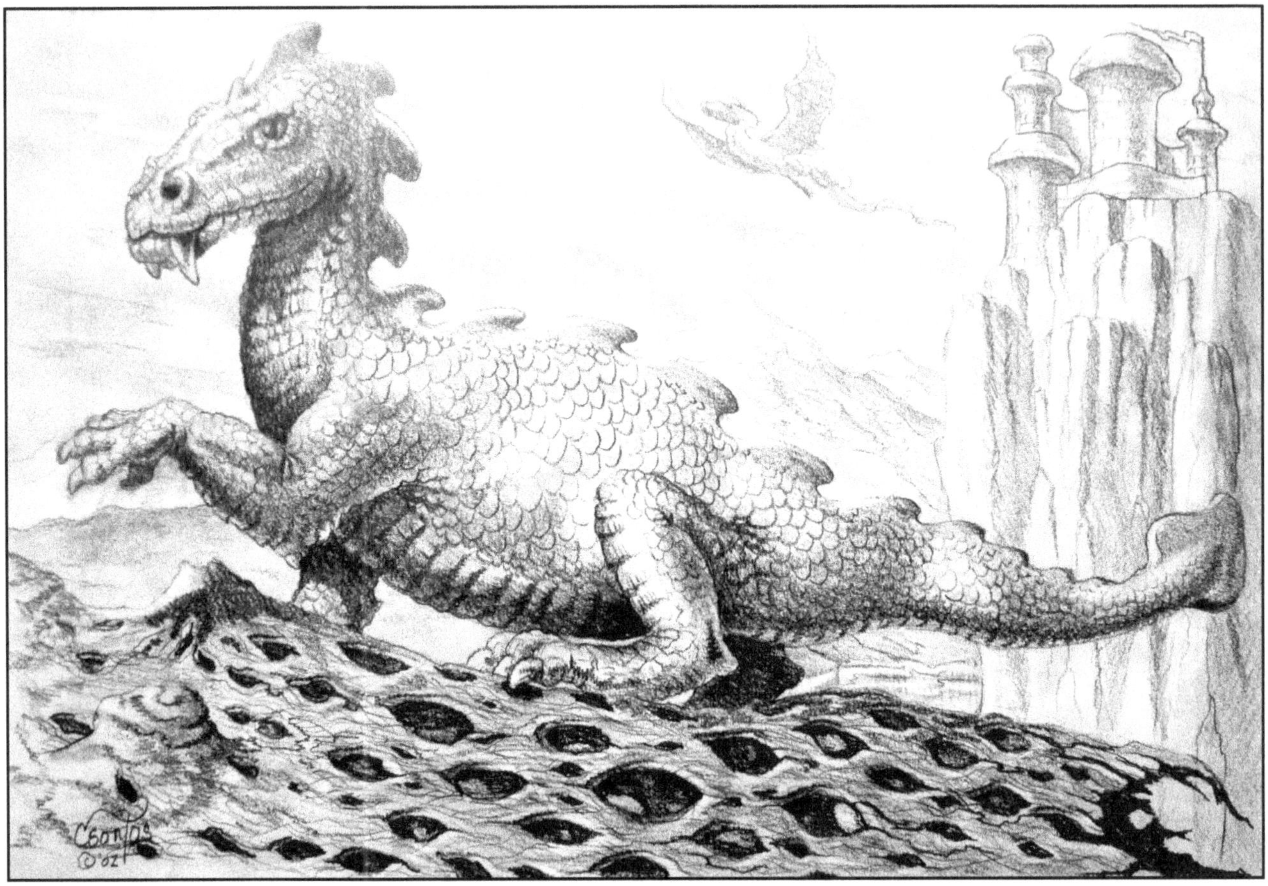

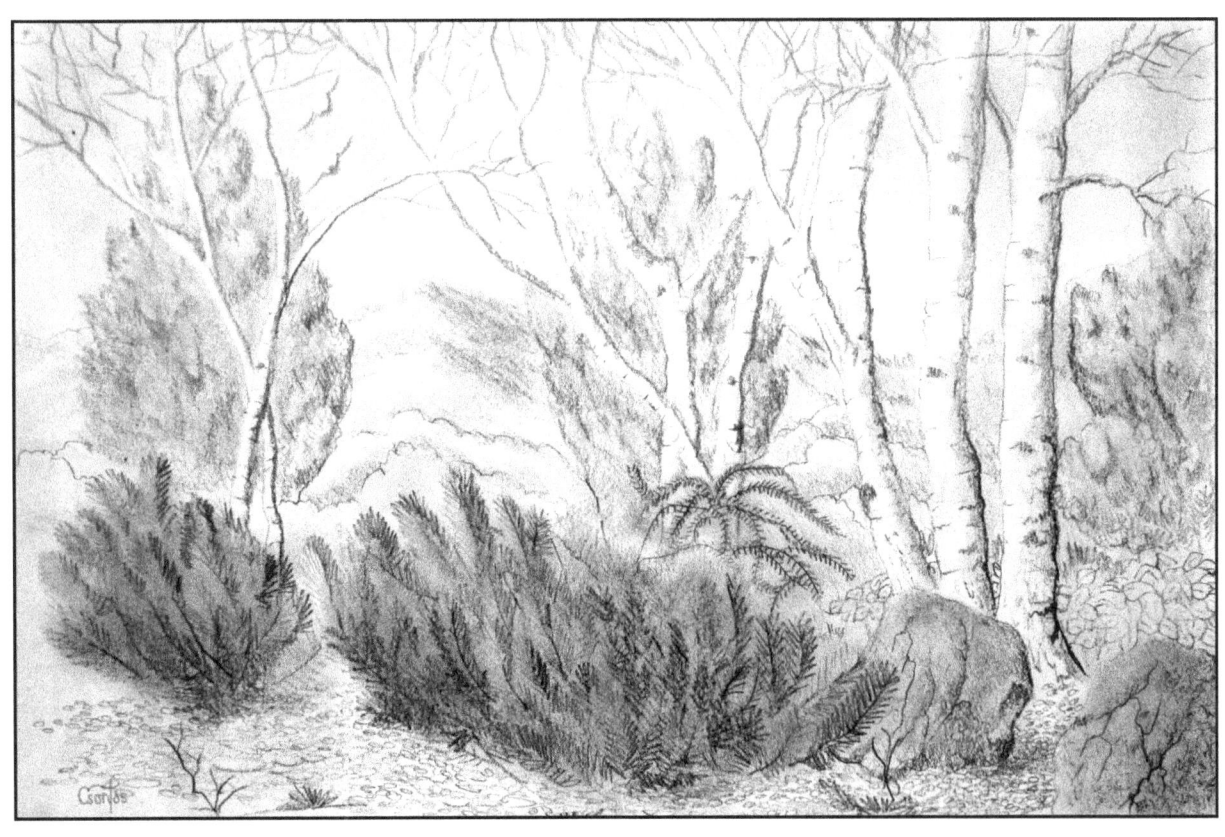

"Dragon Land"
4B pencil on drawing paper.

Landscape study with 4B pencil on drawing paper.

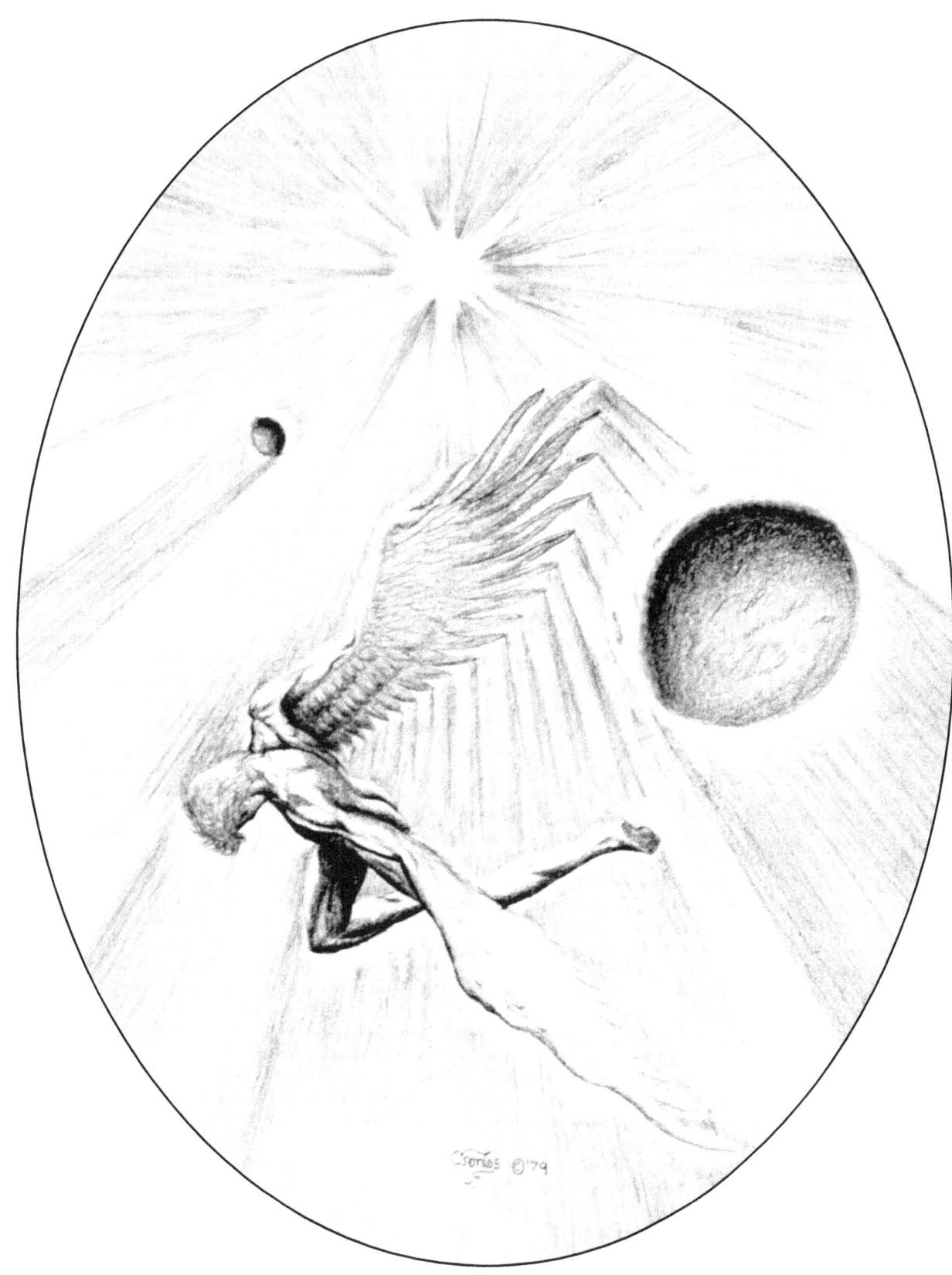

"The Fall"

4B pencil on drawing paper.
I was at an art show in a mall in San Jose, California. We were on the second floor and I kept looking over the handrail at the Koi fish pond below. There was not a lot of people on the second floor and the show was pretty much a wasted effort. So I might of been thinking of jumping over the edge.

Reworking a previous preconceived image.

You will obviously recognize this image from page 46. Well I decided to take my own advice and rework the lighter background sections so that the foreground focus can have more of a prevalent effect. Plus darkening those areas removes the busyness from an excessive amount of similar sized linework. When I did the original back in 1978 I could of made the lighter background areas darker with an ink wash but then the image would of needed a halftone screen overlay before printing. Nowadays however, with direct to plate printing and digital formats, any areas with a less than full black toning can be printed instantly because the image is either changed to pixels or receives halftoning automatically as it is sent to the plate maker. Computers were not on the market yet at that time so any direct to plate printing was not available. For this image I did use the computer to re-tone those areas. I made a selection by using a channel mask in Photoshop. Actually several selections to isolate all the areas. It probably took me about four times as long as it should have because my son borrowed my Wacom tablet (for those of you that don't know, a Wacom tablet is a mouse in the shape of a pen with its own tablet [pad]). I had it set up for my left hand as I used the regular mouse in my right hand. I was quite fast with it but my son needed it for his own artwork.

Anyhow after the areas were selected I filled them with a 60% gray and then used the rough pastels filter. After that I used the motion blur filter to angle the smudges in the same direction as the areas themselves. To finish it up I used the Gaussian blur filter to soften everything I did up to that point.

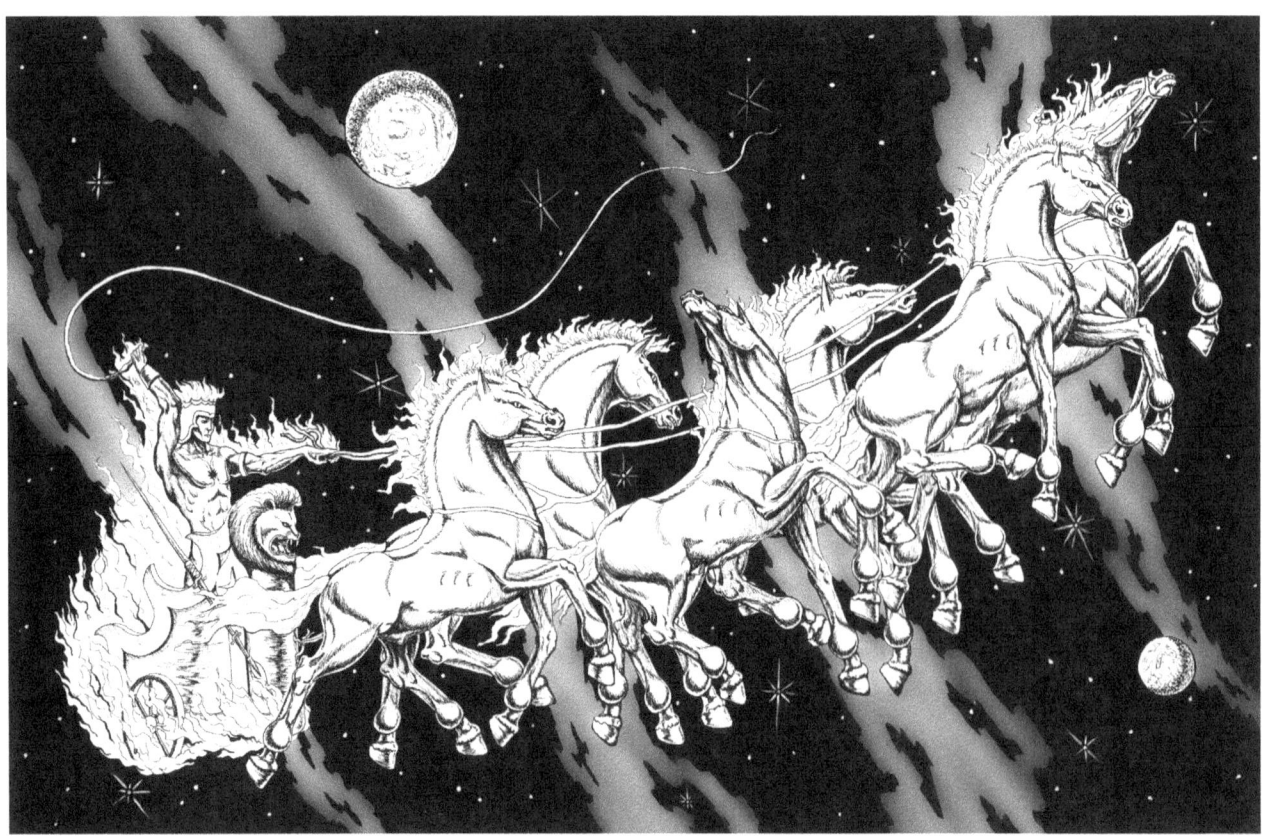

"The Flaming Chariot"

Reworked on the computer to make the background recede away from the foreground focus. Now it looks like it should be colored. I'll put that in my next book, 'Coloring Black and White Images'. Regardless of that, I have to admit it does seem to look better. Another example of visualizing after the fact. Even years later.

Visualizing with pencil and ink.
Spontaneous technique number three.

So far in this book I have yet to come up with a reasonable explanation of how to see imagery in the doodles and sketches of spontaneous works. I'm not sure how to answer that. I have a theory as to where some of these images or scenes come from. Sometimes after I come up with an image and sketch it in, I remember certain events or comments from the preceding days, weeks, months or even years before, as I've been mentioning by the illustrations I've shown. For example, after I came up with the image of the "Snake Charmer", I remembered from a few days earlier that I rescued a bull snake from what looked like a piece of a fishing net. The net had gotten tighter and tighter around the snake's body as it must have crawled through it. I had to cut the net away as the snake kept biting me. Fortunately it was only a bull snake.

When I came up with the image 'Where Rain Comes From', it was actually raining outside.

One morning I was out for my usual walk. The night before we had a freak snowfall of about five inches (it was late April, the flowers were coming out and I thought winter was over) as I walked along the path I usually take, I noticed that the path itself was free of snow. For some reason the snow had started to melt only where the path was. I was also thinking about how much snow might have fallen on the mountains by Flagstaff (as I can usually see them from a knoll on my walk) and if the skiing season had been extended.

The initial sketch, which you can see is even more basic than most.

All these thoughts might have been in my subconscious when I got back home and sat down to sketch another image. The image that came out of that particular sketching was 'Tramway'. What is even more bizarre was that the initial sketching was just a few horizontal lines getting smaller and smaller.

Anyhow, I can't really be sure as to exactly where some of the imagery comes from because I don't have any way to prove it, but I do find it very interesting as to what develops. I read once that the subconscious does not know what is real imagery and what is imagined imagery. Which may explain why almost none of my personal scenes I come up with are typical realism.

I also believe it is more challenging to create from one's imagination then to copy a landscape, as I did for the phone book cover. However, the bottom line is to execute the art in a fashion that is professional, which is utilizing the proper technique, and appealing or engaging an emotional response.

The idea laid in with some values. I also tried a few different techniques for the toning of the stonework on the shadow side, such as cross-hatching, scribbling, and curved lines.

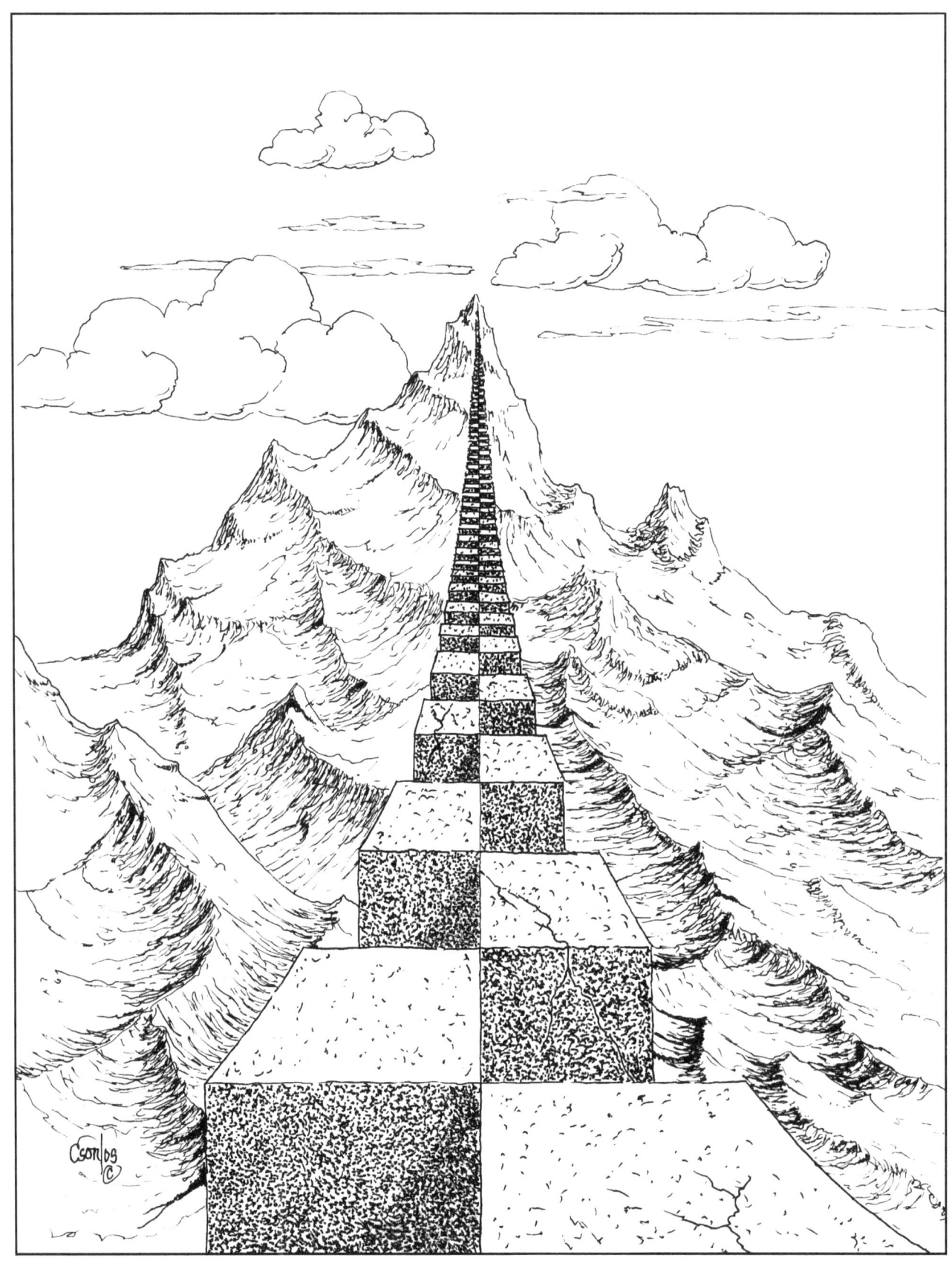

"Tramway"

Ink - pen and brush. Possibly a sub-conscious twist on previous visual stimuli and thoughts. I really love the way I create my personal art. There is something mystical about it and I would not do it any other way.

More samples of spontaneous illustrations.

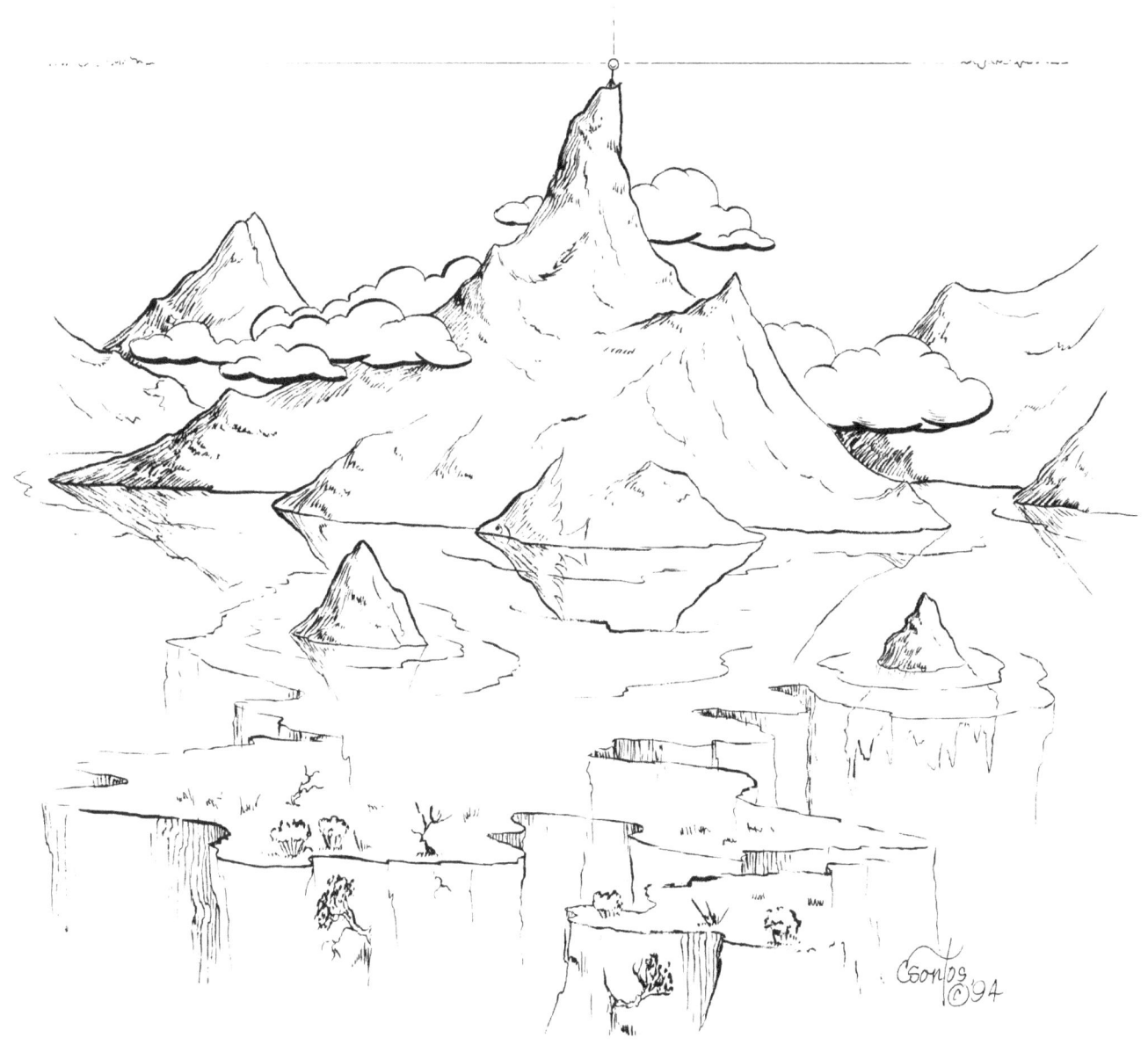

"Symbiosis"
Ink - brush.

It is easy to see recurring imagery in a lot of the pieces. I can only assume that those ideas have made a lasting impression on my mind (as to why, I don't know). For example the little transmission tower at the top of the mountain is the same as the one in "Cosmographical Terrain" on page 68. The pieces were done thirteen years apart.

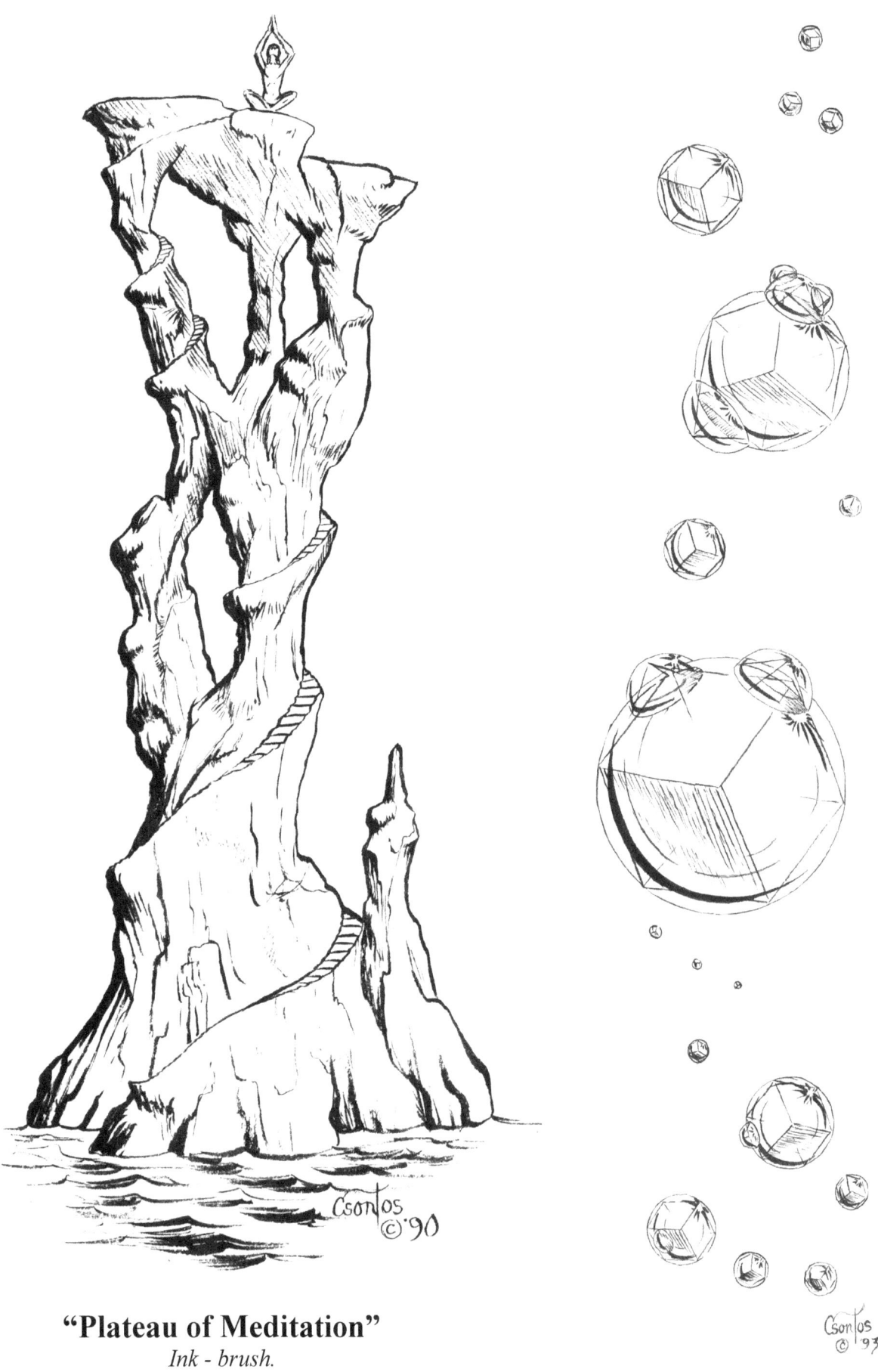

"Plateau of Meditation"
Ink - brush.
I wasn't even meditating at the time I did this
one. Maybe I was thinking about taking it up.

"Levitation"
Ink - pen and brush.

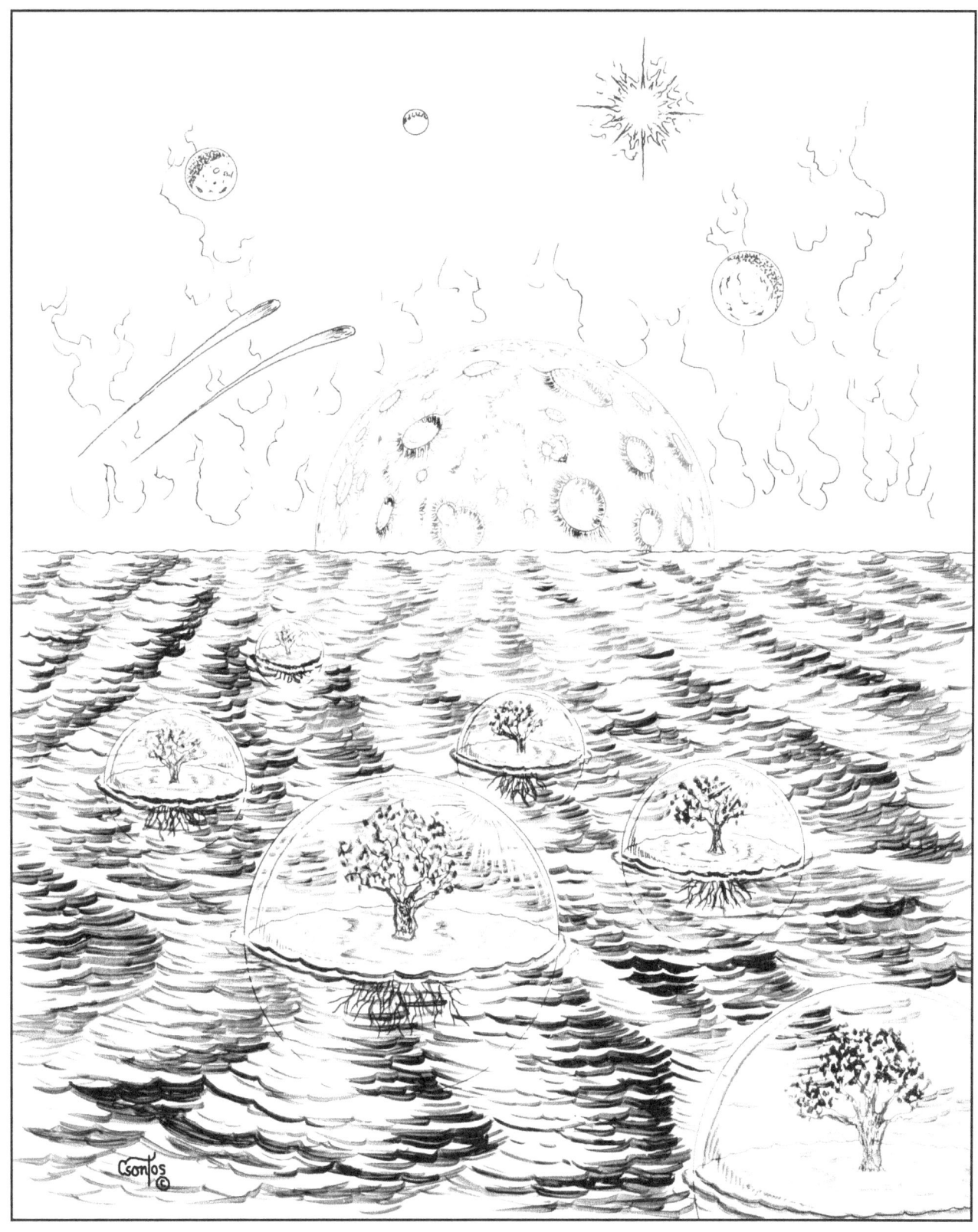

"Hydroponic Tree Farming"

Ink - pen and brush.

I used to do a lot of bubbles as a kid and when I got older I did them again with my son when he was little. I even photographed many different versions and sizes for references for my paintings.

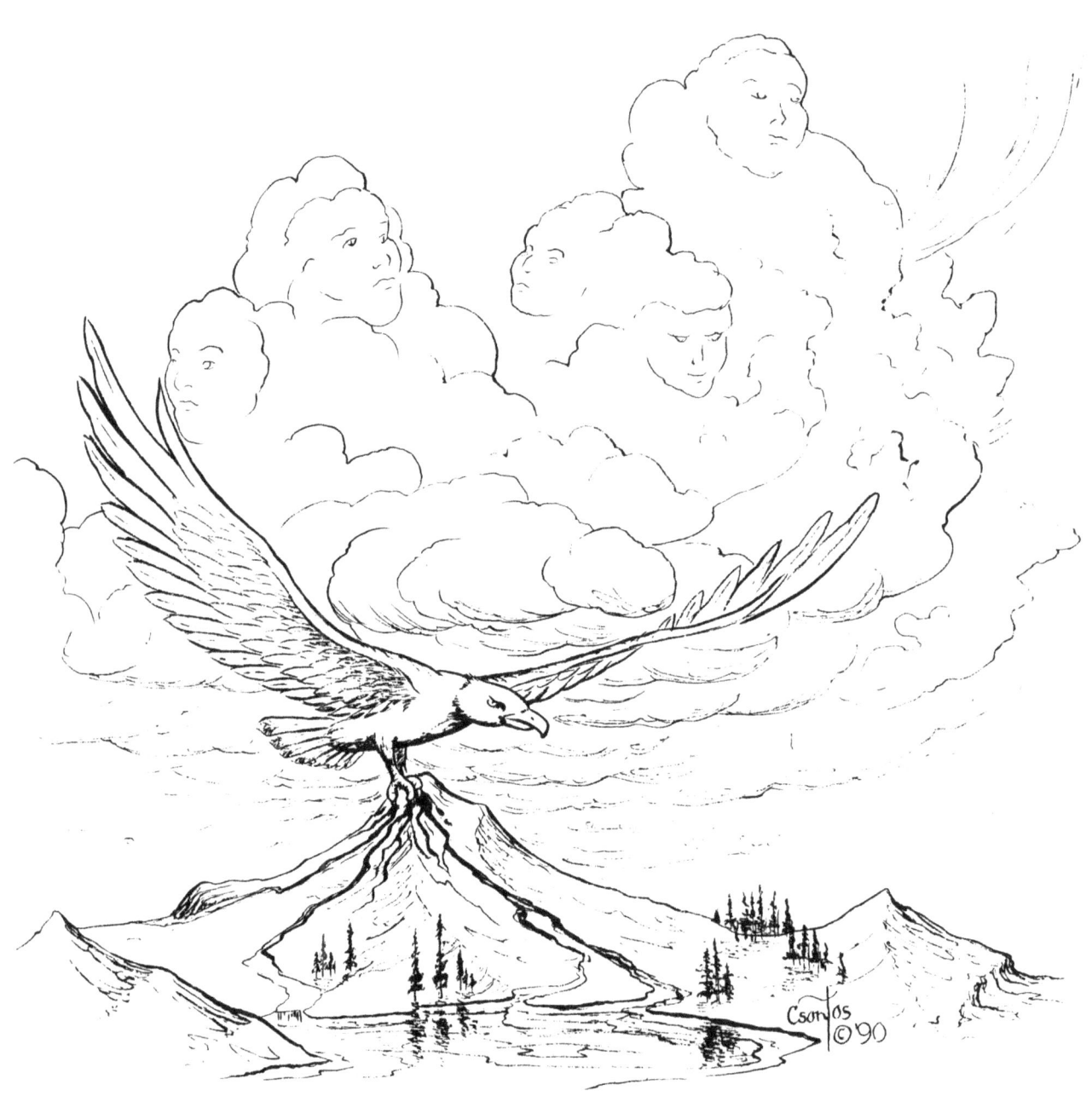

"Ripping The River"

Ink - brush.

Another image where I can remember the though I had as I started to draw. I was thinking of how steams and rivers start and then I remember that the area where they do emerge is probably way up in the mountains where the eagles roam. From those two thoughts came this simple image.

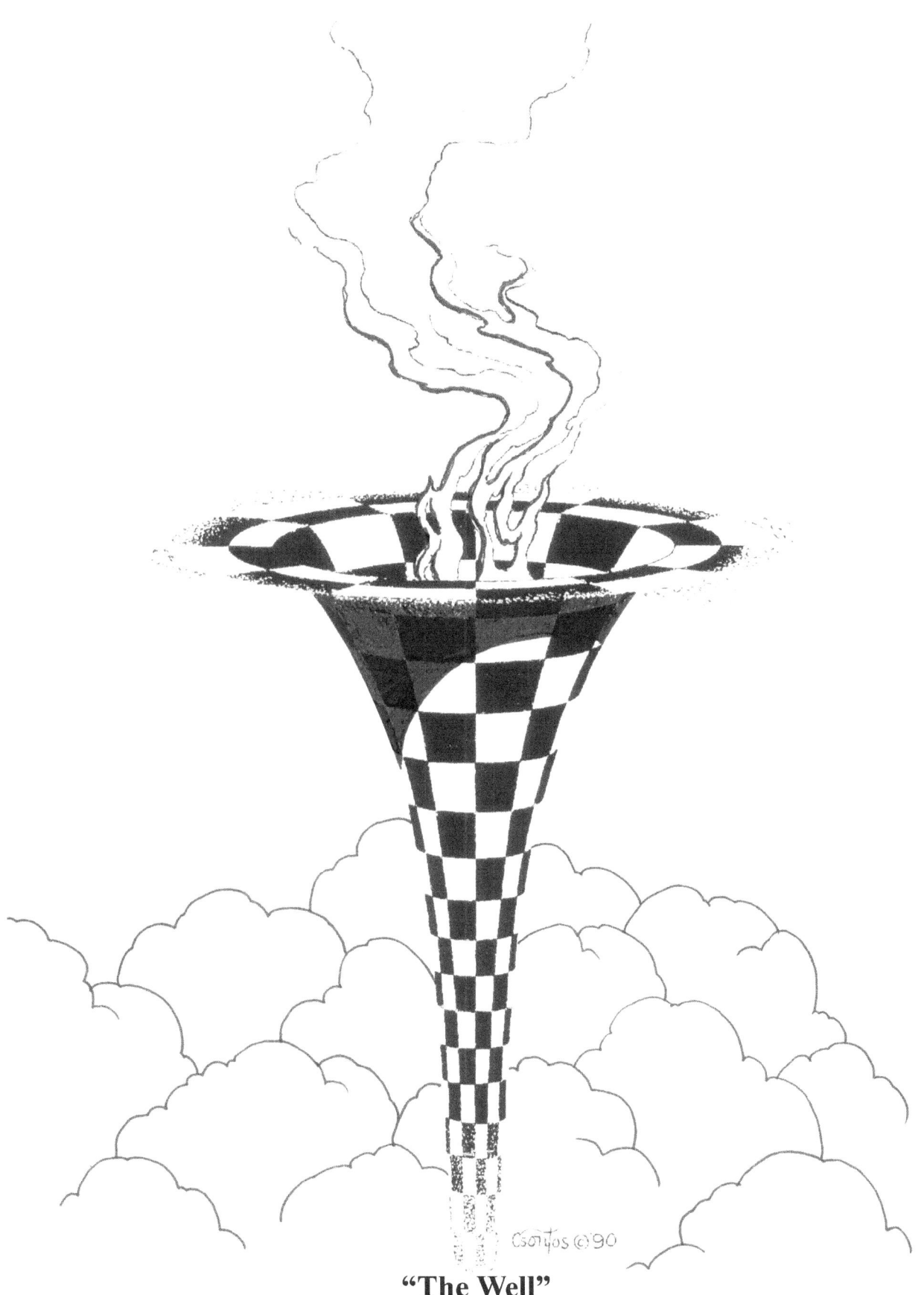

"The Well"

Ink - pen and brush.

This image came to me from basically just a horizontal oval and a vertical line. However, it took me at least three sketches before I could get the curves of the checkered areas to work out as I saw it in my mind. This is one of my favorites. Again with the checkerboards. Hopefully I don't get too redundant.

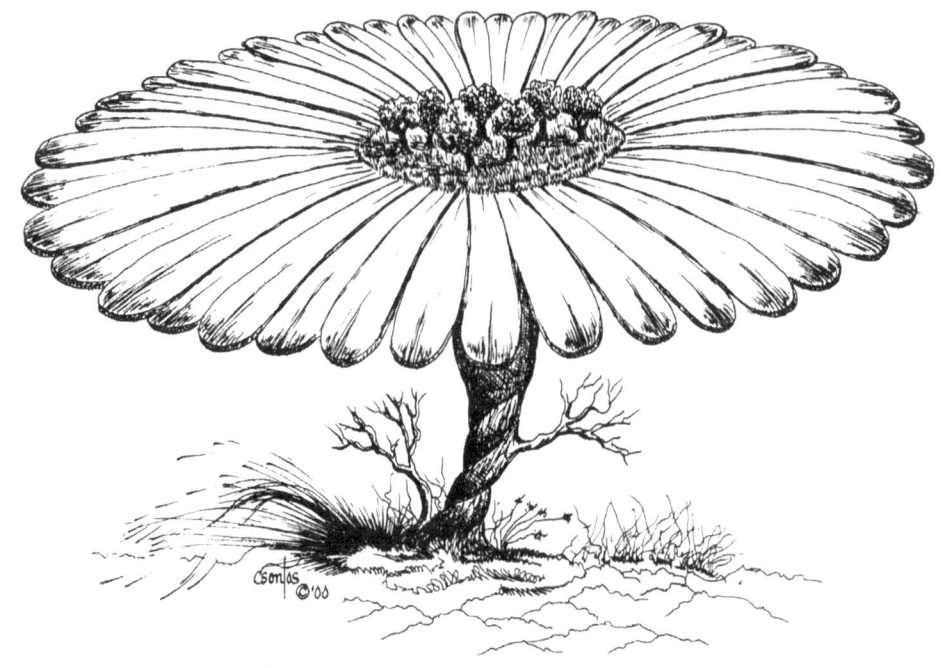

"The Tree is Flowering"

Ink - drawing pen. It's kind of hard to see from the scale of this drawing but the center of the flower is small trees.

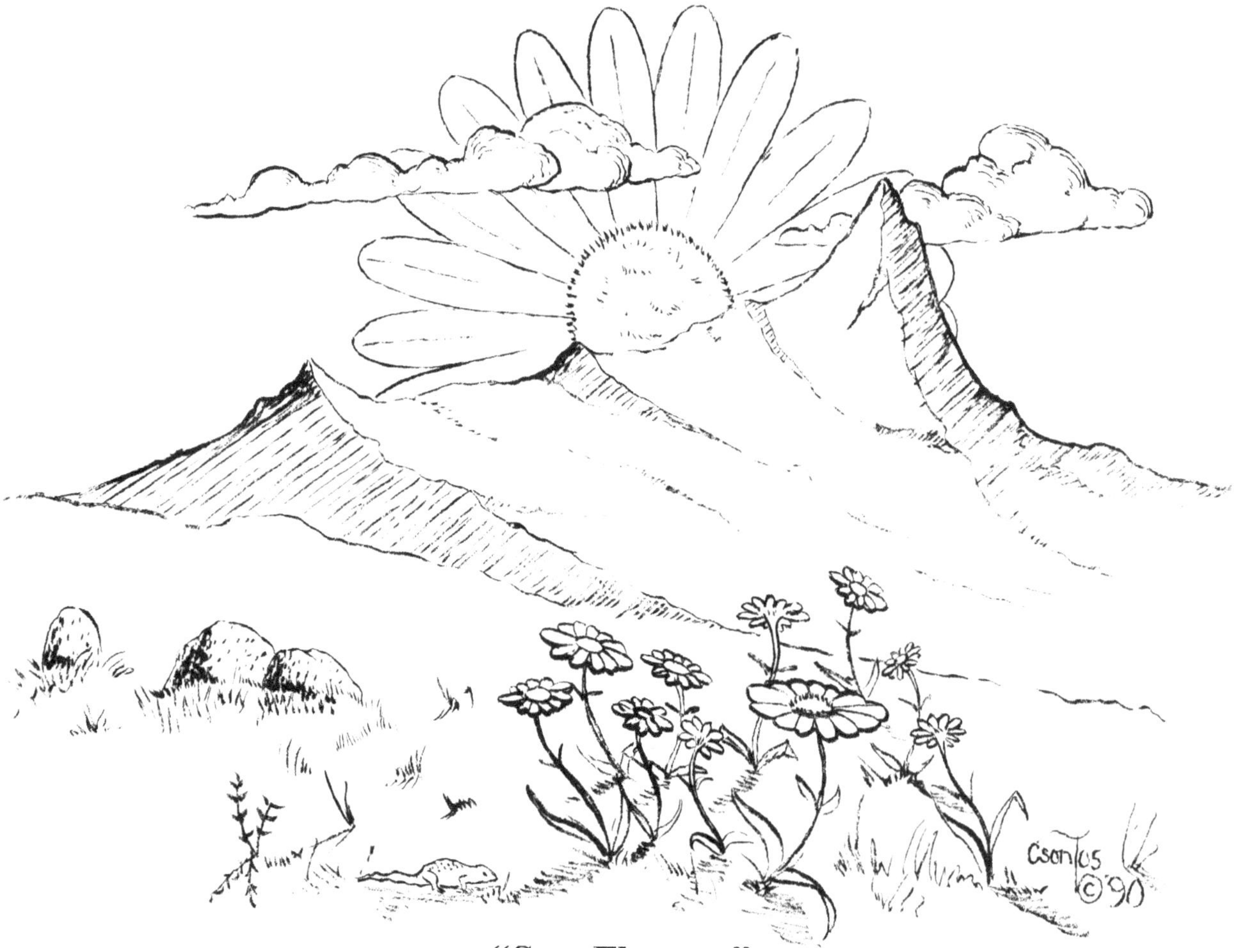

"Sun-Flowers"

Ink - brush. I know exactly where this image came from. Susan was growing sunflowers and one grew up to 10 feet, 5 inches tall. Amazing!

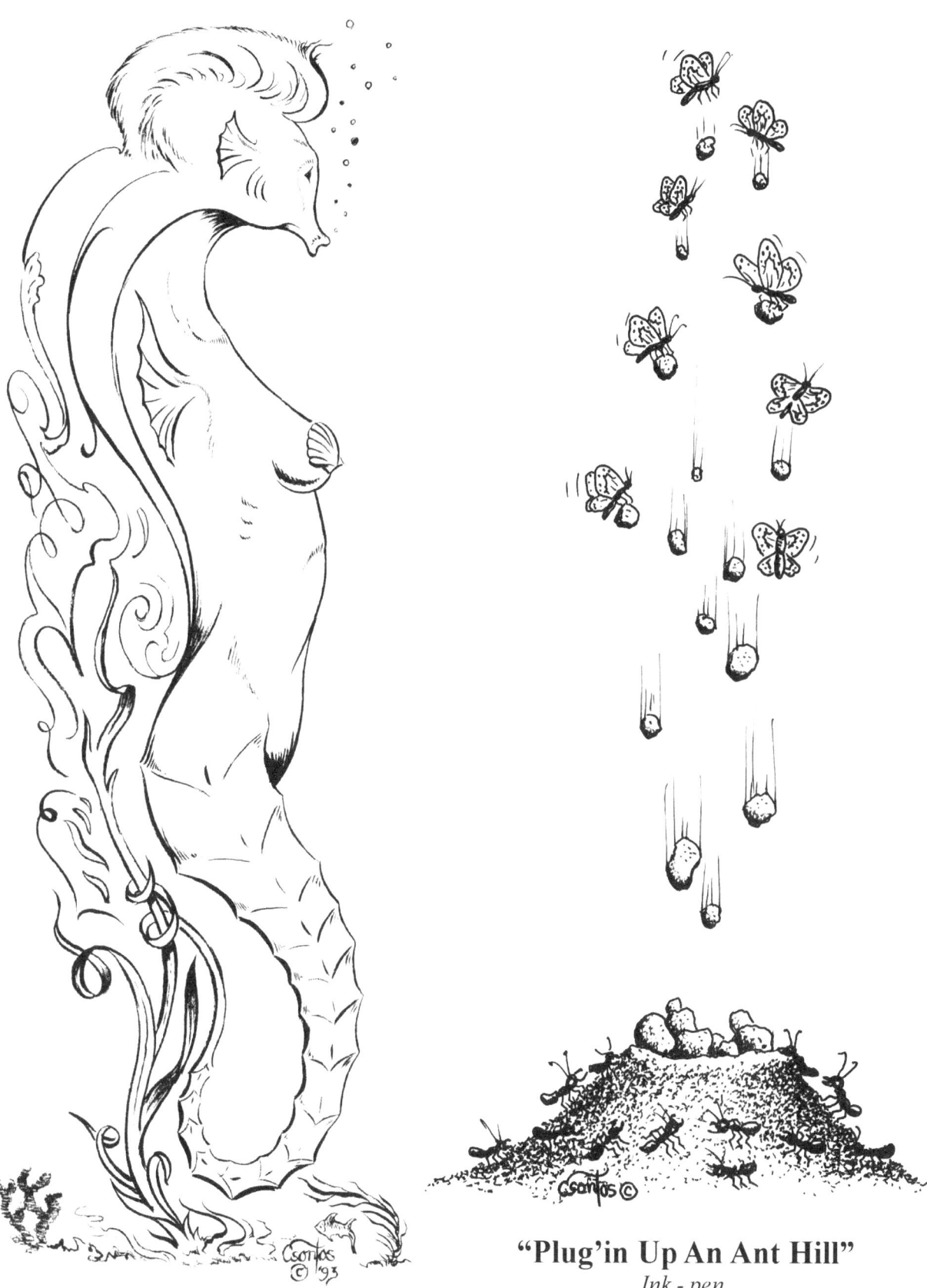

"Sea She-Horse"

Ink - brush. We just got an aquarium and were trying to think of stuff to put into it.

"Plug'in Up An Ant Hill"

Ink - pen.

My son was messing with an ant hill on our property. I constantly get amused at the images that develop from simple every day occurrences.

Visualizing with pencil and ink.
Spontaneous technique number four.

I found the starting aspect of this image very interesting and it seems to correspond with my thoughts of how and where some of the imagery

comes from. The first phase of the sketch is very similar to the starting sketch I made for "The Edge of Space" (page 94), which was basically just an indeterminate dark abstract area. For the image "The Edge of Space", I was just coming off those sci-fi presentation images and I probably still had some outer space stuck in my head.

But for "Where Rain Comes From", it was raining outside of my studio window. I remember thinking that the rain would be good for the oak trees as they were going through their leaf transition and if it doesn't rain at that time they go dormant until it does rain. I have seen the oak trees stop their new leaf growth for up to three months because of drought conditions.

The initial sketch which was nothing more then a dark area. The swirls were drawn in afterwards and gave me the indication of clouds. Once the clouds came to mind then the water just seemed a natural fit for the dark area.

The resulting image which probably came from watching and listening to the rain outside my studio window. The bird shapes are a repetition of the smaller cloud shapes.

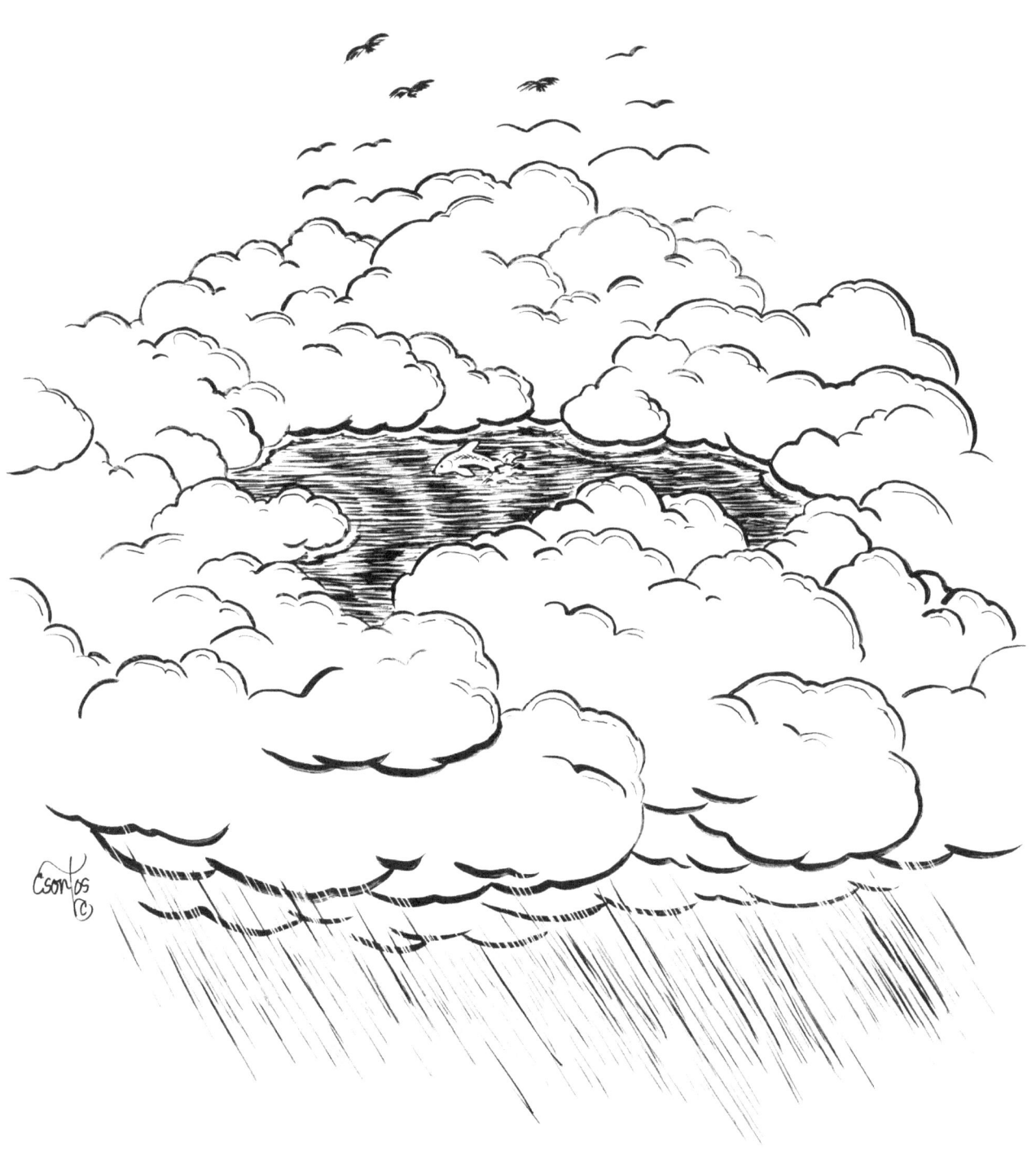

"Where Rain Comes From"
Ink - brush.

Still more samples of spontaneous illustrations.

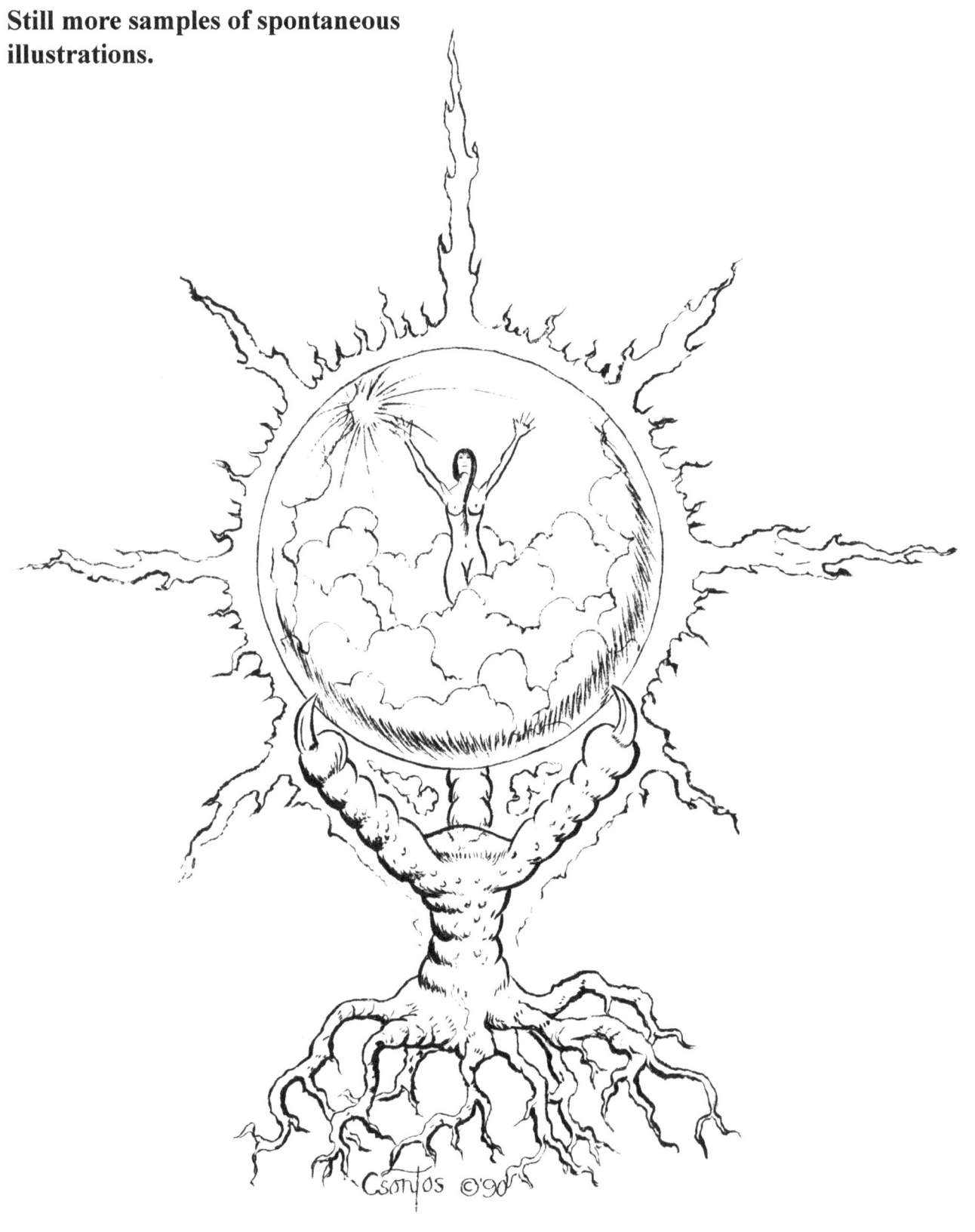

"In-Chanting"
Ink - brush.
I started reading a book on the secret organizations of the ancient (and modern) world. It got a little too heavy for me with all the deity names and rituals some of them went through.

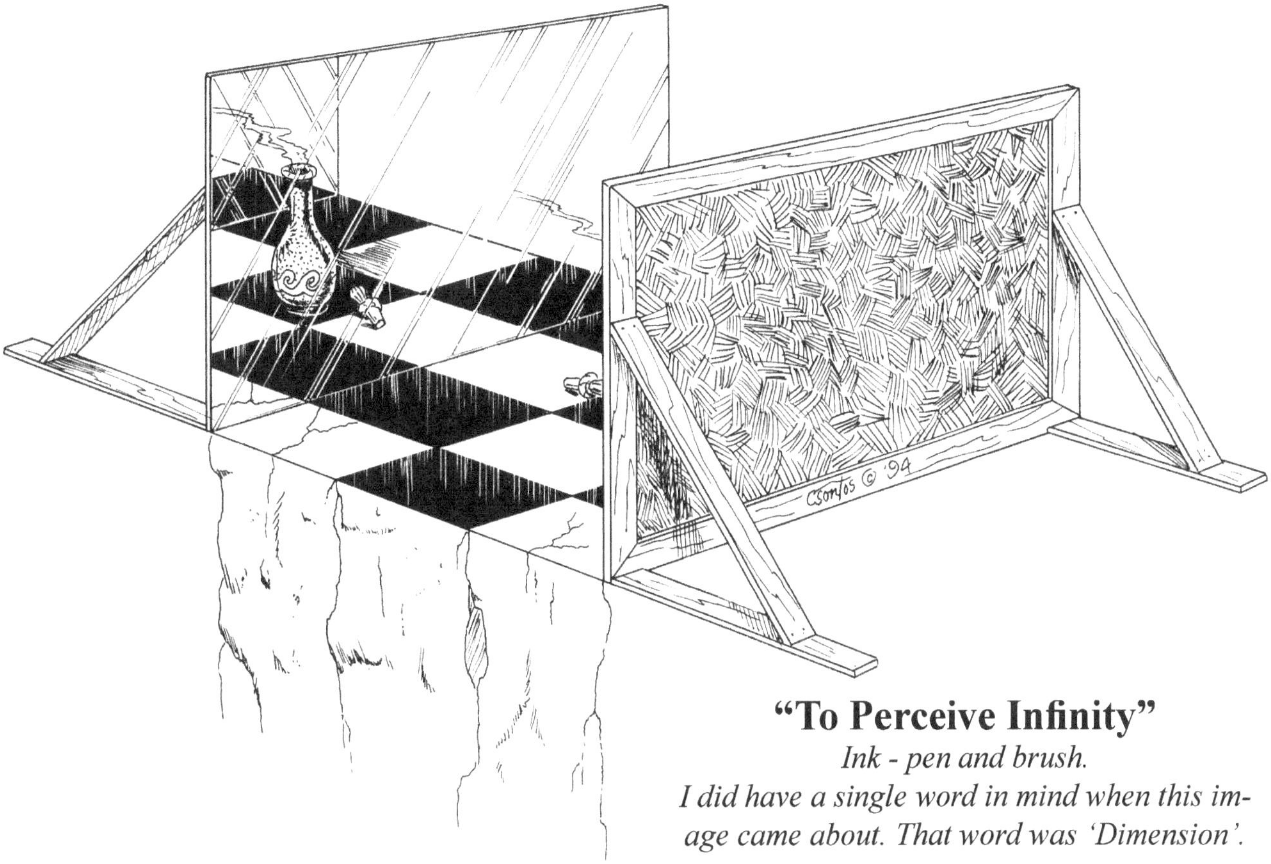

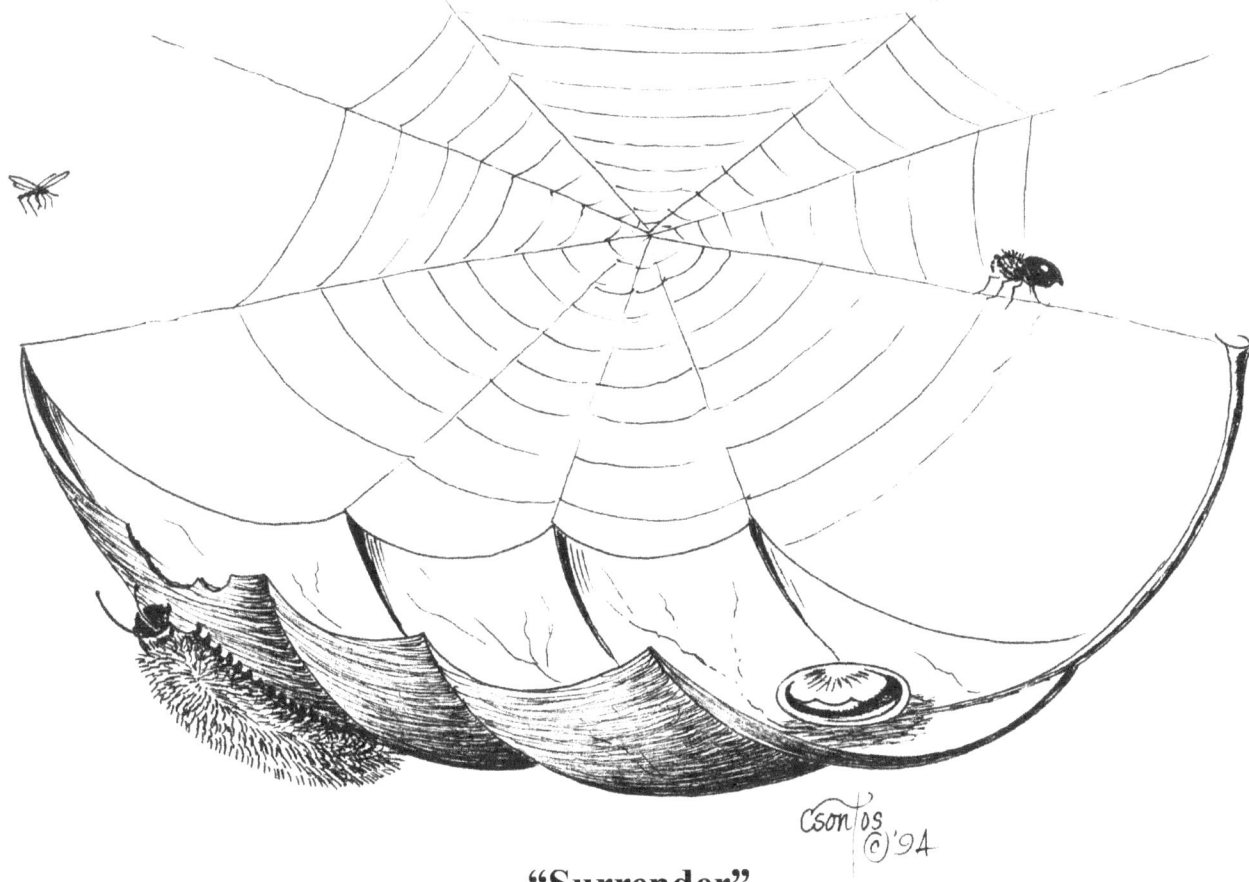

"To Perceive Infinity"
Ink - pen and brush.
I did have a single word in mind when this image came about. That word was 'Dimension'.

"Surrender"
Ink - pen and brush. Another result of taking close-up photographs of the forest floor.

87

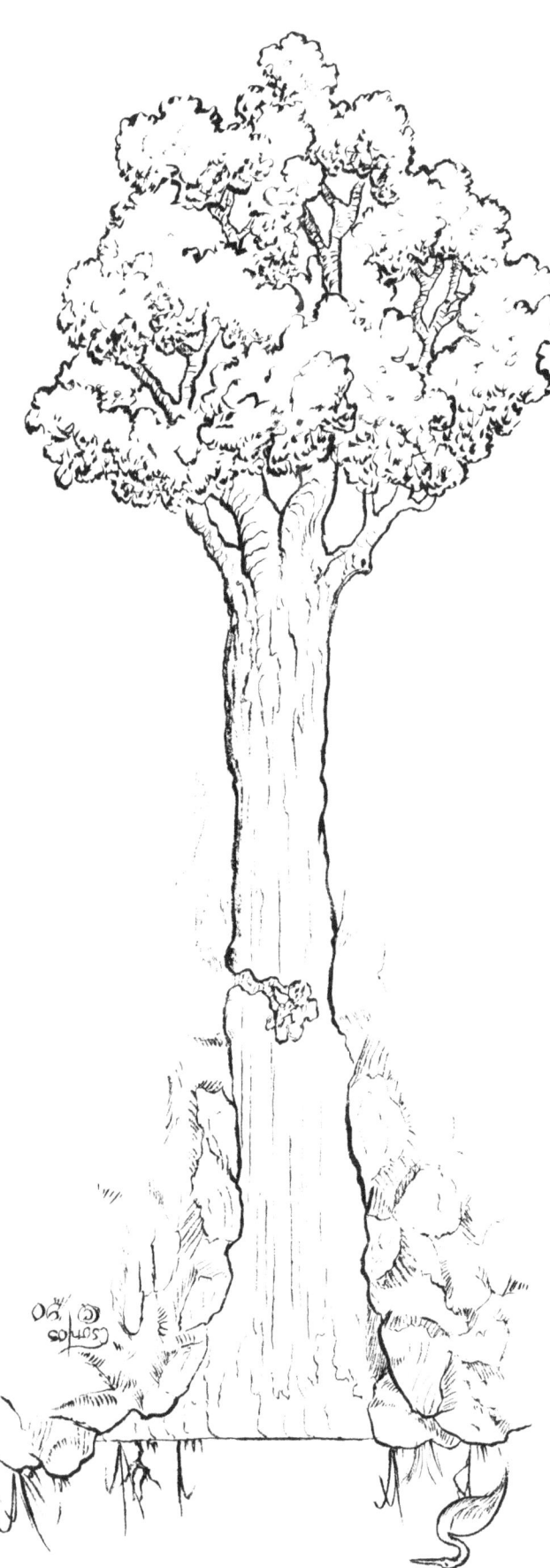

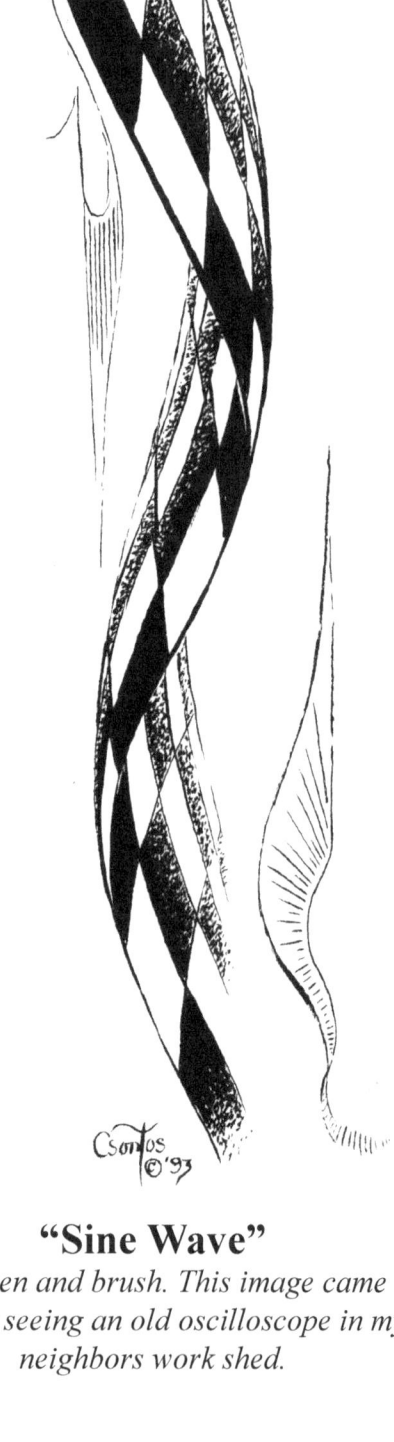

"Hydroponic Cellulose"

*Ink - brush. Another result of turning the
original sketching upside down as I work on it.*

"Sine Wave"

*Ink - pen and brush. This image came
up after seeing an old oscilloscope in my
neighbors work shed.*

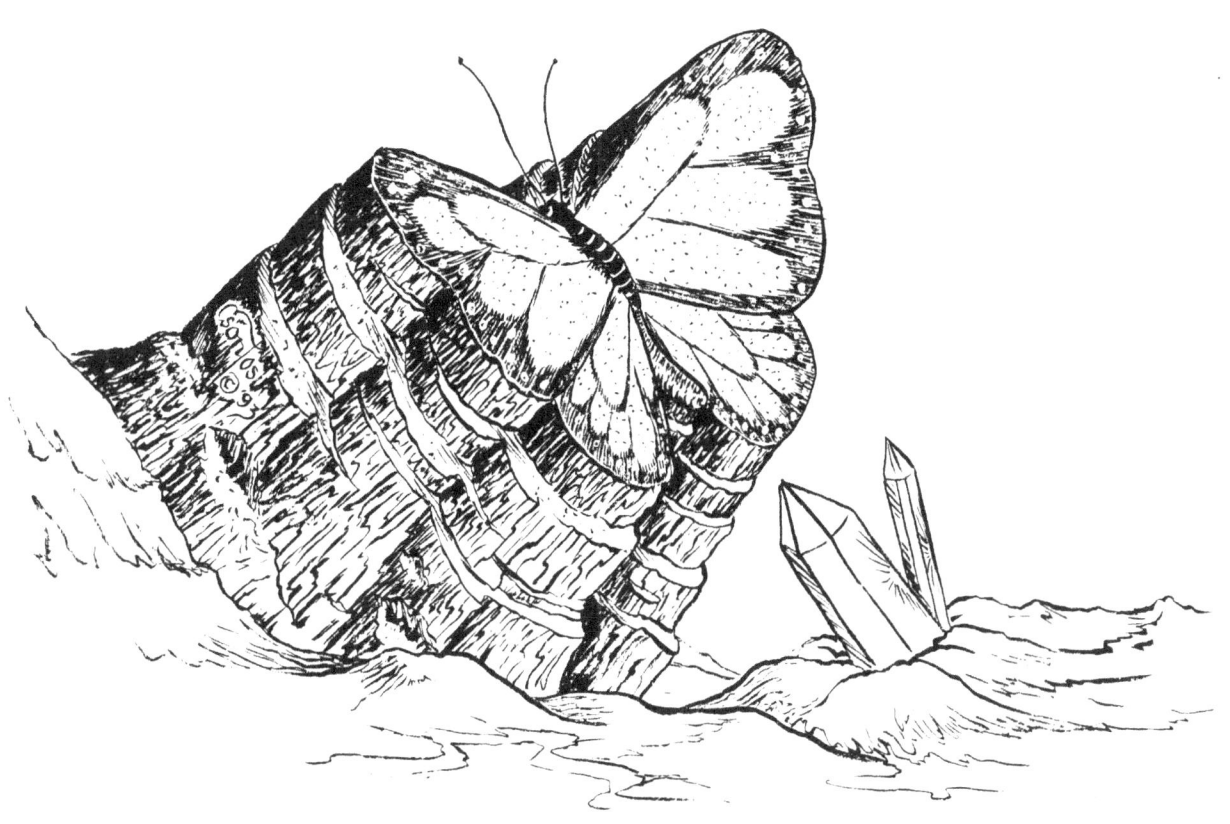

"Fossilized Butterfly"

Ink - brush. This image came about after I saw the movie "Jurassic Park".

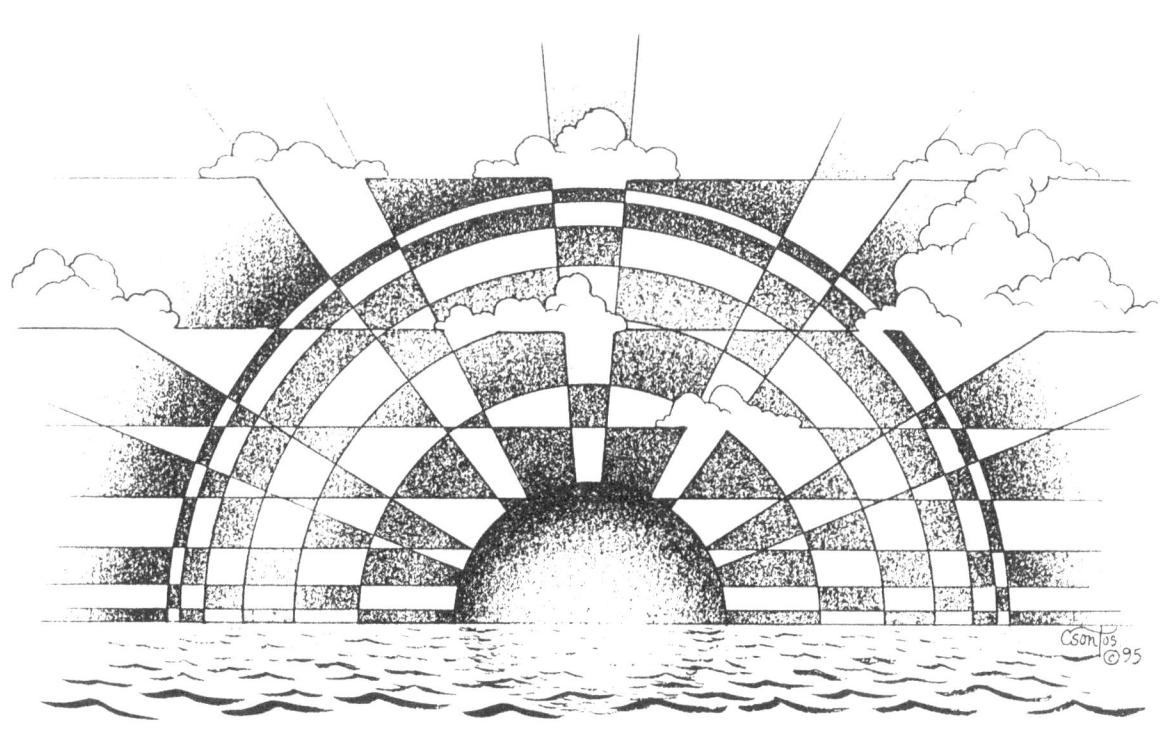

"Optic Sunset"

Ink - pen. I did this piece the day after I saw a perfect ground to ground rainbow on one of my walks.

89

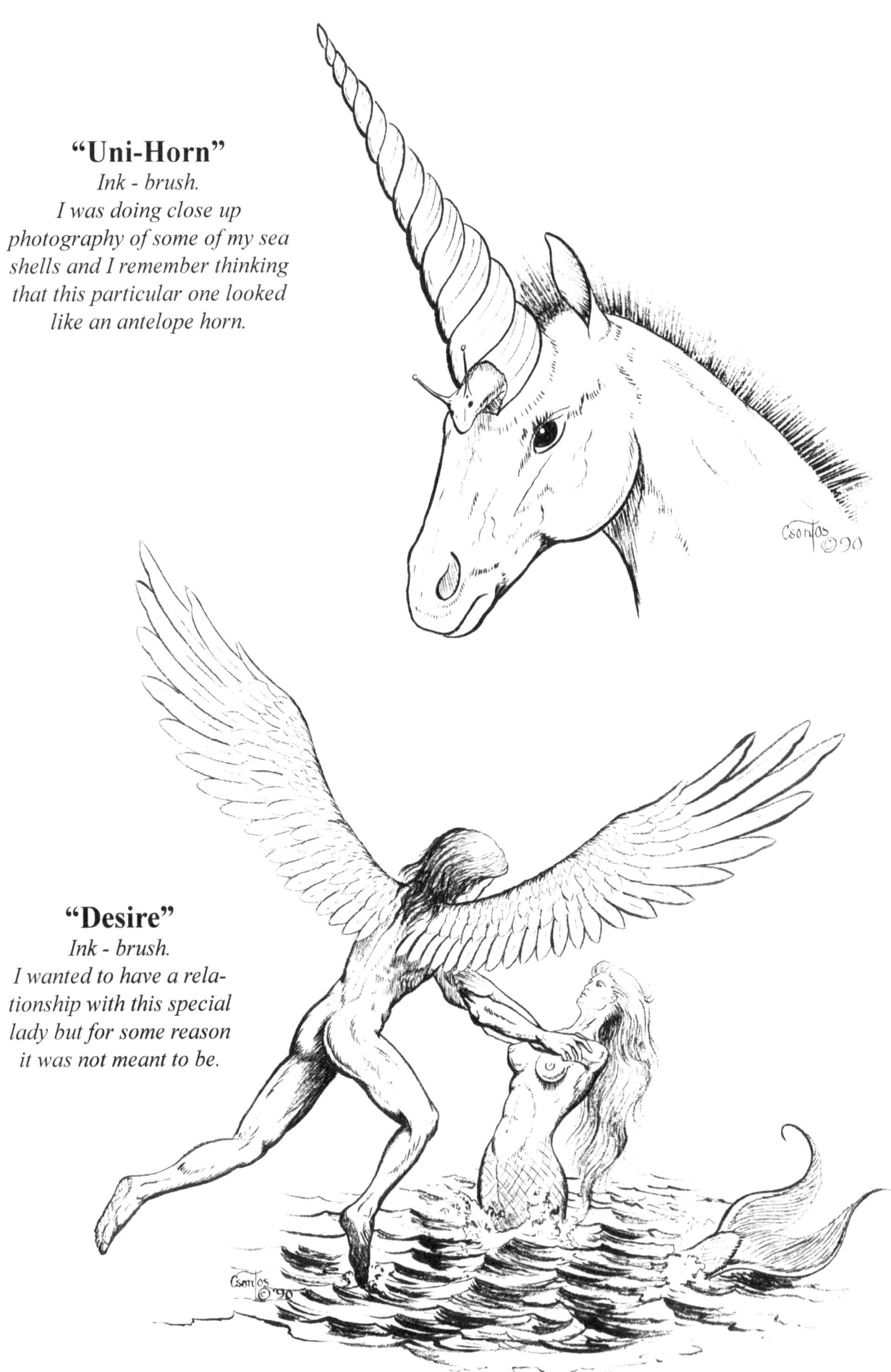

"Uni-Horn"
Ink - brush.
I was doing close up
photography of some of my sea
shells and I remember thinking
that this particular one looked
like an antelope horn.

"Desire"
Ink - brush.
I wanted to have a rela-
tionship with this special
lady but for some reason
it was not meant to be.

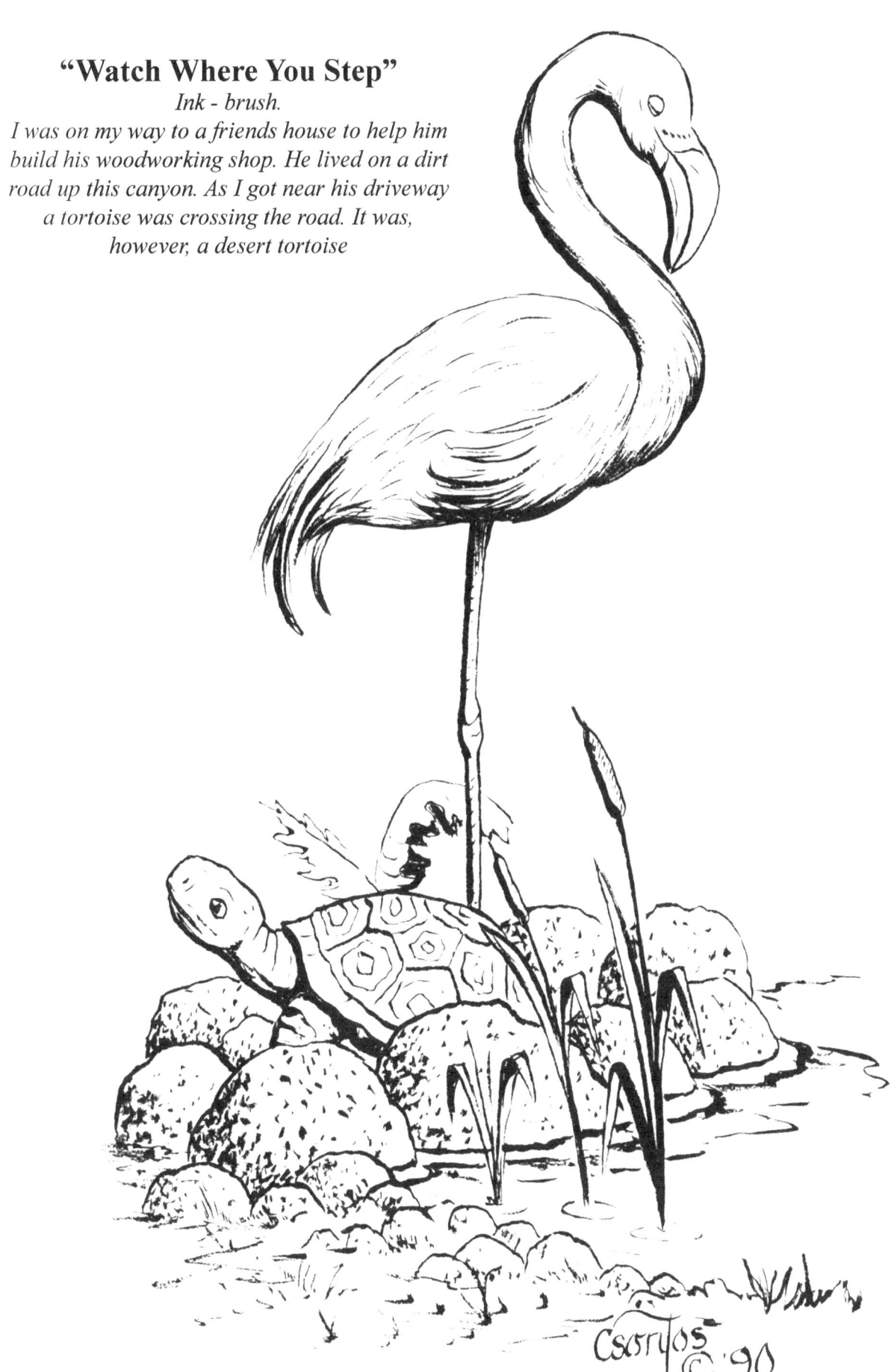

"Watch Where You Step"
Ink - brush.
I was on my way to a friends house to help him
build his woodworking shop. He lived on a dirt
road up this canyon. As I got near his driveway
a tortoise was crossing the road. It was,
however, a desert tortoise

91

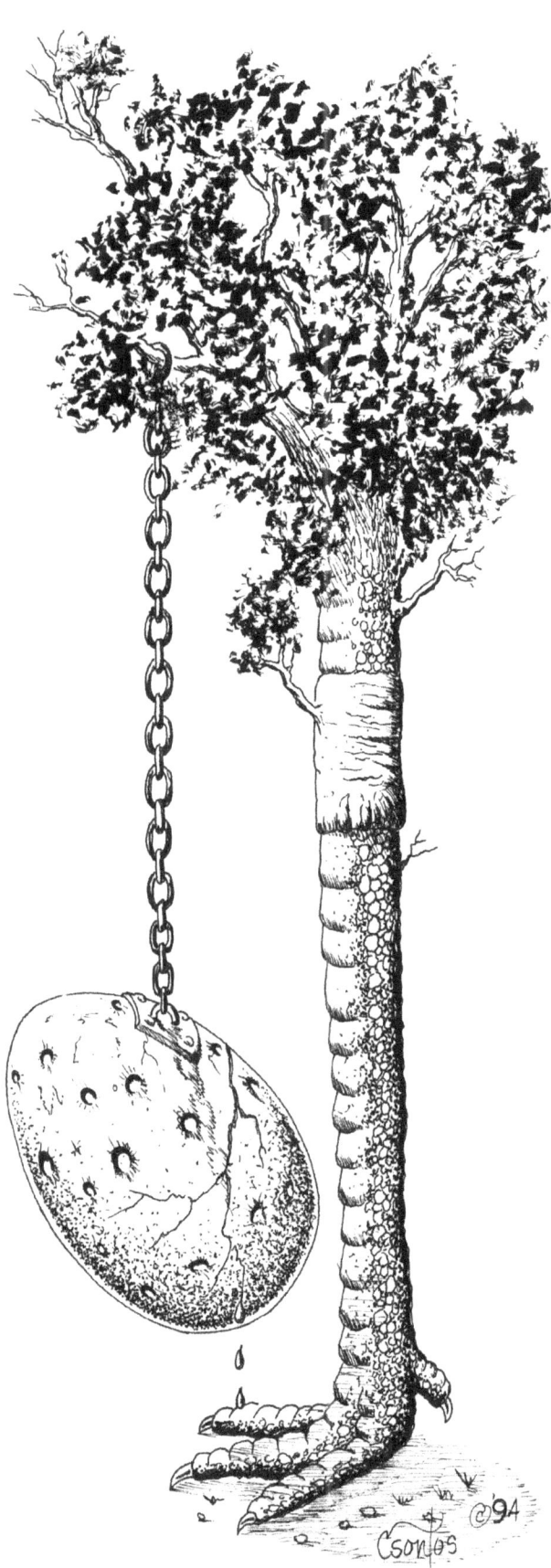

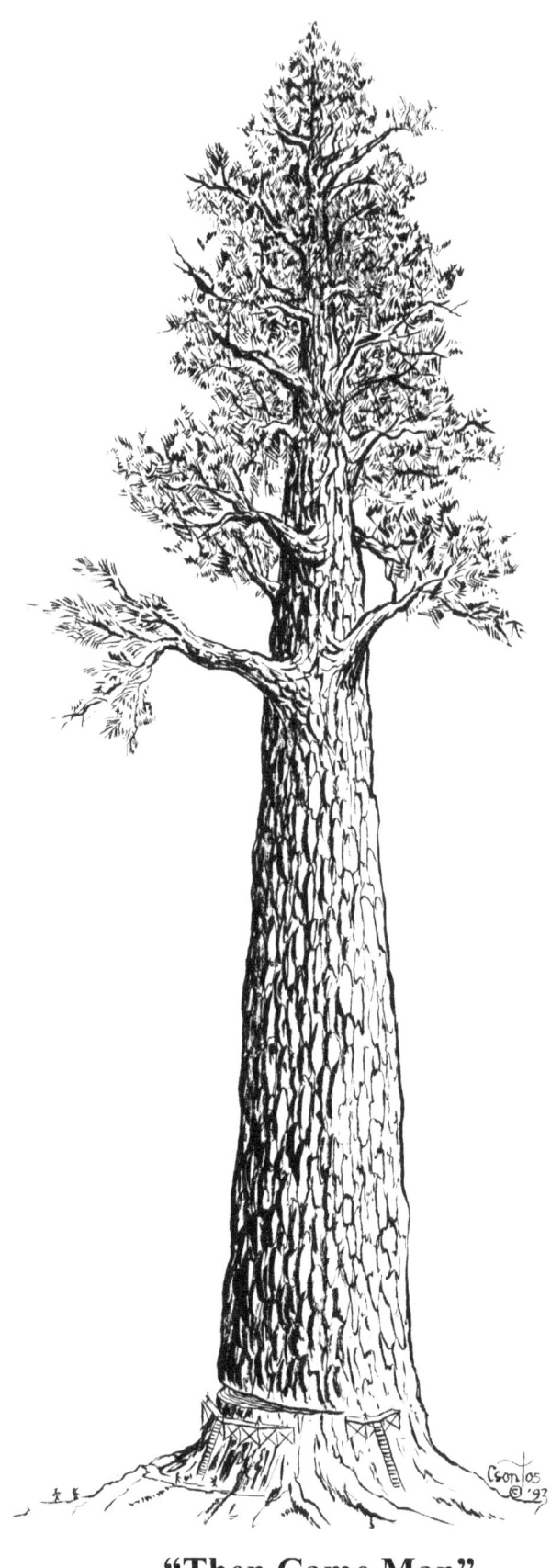

"Chain Reaction"

*Ink - pen and brush. I remember thinking of
the phrase, "Which came first, the chicken
or the egg?"*

"Then Came Man"

*Ink - brush.
I had helped build several decks in a
row, all with redwood. I didn't say I was
proud of it.*

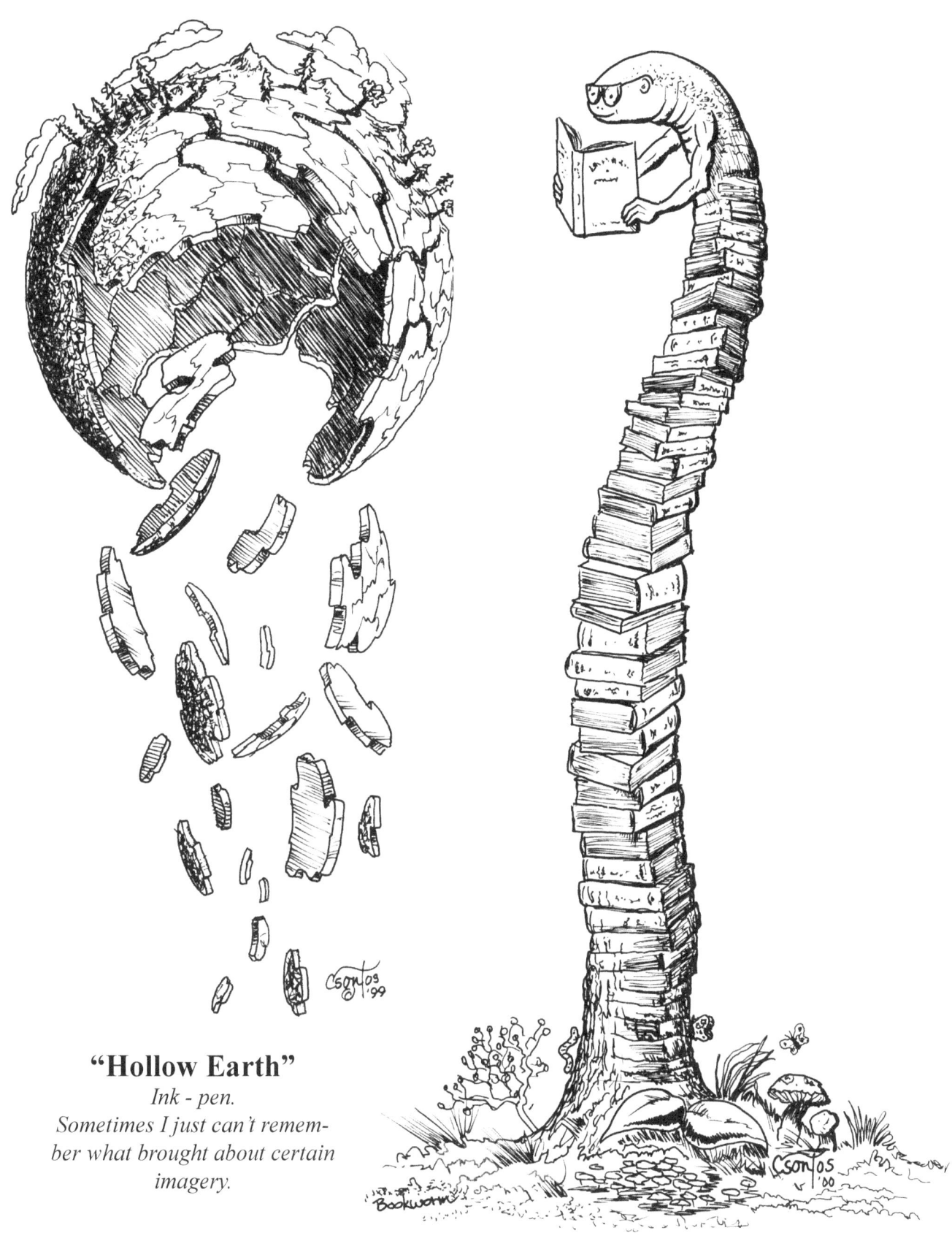

"Hollow Earth"
Ink - pen.
Sometimes I just can't remember what brought about certain imagery.

"Book Worm"
Ink - pen. An art director requested an image that showed an interest in books. Having that single thought in mind gave me this result.

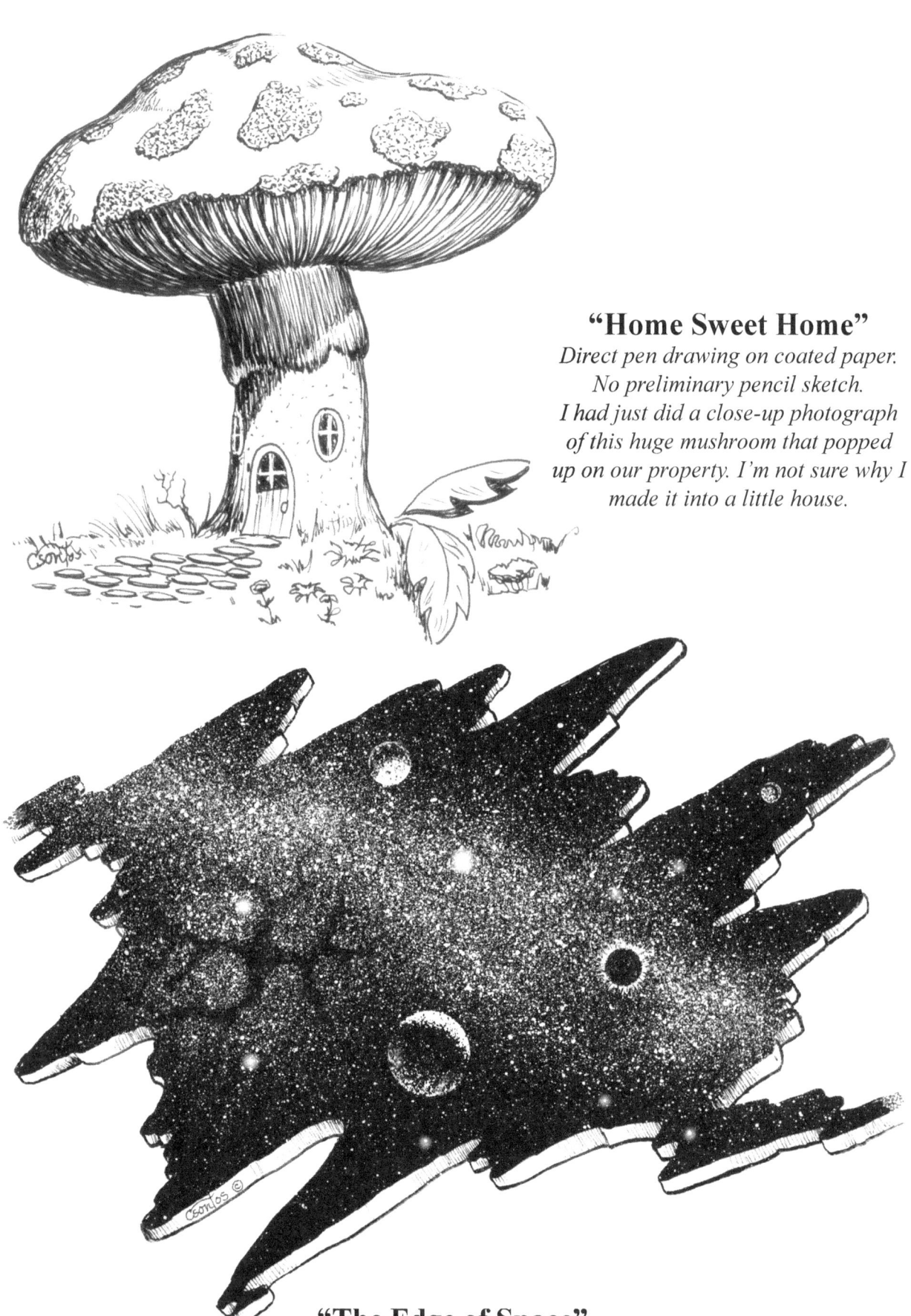

"Home Sweet Home"
Direct pen drawing on coated paper.
No preliminary pencil sketch.
I had just did a close-up photograph
of this huge mushroom that popped
up on our property. I'm not sure why I
made it into a little house.

"The Edge of Space"
Ink - pens and brush; and acrylic paint stippled with an air brush on illustration board. An image where the initial sketch was quite similar to the one for "Where Rain Comes From", but the result is quite different.. Another image where sci-fi was stuck in my head.

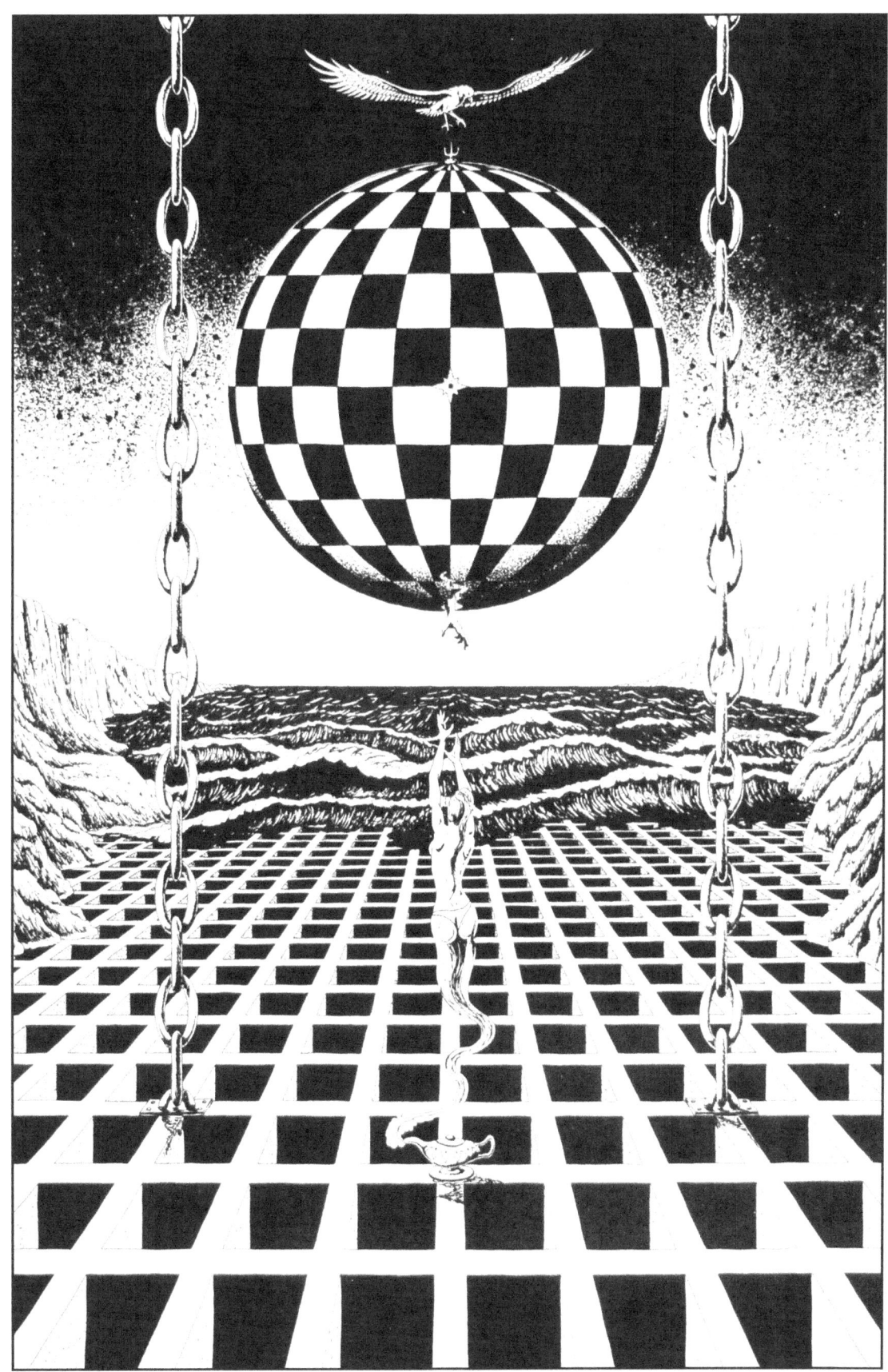

"Sortilegic Deluge"

Ink - pens, brush and sponge on illustration board.. After I came up with this image, the succeeding thought was to see how well I could use ink to portray a deep perspective. In retrospect, I'm not all that crazy about the sponge technique for the sky.

Visualizing with pencil and ink.
Spontaneous technique number five.

This is the last step by step technique layout for this book. For the techniques 3, and 4, (and pages 13-16) I purposely left out a few of the intermediate steps where I just refine the image in pencil before inking. It basically involves re-drawing until the imagery has the anatomical corrections that I feel are necessary for the

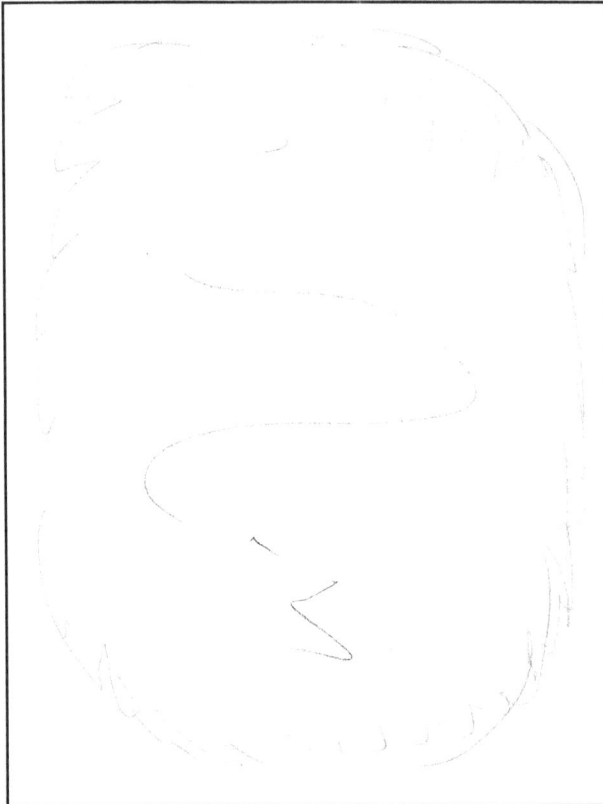

The first stage where I intentionally doodled around the perimeter of the paper.

piece. Whether that anatomy is of people, animals, trees, rocks, plants, or what have you, they should be drawn to such a degree where they are understandably correct or drawn as good as anything else you've seen. These intermediate steps are also the stages where the idea develops more congruence and associated details.

The inking however is another matter. A personal style will come across and develop as experience and practice comes into play. At that point an almost unconscious control will dic-

tate as to what degree to take a subject matter. And also what technique to use, such as pen or brush, or an airbrush stipple, or computer toning and/or whether or not coloring will be involved. And then there is the secondary technique of texturing, which can be pointillism, crosshatching, brush lines (feathering and line weights), scribbling, splattering, sponging, and dry brush, among others.

In visualizing, I believe no two people will see the exact same thing as they study a preliminary spontaneous sketch. Obviously I can only show techniques with what I see. And what I see is based on how and where I was brought up (I took thousands of walks in the woods and climbed trees just as many times); my current age (which is a direct result of my life experiences); and my interests and concerns. I am sure that there are a multitude of other factors as well. The point is, as I've said before, to let the artwork create itself. The brain will compose just about anything if you allow it. It's like looking at an ink blot. Rotating the sketch will change what you see as well. Even if both you and I see the same thing in a preliminary doodling we would see it slightly different.

The second stage where the idea is developing.

The third stage where I am fairly sure of the composition and individual sections.

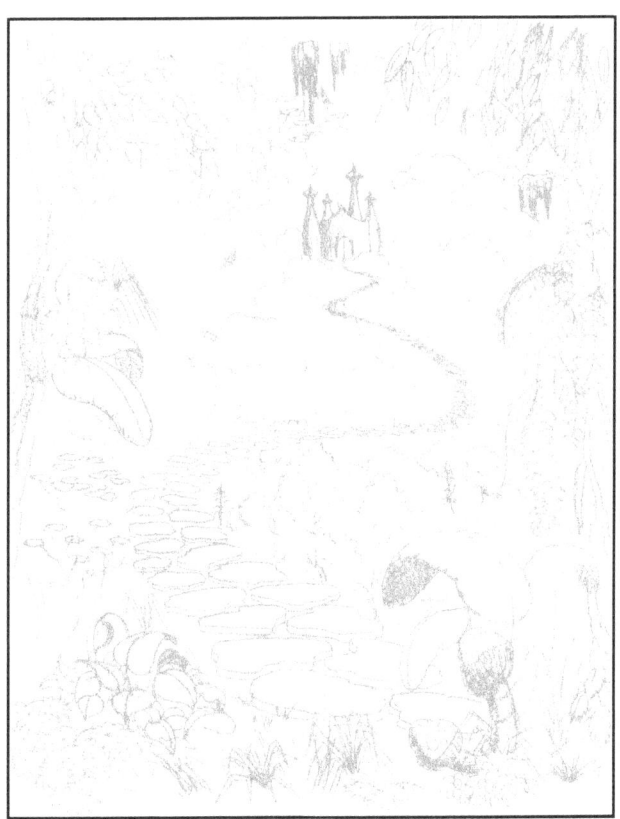

The forth stage where I have begun to add shading to orient my mind's eye to that effect just before inking.

You will see what you expect to see. I know a lady that sees faces in almost every sketch I show her. A lot of people see faces. But as I've mentioned I grew up taking walks in the woods and there weren't too many faces in the woods. Can you tell that from looking at some of the finished pieces? I also played chess and loved magnets as a kid (page 4).

So now you may be asking, "Just what is the point of this spontaneous artwork?" I believe it is to tell a story or expressing oneself. I also believe that art is a basic need of some people. Just like food, clothing and shelter. It must be, because we know that the expression of artwork goes back over 20,000 years. If you as a viewer can appreciate what the artist portrays then it has served a two-fold purpose.

For this piece I intentionally started at the outside of the paper. I have only done that maybe four other times in the past 35 years and it was for logo letterheads. I wanted to see if it would make a difference, knowing that this piece was going to be the last technique section done specifically for this book. It did end up being quite detailed.

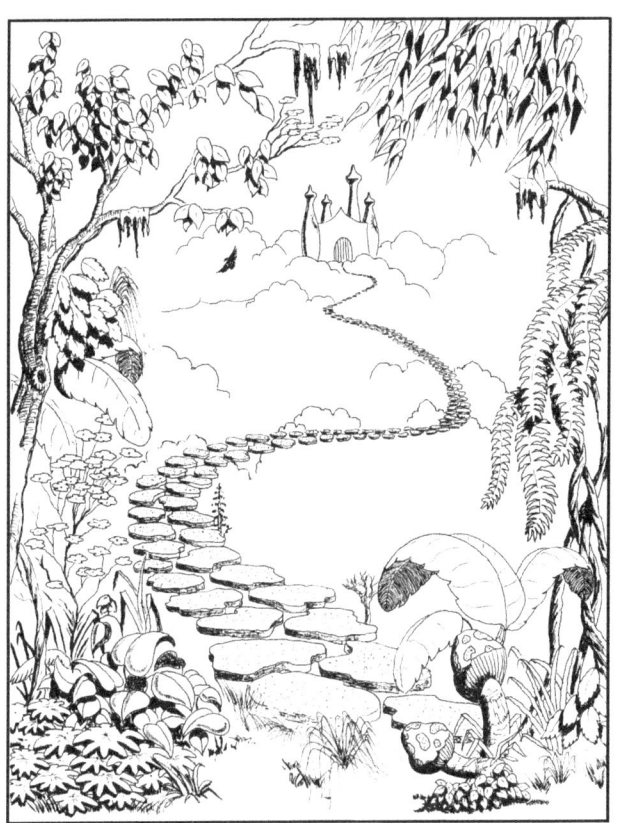

The inking about 40% underway.

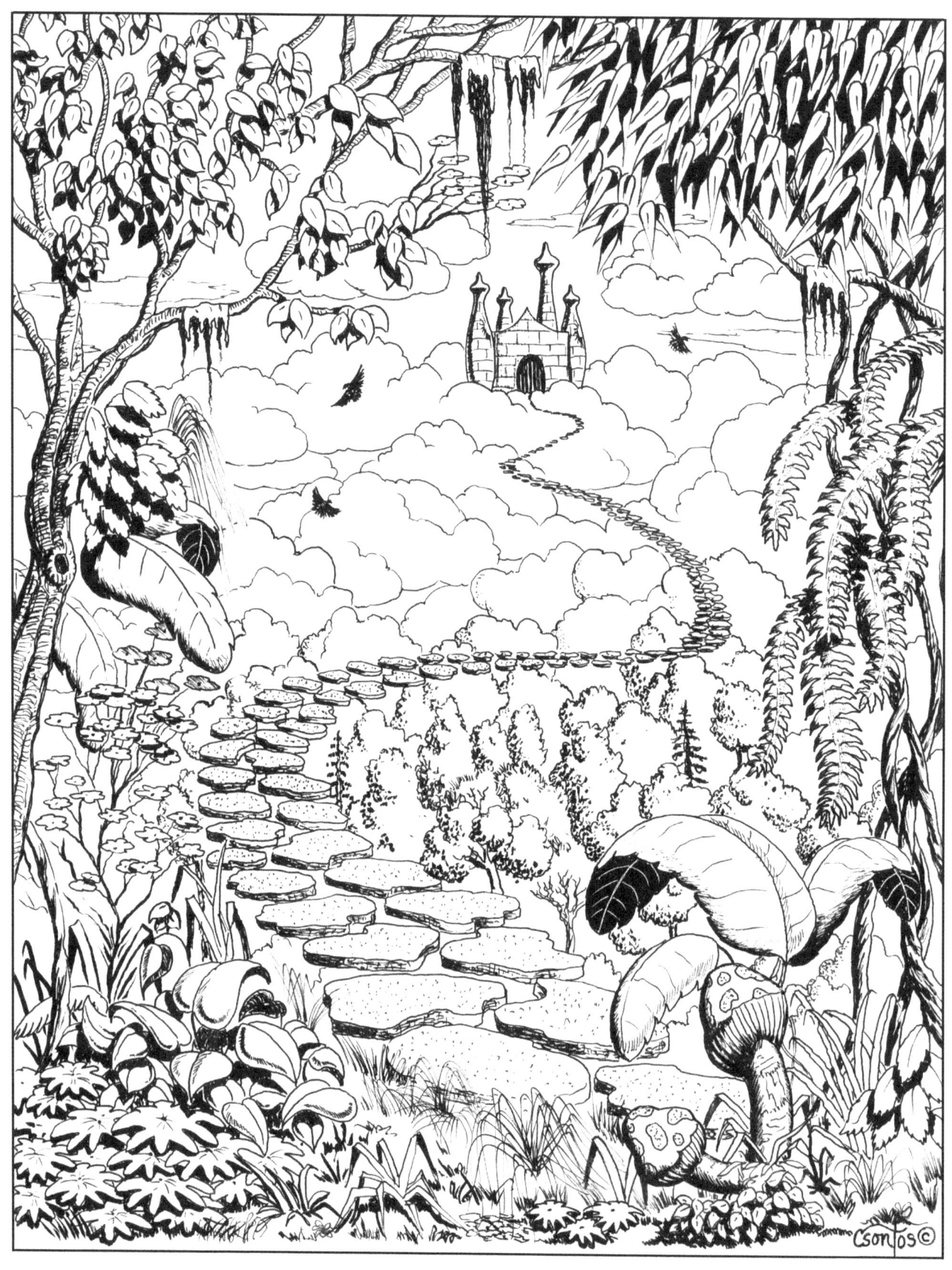

"On the Way to Camelot"
Ink - pens and brush.

Yet still more samples of spontaneous illustrations.

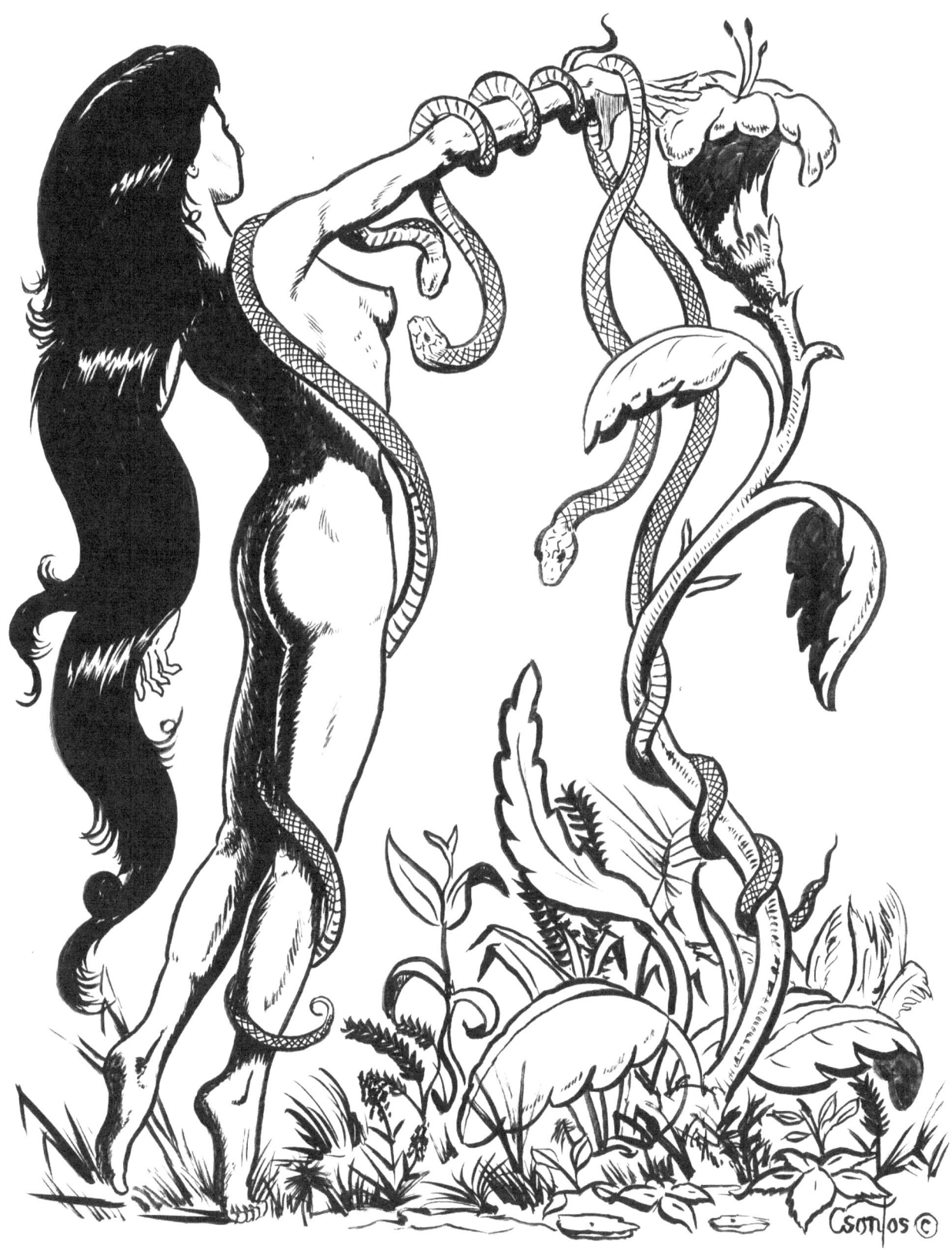

"Snake Charmer"

Ink - brush. As I mentioned earlier, I believe this was the result of my rescuing a bull snake from what looked like a fishing net.

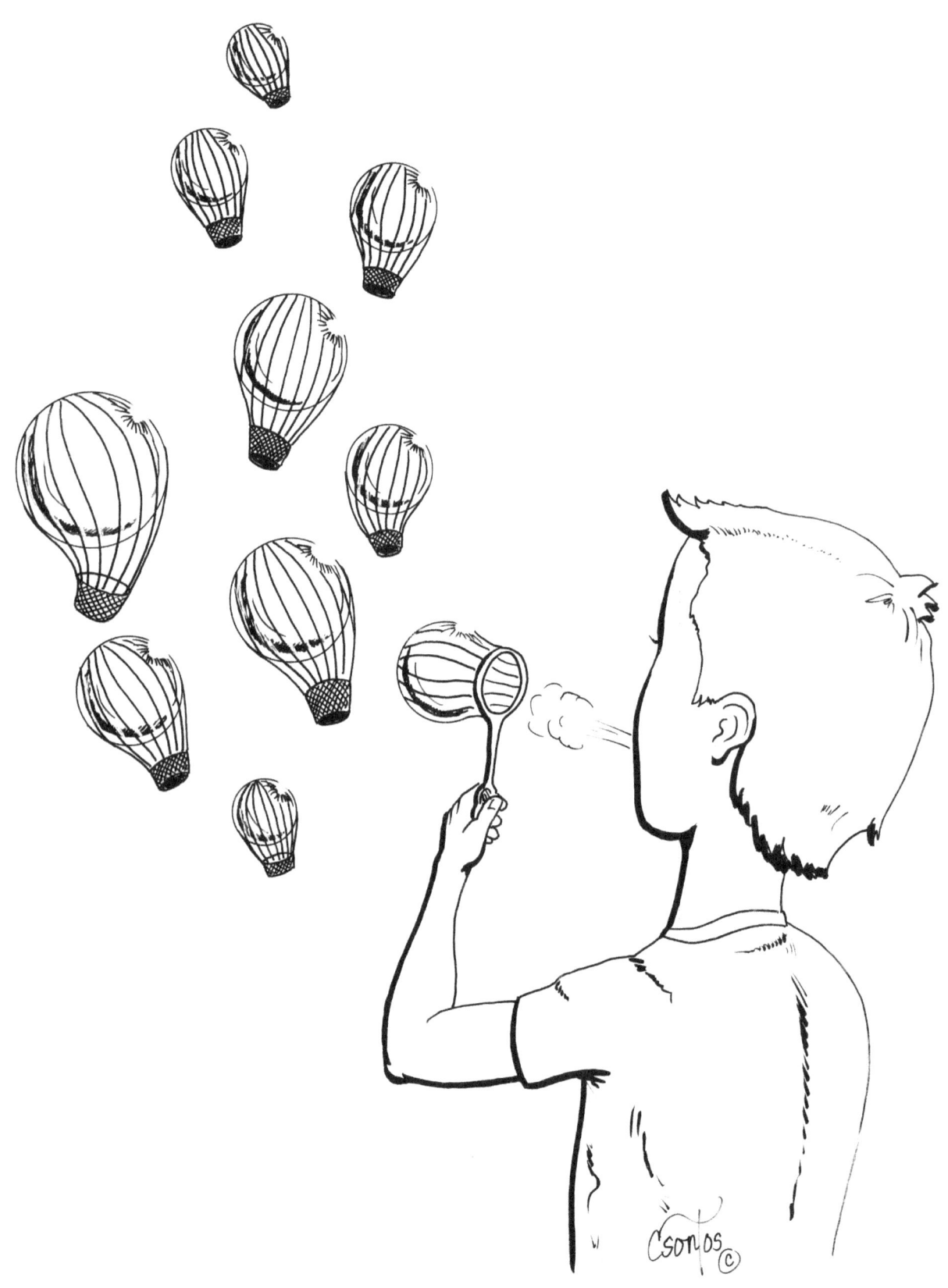

"Hot Air Bubbles"

Ink - pen and brush. This image came about the day after we took a trip to Tucson. As we got about ten miles north of Phoenix there was obviously a hot air balloon gathering going on. We counted about 25 of them.

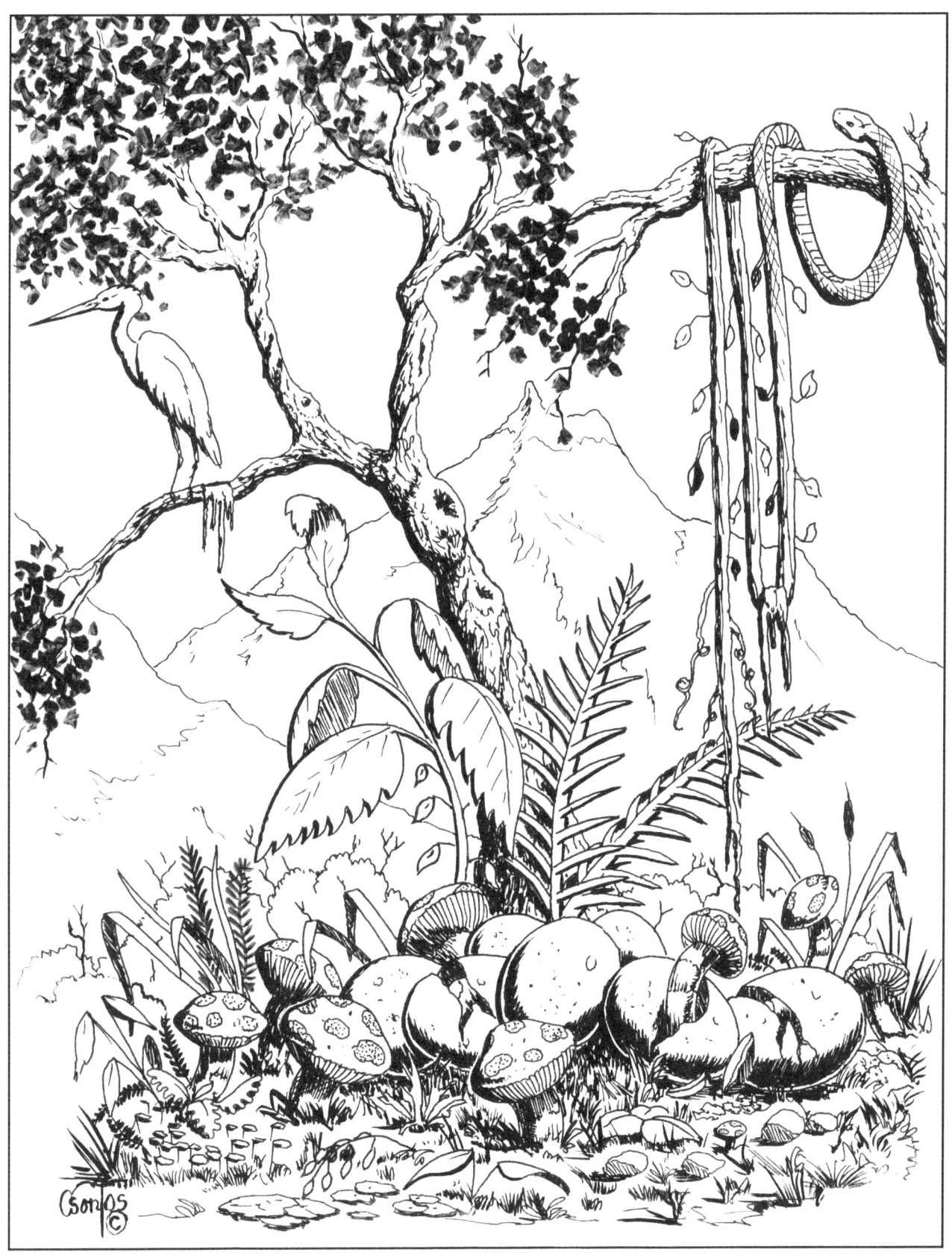

"Hatchlings"

Ink - pen and brush. I think this image and the one on page 103 are the result of me trying to grow a simple garden. The plants all started early indoors and then when it came time to put them in the garden the weather turned incredibly hot. Not to mention that our well went dry at the same time. Needless to say the garden failed miserably.

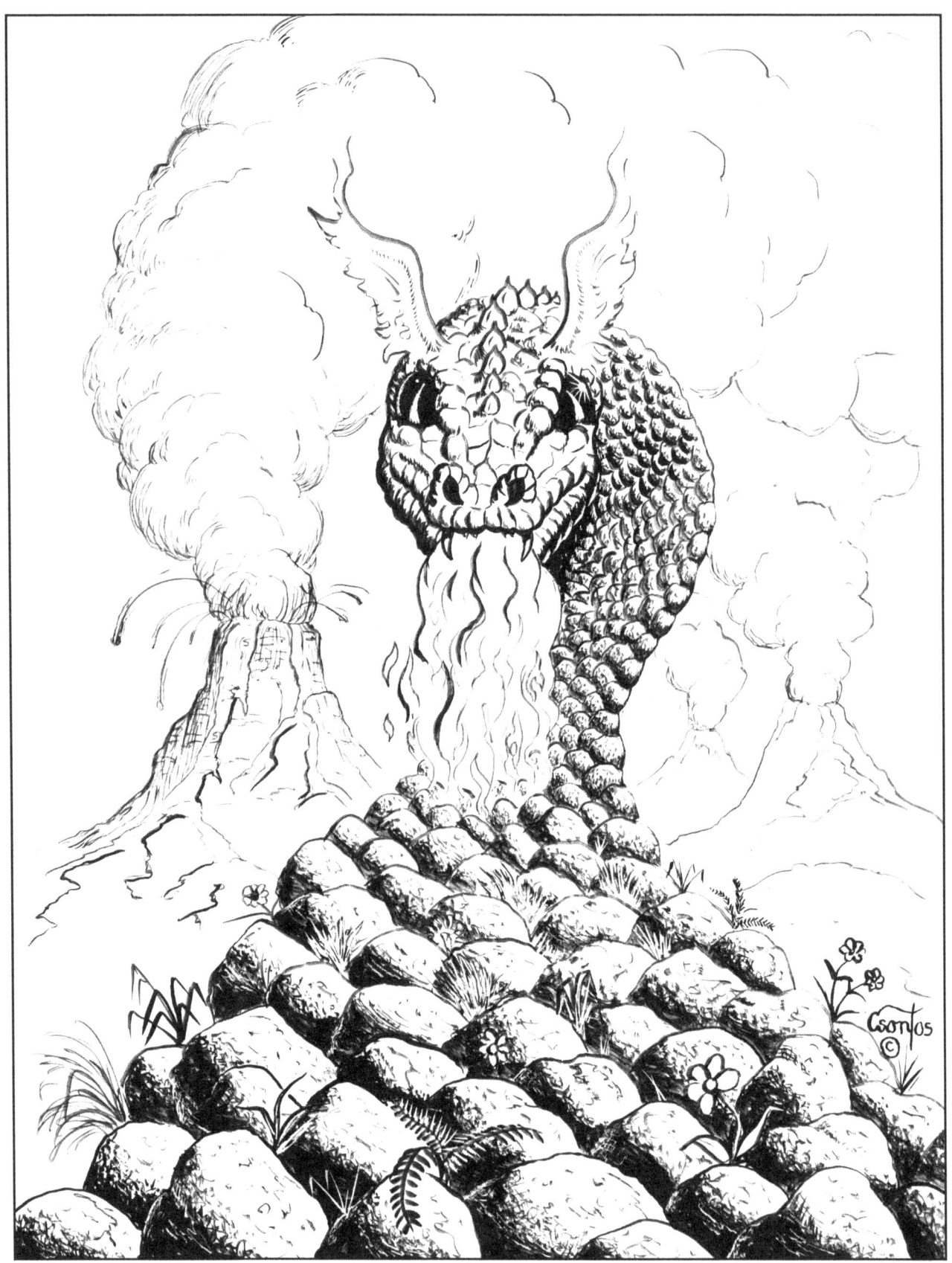

"Where Lava Comes From"

Ink - brush. When this image came about I was working on a similar theme in a painting. When that happens I usually try to abandon the idea and start over but this time I elected to continue because I wanted to see how the rocks would look with a brush technique.

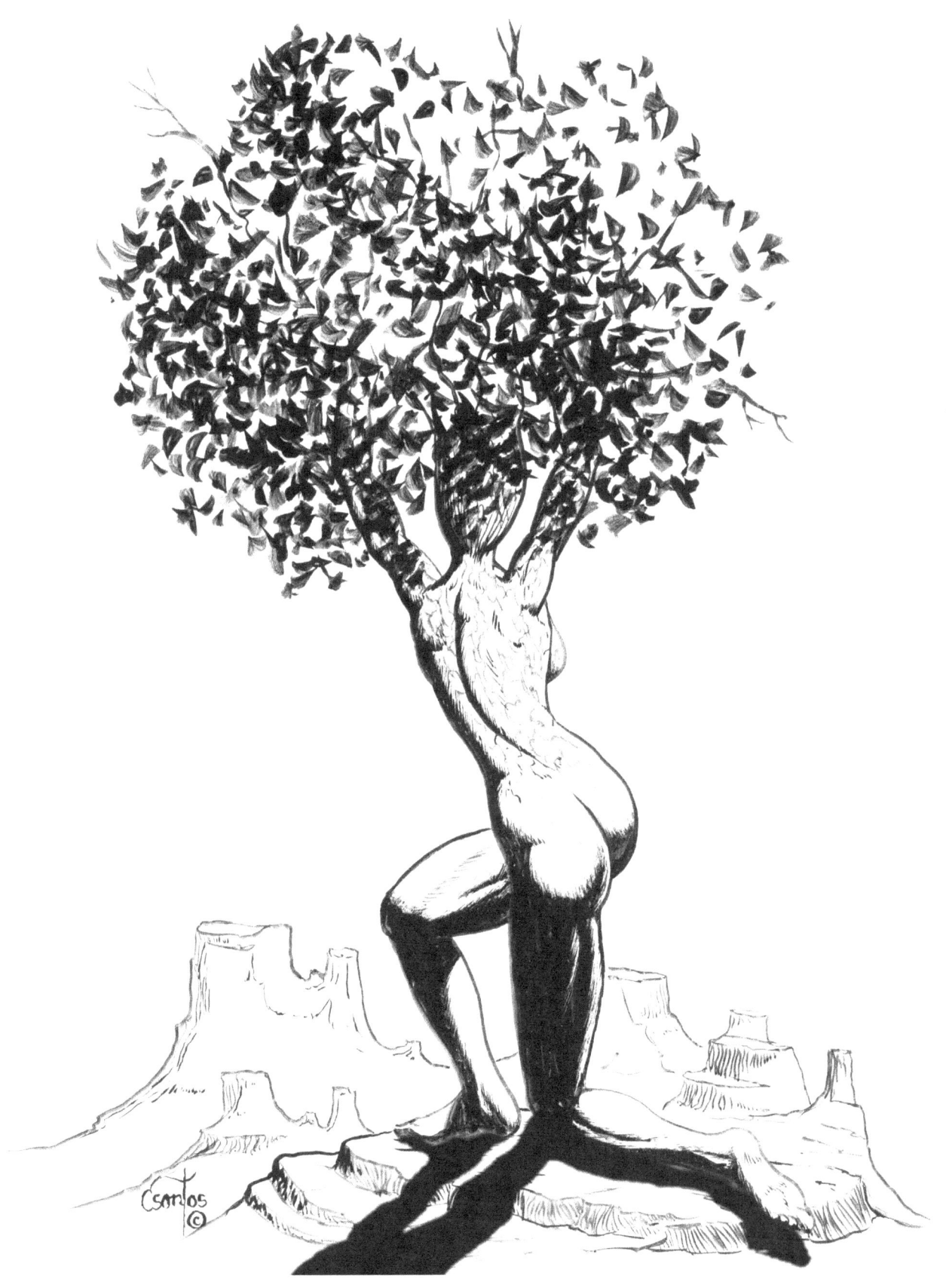

"A Place to Flourish"

Ink - brush with computer touch-up. It seems like the only way a plant can mature and thrive in a hot dry climate is in a drawing.

Artist Bio...

Well, if you really want to know...

Born February 2, 1951 - Manhattan, NY

Within a few months after I came into this world my family moved to a 300 acre farm in upstate New York. Nothing better could have ever happened to my childhood. I will be eternally grateful to my Dad for wanting to make that move. I explored every nook and cranny of the forest and could actually sit so still animals could come right up to me and not even know I was there, until I started laughing.

My formal art education did not begin until I was 16. Sadly, being brought up in the country, institutions for art training did not exist. So I had to improvise and use the margins and back pages of my notebooks for my art lessons. More then once I was told that artwork should not be done unless I was completely finished with class work. Where in actuality I would make sure the art was done before the class work would even get started. You have to categorize your priorities for stress relief.

From 1967 to 1970 I had two years of architectural and mechanical drawing and one year of geometrical and technical design. I still use that knowledge to this day as I occasionally design and make furniture.

From 1971 to 1976 I moved to the Schenectady area and studied various forms of linear design, light and shade, composition and other aspects of fine art. I took all the art curriculum at the local community college except for history of art. I did scan the book in the college bookstore and came up with my own opinion that it was too opinionated. Thinking that art is doing not criticizing. And who really knows what is in the mind of an artist. Especially dead artists.

In 1976 I approached several galleries and museums and inquired about representation. But then I got the itch to move and traveled to Arizona where I got involved with doing art shows. I traveled through the southwest to do other shows and still occasionally approached galleries. I had several paintings reproduced by lithography companies for posters and lithographs for national distribution.

From 1976 to the late 90's I made hundreds of studies of objects and took thousands of photographs for references.

For years I continually experimented with my art trying to find out what was my real role in this creative process. Later I realized that this time period was actually the development of a personal

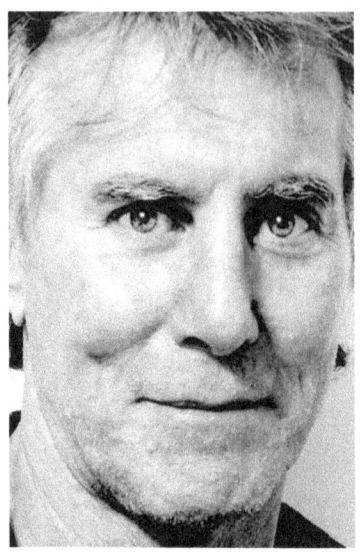

Mug shot.

approach to art. I assume I practiced at drawing and painting until I felt I was ready for... something. Now that I'm all grown up (physically) I stick to what I enjoy. I did fantasy and science fiction, still life and landscapes, some portraits and decor pieces. I also did thousands of commercial art layouts and illustrations. But at any time when there was a quiet time between the necessities of survival I did a spontaneous surrealistic or perceptive work of art. And it took a few years for me to realize this is what I am supposed to be doing. It must be, because I continually return to that style for some unknown reason. I am unable to even think of doing any other type of art as a means of a gratifying self expression. I even dream almost the exact same things I paint. I did other forms of art because they brought me money. I do what I enjoy because it seems to bring fulfillment.

I have been given the privilege of being able to do various forms of art in this life. It is this achievement alone that makes me believe art is my purpose.

Michael Csontos